PROFILES IN WORLD HISTORY

Significant Events and the People Who Shaped Them

DISCARD

Volume 3: *The Crusades to Building Empires in the Americas, 1095-1500*

Crusades and Mongol Expansion
Saladin, Genghis Khan, Innocent III, Alexius V
Religion and Reason in the Middle Ages
Averroës, Maimonides, Thomas Aquinas
Beginning of Constitutional Government in England
Thomas Becket, King John
Muslim Influences on Empires in West Africa
Al-Bakri, Sundiata, Mansa Musa
Exploring the East
Marco Polo, William of Rubrouck, Ibn Battutah
Building Empires in Europe and Asia
Timur Lenk, Mehmed II, Ivan the Great, Babur
Building Empires in the Americas
Topa Inca Yupanqui, Moctezuma I

Volume 4: *The Age of Discovery to Industrial Revolution, 1400-1830*

Beginnings of the Age of Discovery
Cheng Ho, Vasco da Gama, Jacques Cartier
Religious Reform
Desiderius Erasmus, Guru Nanak, Ignatius of Loyola, Martin Luther
Revival of Science
Leonardo da Vinci, Tycho Brahe, Johannes Kepler
Revival of Literature
Francis Bacon, Miguel de Cervantes, William Shakespeare
Rise of Nationalism
Suleiman the Magnificent, Hideyoshi Toyotomi, Catherine the Great
Enlightenment
John Locke, Voltaire, Jean-Jacques Rousseau
Industrial Revolution
Charles Townshend, Richard Arkwright, James Watt

CHICAGO PUBLIC LIBRARY
ICLE PARK BRANCH
N. OKETO

PROFILES IN
WORLD HISTORY

Issues of Human Survival to Middle East Peace Process

1950
Pablo Neruda wins Soviet International Peace Prize.

1963
Robert Mugabe organizes the Zimbabwe African National Union.

1974
Donald Johanson discovers Lucy, a three-million-year-old skeleton.

1975
Bill Gates organizes Microsoft Corporation.

1977
Vaclav Havel helps write Charter 77, protesting the lack of civil rights in Czechoslovakia.

1985
Mikhail Gorbachev becomes leader of Soviet Union, begins reforms.

1990
Gorbachev wins Nobel Peace Prize for helping arrange arms reductions, ending the cold war.

1991
Soviet Union is dissolved; Boris Yeltsin becomes president of Russia. Lech Walesa becomes president of Poland.

1992
Rigoberta Menchu wins Nobel Peace Prize.

1993
Vaclav Havel becomes president of Czech Republic.

1994
Yasir Arafat, Shimon Perez, and Yitzhak Rabin share Nobel Peace Prize. Toni Morrison wins Nobel Prize for Literature.

1994
Nelson Mandela becomes first black president of South Africa.

PROFILES IN WORLD HISTORY

Significant Events and the People
Who Shaped Them

Issues of Human Survival to
Middle East Peace Process

JOYCE MOSS
and
GEORGE WILSON

AN IMPRINT OF GALE RESEARCH
AN INTERNATIONAL THOMSON PUBLISHING COMPANY

CHICAGO PUBLIC LIBRARY
ORIOLE PARK BRANCH
5201 N. OKETO   60656

PROFILES IN WORLD HISTORY
Significant Events and the People Who Shaped Them

VOLUME 8: ISSUES OF HUMAN SURVIVAL TO MIDDLE EAST PEACE PROCESS

Joyce Moss and George Wilson

Staff

Carol DeKane Nagel, *U•X•L Developmental Editor*
Julie L. Carnagie, *U•X•L Assistant Editor*
Thomas L. Romig, *U•X•L Publisher*

Shanna P. Heilveil, *Production Assistant*
Evi Seoud, *Assistant Production Manager*
Mary Beth Trimper, *Production Director*

Barbara A. Wallace, *Permissions Associate (Pictures)*

Mary Krzewinski, *Cover and Page Designer*
Cynthia Baldwin, *Art Director*

The Graphix Group, *Typesetting*

This publication is a creative work fully protected by all applicable copyright laws, as well as by misappropriation, trade secret, unfair competition, and other applicable laws. The editors of this work have added value to the underlying factual material herein through one or more of the following: unique and original selection, coordination, expression, arrangement, and classification of the information. All rights to this publication will be vigorously defended.

Copyright © 1996
Joyce Moss and George Wilson

All rights reserved, including the right of reproduction in whole or in part in any form.

∞™ This book is printed on acid-free paper that meets the minimum requirements of American National Standard for Information Sciences—Permanence Paper for Printed Library Materials, ANSI Z39.48-1984.

ISBN 0-7876-0464-X (Set)
ISBN 0-7876-0465-8 (v. 1)   ISBN 0-7876-0469-0 (v. 5)
ISBN 0-7876-0466-6 (v. 2)   ISBN 0-7876-0470-4 (v. 6)
ISBN 0-7876-0467-4 (v. 3)   ISBN 0-7876-0471-2 (v. 7)
ISBN 0-7876-0468-2 (v. 4)   ISBN 0-7876-0472-0 (v. 8)

Printed in the United States of America

I(T)P™ U·X·L is an imprint of Gale Research,
an International Thomson Publishing Company.
ITP logo is a trademark under license.

Contents

R01226 89172

CHICAGO PUBLIC LIBRARY
ORIOLE PARK BRANCH
5201 N. OKETO   60656

Reader's Guide vii
Acknowledgments ix
Picture Credits xi

Issues of Human Survival 1

Paul VI **4**
William McNeill **14**
Paul Ehrlich **20**

Scientific and Technological Breakthroughs 26

Donald Johanson **30**
Edward O. Wilson **38**
Bill Gates **46**

Literature as a Political Tool 56

Pablo Neruda **60**
Toni Morrison **68**
Rigoberta Menchu **76**

Ending the Cold War 84

Mikhail Gorbachev **88**
Vaclav Havel **98**
Lech Walesa **108**
Ronald Reagan **116**
Boris Yeltsin **126**

Winning African Independence 136

Robert Mugabe **142**
Jomo Kenyatta **152**
F. W. de Klerk **162**
Nelson Mandela **170**

Middle East Peace Process 180

Hussein I **186**
Yasir Arafat **196**
Shimon Peres **206**

Bibliography **217**
Index **219**

Reader's Guide

Profiles in World History: Significant Events and the People Who Shaped Them presents the life stories of more than 175 individuals who have played key roles in world history. The biographies are clustered around 50 broad events, ranging from the Rise of Eastern Religions and Philosophies to the Expansion of World Powers, from Industrial Revolution to Winning African Independence. Each biography—complete in itself—contributes a singular outlook regarding an event; when taken as cluster, the biographies provide a variety of views and experiences, thereby offering a broad perspective on events that shaped the world.

Those whose stories are told in *Profiles in World History* meet one or more of the following criteria. The individuals:

- Represent viewpoints or groups involved in a major world event
- Directly affected the outcome of the event
- Exemplify a role played by common citizens in that event

Format

Profiles in World History volumes are arranged by chapter. Each chapter focuses on one particular event and opens with an overview and detailed time line of the event that places it in historical context. Following are biographical profiles of two to five diverse individuals who played active roles in the event.

Each biographical profile is divided into four sections:

- **Personal Background** provides details that predate and anticipate the individual's involvement in the event

• **Participation** describes the role played by the individual in the event and its impact on his or her life

• **Aftermath** discusses effects of the individual's actions and subsequent relevant events in the person's life

• **For More Information** provides sources for further reading on the individual

Additionally, sidebars containing interesting details about the events and individuals profiled are interspersed throughout the text.

Additional Features

Portraits, illustrations, and maps as well as excerpts from primary source materials are included in *Profiles in World History* to help bring history to life. Sources of all quoted material are cited parenthetically within the text, and complete bibliographic information is listed at the end of each biography. A full bibliography of scholarly sources consulted in preparing each volume appears in each book's back matter.

Cross references are made in the entries, directing readers to other entries within the volume that are connected in some way to the person under scrutiny. Additionally, each volume ends with a subject index, while Volume 8 concludes with a cumulative subject index, providing easy access to the people and events mentioned throughout *Profiles in World History*.

Comments and Suggestions

We welcome your comments on this work as well as your suggestions for individuals to be featured in future editions of *Profiles in World History*. Please write: Editors, *Profiles in World History*, U·X·L, 835 Penobscot Bldg., Detroit, Michigan 48226-4094; fax to 313-961-6348; or call toll-free: 1-800-877-4253.

Acknowledgments

The editors would like to thank the many people involved in the preparation of *Profiles in World History*.

For guidance in the choice of events and personalities, we are grateful to Ross Dunn, Professor of History at the University of California at San Diego, and David Smith, Professor of History at California Polytechnic University at Pomona. We're thankful to Professor Smith for his careful review of the entire series and his guidance toward key sources of information about personalities and events.

We deeply appreciate the writers who compiled data and contributed to the biographies: Diane Ahrens, Bill Boll, Quesiyah Ali Chavez, Charity-Jean Conklin, Mario Cutajar, Craig Hinkel, Hillary Manning, Lawrence Orr, Phillip T. Slattery, Colin Wells, and Susan Yun. We'd especially like to thank Jamie Mohn and Cheryl Steets for their careful attention to the manuscript.

Thanks also to the copy editors and proofreaders, Sonia Benson, Barbara C. Bigelow, Betz Des Chenes, Robert Griffin, Rob Nagel, and Paulette Petrimoulx, for their careful attention to style and detail. Special thanks to Margaret M. Johnson, Judith Kass, and John F. Petruccione for researching the illustrations and maps.

And, finally, thanks to Carol Nagel of U·X·L for overseeing the production of the series.

Picture Credits

The photographs and illustrations appearing in *Profiles in World History: Significant Events and the People Who Shaped Them*, Volume 8: *Issues of Human Survival to Middle East Peace Process* were received from the following sources:

On the cover: **Reuters/Bettmann:** Bill Gates, Boris Yeltsin; © **Kate Kunz:** Toni Morrison.

AP/Wide World Photos: pp. 21, 39, 42, 49, 51, 73, 99, 103, 105, 114, 122, 149, 155, 171, 178, 183, 199, 202; **Archive Photos:** pp. 9, 95, 120, 207; **Archive Photos/Popperfoto:** p. 197; **The Granger Collection:** pp. 5, 11, 190; © **Kate Kunz:** p. 69; **Lutfi Ozkok:** p. 61; **Newsweek:** p. 71; *New York Times Book Review:* p. 59; **Reuters/Bettmann:** pp. 47, 77, 92, 109, 112, 127, 130, 132, 140, 143, 168; **Reuters/Bettmann Newsphotos:** p. 163; **United Nations:** pp. 15, 22; **UPI/Bettmann:** pp. 31, 32, 89, 146, 157, 153, 187, 193, 212.

Issues of
Human Survival

1957
▼
Pope **Paul VI** (at the time Cardinal Giovanni Montini) organizes the Great Mission of Milan.

1964
▼
McNeill is awarded the National Book Award for History.

1963
▼
William McNeill publishes *The Rise of the West.* Montini becomes Pope Paul VI.

1960
▼
Montini lauds treaties reducing nuclear testing and nuclear weapons.

1966
▼
Paul Ehrlich and his wife Anne visit India.

1968
▼
Ehrlich publishes *The Population Bomb.* Paul VI publishes *Humanae Vitae,* reaffirming the Catholic Church's stance on birth control.

1969
▼
The Ehrlichs launch Zero Population Growth.

1976
▼
McNeill publishes *Plagues and Peoples.*

1970
▼
Ehrlich publishes *Population, Resources, Environments: Issues in Human Ecology.*

ISSUES OF HUMAN SURVIVAL

World War II ended with a world in confusion. The old colonial ties had been broken forever, leaving millions of people in Africa and Asia to invent new societal structures within which to solve problems of overpopulation and starvation. The problem's were aggravated by the industrial West, which was consuming far more of the world's energy and natural resources than the newly formed and lesser-developed countries. Furthermore, hundreds of years of land mismanagement and population growth had reduced nations such as India and Ethiopia to near starvation.

History, a different perspective. Earlier in the twentieth-century, historians such as Fernand Braudel had warned that providing enough food and curbing the spread of diseases were global matters, that everything that occurs anywhere on the earth is a concern of all the people. Braudel had written of history in global terms—attempting to bring together all human knowledge under the umbrella of history. In the 1960s and 1970s a number of people from all points of view began to share a broad view of the human predicament, its worldwide interconnectedness and its relation to history and the future. While some searched for solutions to immediate problems, others began to see the need to act in the present to preserve any human future at all.

William McNeill at the University of Chicago began both to identify current and historical problems and to suggest that solutions required different social structures and world teamwork. McNeill revived interest in world history when he published *The Rise of the West* (1963), in which he built a story of history not around events and individuals but around great world influences, such as the needs of economies, plagues and diseases, and power. This book and his later writings depict Western industrialization both as a tool for uplifting the human status, and as a tool so overused it has reversed its purpose.

Champion of the poor, opponent of war. A highly visible leader of the twentieth-century, Pope **Paul VI** championed the oppressed everywhere and took up the crusade for what he believed were the world's most pressing issues—war, poverty, and overpopulation. World War II had shown the tragedy of modern warfare and its use of atomic weapons. Paul IV campaigned vigorously for a reduction in world weaponry and for abolishing nuclear weapons. He was also torn by the explosion in population that threatened the psychological and physical stability of nations, particularly less-developed ones. The pope, however, was bound by Catholic doctrine and took a position on the issue of population very different from that of historians and scientists.

Buying time: The population explosion. Governments and scientific groups began to attack the world's disease and hunger problems with massive immunization projects and experiments designed to produce more food. For the most part, these proved to provide only short-term solutions where more serious and far-reaching ones were needed. Scientists like **Paul Ehrlich** and Garrett Hardin took up the call for action. Ehrlich and his wife, Anne, visited India and observed firsthand the horrors of starving people. They returned home to study population growth throughout history. The study was revealing—it indicated that within a relatively short period of time, if left unchecked, human population would explode and there would be one hundred people for every square foot of earth. Although natural solutions not controlled by humans might begin to remedy the population crisis long before it reached that point, the Ehrlichs issued a call to action in a 1967 journal article that became a 1968 book, *The Population Bomb.* The Ehrlichs argued strongly that measures needed to be taken immediately to curb population growth.

That same year, Paul VI issued his *Humanae Vitae,* in which he reaffirmed the church's long-standing opposition to birth control. Neither the pope nor the Ehrlichs believed that the issue of population was the only problem area for humanity, or that it was perhaps even the most important issue. But the Ehrlichs thought that limiting human population immediately was the only way to buy enough time to solve other issues, such as prejudice and war.

Thus the 1960s produced three schools concerned with humanity's problems. McNeill studied and recorded a broader history, believing that human history was evolving and would continue to change, creating perhaps a new set of problems and solutions. Paul VI was most concerned about very immediate issues and not at all interested in altering church positions that he saw as anchors to a changing human society. Paul Ehrlich and his wife Anne (the two worked almost always together), while concerned with issues of race, prejudice, and the threat of nuclear war, focused on buying time for solving these problems through population control.

Paul VI

1897-1978

Personal Background

The Montini family. Giorgio Montini, the father of Pope Paul VI, was a journalist and activist. From his home in Concesio, near Brescia, at the foot of the Alps in northern Italy, he published a widely read four-page newspaper. He was a devout Catholic who would be called by the church to head the Italian Union, which would lead Catholics back into Italian politics after a long church ban on such activity.

Giorgio married Guiditta Alghisi, a quiet, equally religious young woman of the Italian nobility. To these two was born a son on September 6, 1897, Giovanni Battista Enrico Antonio Maria Montini (the future pope). Giovanni was a physically weak child, and his mother's strength had been drained by his birth. Church tradition at the turn of the twentieth-century called for infant baptism within a few hours of birth, but the baby Giovanni was so feeble that his initiation into the church was delayed for four days.

The frailty of both mother and son continued so that it soon became necessary to place Giovanni in the care of a woman who would nurse the baby and take full care of him. Giovanni was sent to live with the family of Clorinda Peretti. Of course, his parents were frequent visitors and helped make all decisions about his upbringing.

Education. When he was old enough, Giovanni was enrolled in the Casare Arici Institute, where he studied until he

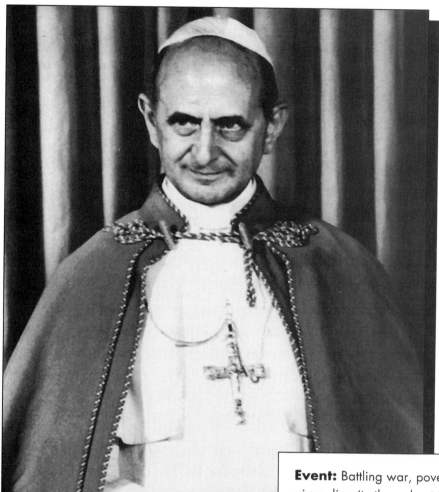

▲ **Paul VI**

Event: Battling war, poverty, and religious disunity throughout the world.

Role: Giovanni Battista Montini was elected Pope Paul VI, following John XXIII, one of the most popular popes of all time. An activist like his father, Paul VI fought for reform within the church and for control of war and elimination of poverty. He recognized the population explosion as a great world issue but refused to bend the centuries-old church traditions that might have helped reduce rapid population growth.

was seventeen years old. He then studied for two years at the Liceo Arnaldo do Brescia. Giovanni had continued to suffer persistent weakness and illnesses. In all those years, he had not attended school with any regularity, staying home most school days and being taught by one tutor or another. Still, at age nineteen, he graduated from the Liceo with highest honors.

Giovanni's education had aimed him toward a preparatory school at Padua and then the university there. It was intended that he would enter the legal profession. Giovanni, however, had long entertained another idea—he would become a priest. The normal path to this goal was to leave family and friends and live an austere life in a monastery. Giovanni's poor health, which included frequent attacks of severe asthma, however, had eliminated him from the wartime draft and certainly did not allow for a life in the damp, dark monastery. It was arranged that he would attend classes at the monastery and live at home.

The Brothers Montini

The child Giovanni, who would later become head of the largest Christian denomination, was the second of three sons born to Giorgio and Guiditta Montini. The oldest by one year was Ludovic, who would become a member of the Italian Parliament. Giovanni would become a priest and then pope. The youngest, Francisco, would become a doctor and a leader of the Italian resistance movement. All shared their parents' enthusiasm for action and their interest in other people.

For three years, Giovanni attended classes with the other priests in training while enjoying the benefits of staying at home and observing his parents at work. His father had never ceased his activism and had long campaigned for the church to lift the ban on participation in politics. When that ban was finally lifted, Montini was asked to take charge of a union organized to encourage Catholics to take part in politics. Thus, Giovanni earned the right to become a priest while continuing to experience life outside the church.

On May 20, 1920, Giovanni was ordained and soon held his first mass in the Sanctuary delle Grazie in Brescia. He would be a priest in nearby Verolanuova for only a short time. Bishop Gaggia, who had ordained him, had other plans for the frail, young priest. On November 20 Gaggia sent Giovanni from his home area to Rome, where he was to become a student living at Lombard College and studying philosophy at the Gregorian University of the Jesuits. He was also to study at the University of Rome.

Pope Pius XI took office in 1922 and appointed Cardinal Pietro Gasparri as his secretary of state with Monsignor Guiseppe Pizzardo as his assistant. Pizzardo had new ideas for the bright young priest from Brescia. Giovanni was already studying for two doctorates, but now he was to attend the Pontifical Academy of Noble Ecclesiastics to prepare for a career of diplomatic service for the church.

In 1923 Giovanni completed his studies and was sent immediately to Moscow to serve as second secretary there. Recalled within the year, Giovanni, now known as Don Battista, became student adviser of the University of Rome. He was soon an aide in the office of the Vatican secretary of state. Don Battista would maintain his base at Rome, serving the central government of the Catholic Church until 1954. In that period, he would become a very close adviser to Pope Pius XII, so close that some believed he would one day become the pope's secretary of state himself.

Instead, in 1954 the aged and feeble pope assigned Don Battista, now known as Father Montini, to be archbishop of Milan. After serving thirty years in the Curia, the central administrative body of the Catholic Church, Montini was being assigned to a position his friends thought was a Catholic Siberia.

> ## A Memory of Giovanni the Student
>
> "He was the best of us all, and we stood in awe of him, even though he was as thin as a toothpick.... What I remember most about him was his vocabulary. He had a way of expressing himself, even with us, so proper and precise, sticking to the point, a style none of us shared" (Clancy, p. 16).

Participation: Battling War, Poverty, and Religious Disunity Throughout the World

Archbishop of Milan. Milan was a busy industrial center that had grown by a one-third of a million people during World War II. The factory workers there had been ready listeners to Marxist recruiters. As a result, there was a large number of workers with Catholic upbringings who had become atheists and Marxists. Some of these lapsed Catholics had not attended a church for two decades.

Archbishop of the workers. Quietly, as was to be his style throughout his life, Archbishop Montini overcame his own disappointment at the assignment. He began vigorous efforts to rebuild the importance of the church in the lives of Milan workers. He reorganized his own archdiocese administration so that his aides were more available to talk and work with the people. The archbishop personally began to visit factories and businesses, never putting down those who believed in communism, but always teaching about the love of God and his importance to all people. He hired an architectural firm to design a church building that was quick and economical to erect, then ordered that the plans be used wherever a new church was needed for the expanding population. The new churches had playgrounds for children and quiet rooms in which older people could talk and meditate. Montini believed that each church site should be the community center for the workers.

As the new construction was increasing the visibility of Catholicism in Milan, the archbishop set out to make sure the new buildings were occupied. He continued to visit factories and talk with the workers, who gradually came to accept him for his honest and forthright speech. Montini talked about God and about human unity and equality.

Montini was a practical leader. Besides preaching and teaching, he organized a central office to handle the charitable work of the church in Milan and opened its doors so that anyone in need could be helped. When he visited factories, he showed a great interest in what the workers were doing and shared their pride in their work. And he set the tone for his future world service by speaking out against those who wanted to condemn people of other Christian sects or non-Christian religions, including Jews. To Montini all were brothers under God.

"Mission to Milan"

In 1957 Pope Paul VI, then archbishop, organized a "Mission to Milan." Nearly thirteen hundred priests, borrowed from all over northern Italy, gathered for a month to talk to the people wherever small groups could be gathered. The priests included twenty "flying priests" who scurried around Milan on motorcycles, jumping off at busy intersections to "open every heart to God" (Clancy, p. 117).

Paul VI traveled throughout the world to work toward world peace, religious unity, and the elimination of poverty.

Montini's work was successful. By the time he was recalled to Rome, only fifty-four thousand of the nine hundred thousand workers of the Milan area were members of the Communist Party. The rest were, for the most part, secure in the Catholic Church. He had accomplished the rebirth of the church without directly attacking any other beliefs.

A new pope. On October 9, 1958, Pope Pius XII, who had been called the pope of peace because of his antiwar efforts, died. He was replaced by Angelo Roncalli, Pope John XXIII. Already seventy-eight years old, John XXIII proved to be a world champion, advancing Catholicism throughout the world and pressing for peace and unity among all religions. Montini was an archbishop, but not yet a cardinal. He had no vote in selecting the new pope, but was pleased that the cardinals had selected a man who shared many of his own ideas. Not long after he was elected, John XXIII made Montini a cardinal and asked him to return to Rome once a year on the coronation date to administer communion to the pope. Cardinal Montini faithfully made the trip to Rome each year until John XXIII died in 1963. Montini was elected to be John's successor and was crowned Pope Paul VI.

A pope for the world. The new pope immediately began the work of reorganizing the church for greater world service. Paul VI's first act was to reform the church's central administration, the Curia. Traditionally a stronghold of Italians, the Curia was broadened to give more representation to Catholics from other countries. Then Paul indicated the direction his leadership would take by announcing that he would make a pilgrimage to the Holy Land (area comprising parts of modern Israel, Jordan, and Egypt). That trip gave him the opportunity to demonstrate his hope that some day all Christians, and then people of all religions, would come together in unity. In 1964 the pope began the healing process among Christians by meeting with Eastern Orthodox Church patriarch Athenagoras I in Jerusalem. This was the first meeting of the two leaders since the Eastern Orthodox Church broke away from the Roman papacy in 1054.

The papal platform. Paul worked persistently toward three objectives: world peace, religious unity, and the elimination of poverty. He traveled throughout the world to accomplish these

▲ Paul VI addressing the United Nations General Assembly, October 4, 1965. At the same time he was reorganizing the church leadership to bring newer ideas into action, Paul demonstrated his unwillingness to stray from old church positions in his stance on birth control.

goals, which became the topics of his encyclicals (papal letters written to all bishops), and, which were taken as directions to Catholics everywhere. In these encyclicals, the pope pleaded for world peace, opposed discrimination, and suggested actions. The wealthy, for example, were told in a 1967 encyclical that they had an obligation to help the poor. A year before, another paper had called for organizing a world peace conference.

Paul was, however, bound by Catholic tradition. When an issue concerning priests arose in 1967, he reaffirmed the church stance that priests should not marry or have sexual relationships. He also opposed new Italian laws permitting easier divorce. But even in matters of tradition, he sometimes proved flexible. For example, in 1966 he ruled that Catholics who married non-Catholics outside the church would no longer have their marriages unrecognized. Then, when he visited Latin America and saw the poverty there, he relaxed his antiwar position, stating that revolution was sometimes justified to correct the world's ills.

In general, Paul tried to make the Catholic Church more democratic. He expanded the number of cardinals to gain a fairer worldwide representation and brought archbishops and bishops into the decision-making processes.

World population and birth control. Perhaps one of Paul's greatest dilemmas was in the area of world population. He was an outstanding scholar and observer, realizing very early that the explosion in world population was potentially a great problem. If it continued its rapid growth, the burgeoning population could only lead to more starvation and more separation between those who had everything and those who had nothing.

As early as 1964, Paul appointed an elite commission to investigate birth control and population. He struggled with this issue for several years. Finally, however, Catholic tradition as defined by past popes won out over the population crisis. In 1968 he issued perhaps his most famous encyclical, *Humanae Vitae.* In it he warned against taking easy steps (such as birth control) to control world population. Birth control devices and procedures were not, he decided, acceptable to the church. Even the so-called rhythm method—an effort to synchronize sexual activity with periods when women are less likely to conceive babies—should not be overused.

Aftermath

Until his death, Paul VI continued to call for world peace and for the elimination of poverty. He also continued his world travels to accomplish these goals. In 1970, at age seventy-three, he completed a world tour that took him twenty-eight thousand miles in nine days. Not all of his messages were well received. On his visit to Bolivia, he was almost assassinated. Undaunted by this experience, the pope traveled to the Soviet Union the next year, visited Marshal Tito, the Communist leader of Yugoslavia, and paid a visit to Cardinal Mindszenty in Communist-controlled Hungary.

At the same time he was reorganizing the church leadership to bring newer ideas into action, Paul demonstrated his unwillingness to stray from old church positions in his stance on birth control. He spoke often and passionately about unity of all Christians, and on a trip to Asia expanded that plea to include all religions. Yet he was not prepared to yield any Catholic independence by uniting with the World Council of Churches, a union of Protestant denominations. He also changed the church structure permanently by ruling that cardinals over the age of eighty would no longer be eligible to vote for new popes. Later he declared that bishops and priests should be prepared to retire at age seventy-five.

Paul's work to open the Catholic Church to the world met with some success. When he died in 1978, a new pope was chosen from Poland, not from Italy. The ancient teachings of the church against uncharitableness, for the sacredness of marriage, and against all forms of birth control continued under the new pope.

For More Information

Clancy, John G. *Apostle for Our Time: Pope Paul VI.* New York: P. J. Kennedy and Sons, 1963.

Gordon, Thomas, and Max Morgan-Witt. *Pontiff.* Garden City, New York: Doubleday, 1983.

Hardin, Garrett. *Population, Evolution, and Birth Control: A Collage of Controversial Ideas.* San Francisco: W. H. Freeman, 1969.

Hatch, Alden. *Pope Paul VI.* New York: Random House, 1966.

William McNeill

1917-

Personal Background

Toronto. William S. McNeill's grandfather, also named William McNeill, grew up on Prince Edward Island in the Gulf of St. Lawrence at a time when that island was resisting becoming part of British Canada. He became speaker of the House of Parliament on the island and was a leader in the resistance against Canada and Great Britain. Nevertheless, some of his children moved to British Canada. The younger William McNeill was born in the far-western city of Vancouver on October 31, 1917. Before he became of school age, however, the family moved to the much larger city of Toronto.

McNeill attended Hudson Street School. As with most schools of that day, patriotism was a keynote of the school and heavily influenced the curriculum. Students rose each morning to sing the national anthem, "O Canada", and then worked through history lessons about British heroes—history lessons that McNeill later recalled made little mention of the French and Indians who played such a large part in settling the nation. The school history courses were in direct contrast to McNeill's personal experiences, for he spent each summer on his grandfather's farm. The area around the farm, like most of eastern Canada, was home to many French people—a living witness to their active role in founding the country.

The University of Chicago. Upon graduation from high school, McNeill left Canada to attend the University of Chicago.

▲ In *The Rise of the West* McNeill depicts Western industrialization both as a tool for uplifting the human status, and as a tool so overused it has reversed its purpose.

Event: Defining major issues in the modern world.

Role: Trained as a historian, William McNeill has continuously attempted to put such world issues as nationalism, population, and trade in historical perspective. His studies have led to his championing a "one world" concept.

He graduated with a degree in history in 1938 and in another year earned a master's degree. He then applied to Cornell University to pursue a doctorate and earned that degree in 1947. McNeill then returned to Chicago as an instructor in the history department. He remained there throughout his career as a researcher, teacher, and writer.

Universities frequently persuade outsiders to contribute money to establish "chairs," faculty positions that are then awarded to the most deserving faculty members. McNeill's teaching, research, and writing was soon so impressive that he was honored as the Robert A. Milliken Distinguished Service Professor in 1969.

Participation:
Defining Major Issues in the Modern World

Early writing. From the beginning of his term at the University of Chicago, McNeill used writing as a powerful tool in presenting his ideas about world history. His books began with a seemingly local issue in *Greed Dilemma: War and Aftermath,* but quickly began to present all the issues of world history, past and present, as if each major event casts its effect throughout the whole world.

Rather than viewing history as a series of alarming events like wars, or as a parade of famous characters, McNeill views it as a continuous story. His *History Handbook of Western Civilization* (1948), *America, Britain, and Russia: Their Cooperation and Conflict, 1941-1946* (1954), and *Past and Future* (1954) were written from that viewpoint.

In 1963 the University of Chicago Press published McNeill's greatest work to that date, *The Rise of the West: A History of the Human Community. The Rise of the West* was a very wide departure from the textbooks of the day. McNeill drew from all sorts of sources to present evidence for his main idea that throughout the history of humanity people have been attracted to new and potentially more exciting societies or civilizations. These societies served to stimulate their times, attracted others to their way of life, and endured until people were exposed to a new and more interesting society. New civilizations came from discoveries and innovations that made change more attractive: agriculture, the development of government, the growth of bureaucracy, the security of centralized government, the development of irrigation, the domestication of animals, the development of metals (giving rise to, for example, the Bronze Age, and later, the Iron Age), and refinements in religion. All these innovations were welcomed in societies that had peaked. McNeill, in effect, presents history as evolution.

The Rise of the West is really a history of human society, a history in which no single group develops by itself but as part of, as the book's subtitle suggests, "the human community." *The Rise of the West* presented such a clear and novel view of world history that it was awarded the National Book Award for history in 1964.

McNeill's ideas seem to hold true for recent history. He wrote in *The Rise of the West:*

> The rise of the United States and the Soviet Union to world pre-eminence since World War II was indeed only another instance of a familiar historical phenomenon: the migration of military-political power from more anciently civilized but less effectively organized heartlands to regions nearer the frontier. Machine technology, which within recent memory carried western Europe to the apex of its world domination, seems now, like Zeus of ancient fable, to have turned ruthlessly upon its parent (McNeill 1963, pp. 794-95).

Significance. McNeill concludes that modern technology has made it necessary to gather even greater areas under single domination. This might result in global or at least semiglobal governments, although his own view of history does not suggest that great improvements in societies are encouraged by large governments, which tend to become bureaucratic. In fact, McNeill suggests that

McNeill on the Evolution of History

"Civilizations may be likened to mountain ranges, rising through aeons of geologic time, only to have the forces of erosion slowly but ineluctably nibble them down to the level of their surroundings. Within the far shorter time span of human history, civilizations, too, are liable to erosion as the special constellation of circumstances which provoked their rise passes away, while neighboring peoples lift themselves to new cultural heights by borrowing from or otherwise reacting to the civilized achievement" (McNeill 1963, p. 249).

bureaucratic complacency might be the best thing that modern society can expect from its governments—that poorly functioning bureaucracies might be stabilizing influences in a stirring world. (The major twentieth-century accomplishments, he says, seem to be blurring between economics and politics, between peace and war, even between human and nonhuman.) Human engineering—controlling human nature by altering genes and DNA—in this atmosphere of bigger and bigger political-economic communities might make it possible for leaders to develop less independent, and therefore more manageable, people. McNeill warns in the closing chapter about the two-edged nature of power. Still, by and large, McNeill presents a modern world that is full of hope and prepared for either the good or the evil that comes from greater power.

Aftermath

Following the path of such earlier historians as Fernand Braudel, McNeill continues to study and write about history as events entwined in a single global picture. He has written *A World History* (1967) and *The Shape of European History* (1974), continuing to examine history as an evolution of ideas, peoples, and events that, because of its evolving nature, can be useful in predicting future issues.

In 1976 McNeill published another unusual look at history, an investigation into diseases and their roles in changing societies. *Plagues and Peoples* was first inspired by a question: How could the Spanish, with fewer than six hundred men, and not vastly superior weapons, have managed to subdue a highly organized society in the Americas of more than one million citizens? One possible answer—smallpox.

In all his teaching and writing, McNeill presents history not as a sequence of dates and famous characters, but in the ancient Greek meaning of the subject, as an inquiry. In fact, he has invited

---

McNeill's World Outlook

"Men some centuries from now will surely look back upon our time as a golden age of unparalleled technical, intellectual, institutional, and perhaps even artistic creativity. Life in Demonsthenes' Athens, in Confucius's China, and in Mohammed's Arabia was violent, risky, and uncertain; hopes struggled with fears; greatness teetered perilously on the brim of disaster. We belong in this high company and should count ourselves fortunate to live in one of the great ages of the world" (McNeill 1963, p. 807).

his students to read and make their own interpretations of what he has proposed. He believes that his books contribute knowledge only if they cause readers to question, think, and react. The preface to *The Rise of the West* states his intention: "I hope my book may be richly and repeatedly misunderstood" (McNeill 1963, p. vii).

For More Information

McNeill, William H. *History Handbook of Western Civilization.* New York: Harper and Row, 1948.

McNeill, William H. *Plagues and Peoples.* Garden City, New York: Anchor Press, 1976.

McNeill, William H. *The Rise of the West: A History of the Human Community.* Chicago: University of Chicago Press, 1963.

Paul Ehrlich

1932-

Personal Background

Early life. There was no clue in the Ehrlich family that the baby boy born in Philadelphia on May 29, 1932, would become a famous biologist. His father, William, was a salesman and his mother, Ruth (Rosenberg), a teacher of Latin. Still, Paul Ehrlich's interest in animals came early—he claims to have spent his childhood chasing butterflies and dissecting frogs.

Before Ehrlich reached high school age, the family, which included a daughter, Sally, moved from Pennsylvania to Maplewood, New Jersey, a town less than ten miles east of Newark. Ehrlich attended Columbia High School in Maplewood. Sometime in his high school days he read *Road to Survival,* a book by William Vogt that called attention to the problem of supplying food for a growing population. Ehrlich thought that Vogt was clearly saying that if society did not do something about this growing problem, the human population would "go down the drain." He became committed to a career in biology.

Entomology. At age seventeen, Ehrlich graduated from Columbia High and enrolled at the University of Pennsylvania with a major in zoology. For the next eight years he was a college student, earning his first degree at Pennsylvania, then moving to Kansas to earn a master's and a doctorate. Meanwhile, he took every opportunity to work in the field. He joined a party survey-

▲ **Paul and Anne Ehrlich**

Event: Popularizing environmental issues.

Role: Having seen the problems of over-population firsthand on a visit to India, Paul Ehrlich and his wife, Anne, became environmental crusaders—predicting disaster unless civilization changed drastically and immediately. Although they did not see population control as the total solution to environmental crises, the Ehrlichs did consider it the first and best means for buying time to make ecological adjustments.

▲ Slums in the village of Cross Roads, South Africa, 1978. After passing through the squalid, overpopulated Delhi slums, the Ehrlichs began to seriously study the urgency of the overpopulation crisis.

ing biting flies on the Bering Sea and spent some time surveying insects in the Arctic. Ehrlich's research on insects would eventually take him to Africa, Alaska, Mexico, the Pacific Islands, and Asia.

A year after he earned his master's degree, Ehrlich married another researcher in biology, Anne Fitzhugh Roland. (The two would have one child, a daughter, Lisa Marie.) Part of a college teacher's job is to conduct research and write about the findings. Anne often joined her husband in both the research and the writing. For example, when he wrote his early book *How to Know the Butterflies* (1960), Anne was the illustrator.

Ehrlich's college work progressed very well, so well that after he had earned the master's degree he was granted a fellowship by the National Institute of Health to study parasitic mites. He used the fellowship at the University of Kansas and the

Chicago Academy of Science. Ehrlich completed the work for his doctorate in 1957 and two years later joined the faculty of Stanford University. Ehrlich, at six feet two inches, with blue eyes and dark hair, soon developed a relaxed classroom style that was witty but serious. He had a natural flair for dramatics that made him popular as a speaker. His research at the university focused on controlling insect pests with their natural enemies rather than with pesticides. Specifically, he experimented with controlling butterfly caterpillars by using ants. His foreign travels and continued study of biology, however, led him to understand that there was a human population problem.

Participation:
Popularizing Environmental Issues

The awakening. In 1966 the Ehrlich family visited India, staying in Delhi. Returning to their hotel by taxi one night they passed through a section of Delhi slums. The taxi moved slowly because of the masses of people. People were begging, using the streets for bathrooms, herding animals, eating, washing, sleeping, arguing. In this nightmarish scene it appeared that people were everywhere. The experience changed Paul and Anne's intellectual understanding of the population issue into an emotional one, and the Ehrlichs began to study seriously the urgency of the crisis.

Beginning to spread the concern. After more than a year of study, Ehrlich was ready to present his ideas to the world. First he published an article in the British Journal *New Scientist* in December 1967. This article was soon published in the *Washington Post,* a leading U.S. newspaper. Ehrlich's was the voice of doom. World populations had increased rapidly and for many years people had struggled to find ways to feed their growing numbers. But Ehrlich claimed that this struggle was over and lost. He predicted that massive famines would strike human populations between 1970 and 1985.

In this first written work on the population explosion, Ehrlich suggested some unusual stopgap measures: the United States should begin to control its population immediately by placing a tax on diapers and baby foods. Moreover, it should take a leadership role by encouraging other nations to take similar actions. Where the situation seemed hopeless—in India, for example—the United States and other nations should stop encouraging population growth by ceasing to send emergency food supplies.

Ehrlich and Hardin. Other scientists had also come to the conclusion that overpopulation was a major environmental issue that might someday lead humans to the same fate as the dinosaurs. One of these scientists, biologist Garrett Hardin, likened the human situation to living in a lifeboat. There was only limited room in the boat, Hardin concluded, and those of us in it (those living in places with enough food and supplies) should protect ourselves and abandon the people of Africa and Asia, in which the population was already beyond sustainable limits. Ehrlich took a slightly broader view by comparing the earth to a spaceship of unknown dimensions. What we needed to do immediately, he believed, was to determine the optimal capacity of the spaceship—to decide the ideal limit of world population, and then take steps not to exceed that limit. Otherwise, according to Ehrlich, Hardin, and others, no effort to supply more food would be enough.

Going public. Ehrlich followed his initial article with a full-length book, *The Population Bomb* (1968), in which he presented startling evidence illustrating the dangers of overpopulation.

The book brought Ehrlich immediate attention. He was interviewed on late-night television on the *Johnny Carson Show* and publicized in such newspapers as the *Washington Post*. He successfully launched Zero Population Growth, a political action group pushing for concerted measures to bring about population control, including tax incentives to limit family size.

Aftermath

Soon after his initial dramatic presentation of the population problem, Ehrlich began to see this issue as only one (although the major one) of many social issues. In fact, he began to talk about population control as only the beginning—a way to buy time to solve other global issues such as racism and war. Since these other issues were, for the most part, divisive, they might also be considered possible solutions to the population issue, one of two approaches. Humans can, Ehrlich thought, control birth rates or wait for famines, wars, and diseases to control them.

Ehrlich's initial views about population also changed as he realized that no single segment of the population could survive without other segments. The people of Africa and India could not be excluded from the spaceship. Along with population control, the world needed to conserve its environment through wise use of resources. A large part of the problem, as Ehrlich posed it, was the wide difference between "underdeveloped" and "industrialized" peoples in their consumption of world resources.

> ## Ehrlich on Planet Earth
>
> "Spaceship Earth is now filled to capacity or beyond, and running out of food. And yet people traveling first class are, without thinking, demolishing the ship's already overstrained life support systems" (Ehrlich 1970, p. 3).

Ehrlich continues to teach and campaign for ecological sanity. He is an associate of the Center for the Study of Democratic Institutions and a member of the editorial board of the *International Journal of Environmental Science.*

For More Information

Ehrlich, Paul. *The Population Bomb.* Rivercity, Massachusetts: Rivercity Press, 1968.

Ehrlich, Paul. *Population, Resources, Environments: Issues in Human Ecology.* Redwood City, California: W. H. Freeman, 1970.

Rorvik, David M. "Paul Ehrlich." *Look,* vol. 34 (April 21, 1970), pp. 42-44.

Scientific and Technological Breakthroughs

1971

Bill Gates starts Traf-o-Data with Paul Allen.

1959

Lewis and Mary Leakey discover hominid fossils in Olduvai Gorge.

1974

Donald Johanson discovers "Lucy" in Afar Triangle. Ed Roberts unveils home computer kit, the Altair.

1975

Edward O. Wilson publishes *Sociobiology: The New Synthesis.* Johanson excavates "First Family" of hominids. Gates and Allen form Microsoft Corporation.

1992

Wilson publishes *The Diversity of Life.*

1985

Microsoft releases Windows.

SCIENTIFIC AND TECHNOLOGICAL BREAKTHROUGHS

What makes us human? How and when did our humanity begin? How has it developed through time? And how will it carry on into the future? These questions have seemingly always occupied humanity's thinkers, but recently scientists and historians have come up with answers to some of the puzzles of the past, as well as a clarified vision of the future of humanity.

Many qualities separate us from other animals. The ability to produce language is one thing frequently put forward as defining our humanity. Another ability often thought to define us as human is our skill at making tools, at creating and improving technology. We do not have direct evidence of when language first came into being. We do, however, have direct evidence of humankind's early stone tools, dating from about two million years ago.

It was at about this time, anthropologists like **Donald Johanson** believe, that the first humans developed from more apelike ancestors. The earliest species that scientists consider truly human is in fact named for its toolmaking ability: *Homo habilis,* or handy man. Before *H. habilis,* Johanson believes, our ancestors were creatures that walked fully upright like us but had much more apelike heads and faces. Johanson and others have found the fossilized bones of such creatures, called australopithecines ("ah-stray-lo-**pith**-uh-sines"), in Africa, where they and humans are thought to have evolved.

It is not clear whether australopithecines used stone tools. Some tools have been found near australopithecine fossils, but these may have been left there by later humans. Nor is it clear that, as Johanson claims, some australopithecines were the ancestors of modern humans. Johanson's rival Richard Leakey argues that humans go back much further than we now have evidence for, and that australopithecines were "cousins" of humans, not ancestors. Most scientists, however, now tend to side with Johanson.

Johanson's most famous discovery, a female australopithecine skeleton called Lucy, lived over 3 million years ago. Then came *H. habilis* (2.5 million years ago) and *H. erectus* (1.5 million years ago). Modern humans, *H. sapiens,* did not appear until just 250,000 years ago.

By contrast with these lengthy time scales, human civilizations in Mesopotamia, India, China, and Egypt did not begin until about five thousand years ago, around 3000 B.C., when humans first started using metal instead of wood and stone to make their tools and weapons. Since that time, humankind has polished toolmaking skills to a degree that people in other ages could never even have imagined. Tools and technology have put us in space, put our vehicles on distant planets, and extended our vision (through telescopes) to the edge of the known universe. And in the last quarter of the twentieth century, an amazing computer revolution has made much of this same technology available to the average person in the West. One man, **Bill Gates,** seems to have foreseen the whole revolution.

As a teenager in Seattle, Washington, in the 1960s, Gates got hooked on computers, which then were large, expensive, and slow. Gates, however, was convinced that one day they would be not only faster but also smaller and cheaper—in fact, cheap enough to be common items in people's homes and businesses. He also knew that all these computers would have to have programs in order to be useful. A business genius as well as a computer whiz, Gates wanted to write those programs and sell them to the public. Today, his company Microsoft is the world leader in software, and Gates himself is one of the world's richest men. Microsoft programs can be found on nearly all of the world's millions of personal computers. In acting on his vision, Gates helped make it come true.

Technology can indeed be seen as central to both humanity's past and its present. What about its future? Our tools have given us an edge over other animals, but scientists such as **Edward O. Wilson** think that this edge might cut two ways. Our tools include the bulldozers and machetes that today are hacking away at the world's remaining rain forests. Playing a vital role in recycling our atmosphere, the rain forests are also home to a vast number of unknown plants and animals. Beautiful in their own right, they have a stunning richness and variety that are of great value to humanity, especially in developing new drugs to treat diseases.

Biologist Wilson sees it as a dangerous mistake to be throwing away this "biodiversity." Pollution, however horrible, can be cleaned up, but an extinct species is simply gone forever. Who knows which newly extinct plant might have been like the rosy periwinkle, a rain forest flower now used as a tool to treat cancer? The flower's original habitat, the island of Madagascar, is now in danger of being completely stripped of its rain forest. Wilson leads a movement he calls New Environmentalism, which emphasizes the practical value of such habitats for improving human life. Perhaps our road to the future lies in finding our tools in nature's diversity, as we did in the past and as some of us—those who live in the disappearing rain forests, for example—still do.

Donald Johanson

1943-

Personal Background

Childhood. Donald Carl Johanson was born on June 23, 1943, in Chicago, Illinois, where his parents had emigrated from Sweden. His father died when he was two years old. Soon afterward Donald and his mother moved to Hartford, Connecticut, where she supported them by working as a cleaning woman.

Curiosity. As Donald grew up in Hartford, he was lucky enough to find an older man who took an interest in his upbringing, an anthropology teacher named Paul Leser. In Leser's apartment Donald found shelves and shelves of books on anthropology, the study of humankind. Many of the books were about fossils, the bones left behind by once living things that have turned slowly into rock over hundreds of thousands of years. Some fossils are millions of years old, so they act as "documents" that anthropologists and others can use to find out about creatures that lived long before our time. They are found in ancient soil and rock formations and have to be dug out very carefully.

For several decades in the twentieth century, anthropologists had been finding fossils of early hominids, or humanlike creatures, in Africa. These scientists had come to believe that Africa, home of many species of apes, was where early humans first evolved. When Leser went off on trips to Africa, Donald found his own curiosity and excitement stirred up.

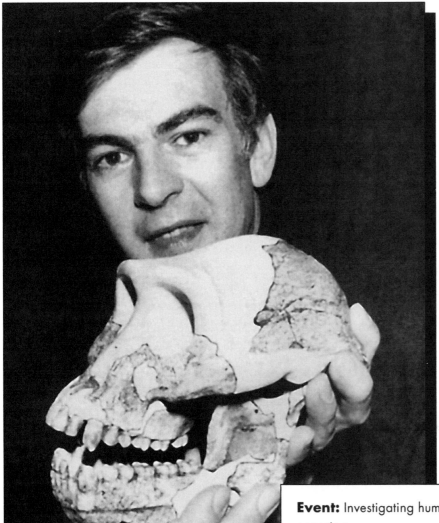

▲ **Donald Johanson and Lucy**

Event: Investigating humankind's early ancestors.

Role: In 1974 young anthropologist Donald Johanson found a partial, humanlike skeleton in Ethiopia that proved to be more than three million years old. It was the fossilized remains of a young female, whom Johanson and his coworkers named Lucy. Johanson has since won wide agreement with his claim that Lucy and her kind were the ancestors of modern humans.

▲ Louis and Mary Leakey digging for bits of bone and tools in Tanzania, July 1961. Excited by Louis Leakey's work, Johanson switched his major from chemistry to anthropology.

Louis Leakey and Olduvai Gorge. Donald knew he wanted to be a scientist when he grew up, but Leser warned him against a career in anthropology. Anthropologists don't make much money, Leser said. So when he began college, at the University of Illinois, Donald chose chemistry as his major. Already, though, in his last year in high school, he had read an article in *National Geographic* that made chemistry seem boring to him. Written by famed anthropologist Louis Leakey, the article described Leakey's discovery in 1959 of a two-million-year-old hominid skull at Olduvai Gorge in Tanzania, Africa. The very name Olduvai Gorge seemed strange and romantic to Donald. A few years later, in 1964, Leakey announced the discovery at Olduvai of an early human skull that was just as old. Leakey's discovery had pushed humankind's presence on the earth back at least one million years earlier than anyone had previously thought.

Excited by Leakey's work, Johanson switched his major to anthropology. After finishing college, he began graduate work at the University of Chicago, under Clark Howell, a leading American anthropologist.

Participation: Investigating Humankind's Early Ancestors

To Africa. Johanson's work as a graduate student was supposed to focus on chimpanzees and what can be learned from studying their teeth. But what he really wanted to do was look at the skulls that had been found in Africa. He needed an excuse. The hominid skulls were still being studied, and Johanson told Howell that he might be able to put together a helpful catalog of them. (The hominid skulls, including teeth, were very similar to those of chimps.) Howell, Johanson wrote later, "fell for that" (Johanson 1994, p. 123) and gave him permission. So in early 1970, a very excited Johanson left for a summer in Africa.

There Johanson met Mary Leakey, Louis's wife, and the Leakeys' son Richard. Both were also leading anthropologists (it was Mary who had actually found the famous hominid skull in 1959). Johanson spent some time helping at a "dig" that Howell was leading at Omo, Ethiopia, getting used to camp life and watching as the scientists handled the fossils that were found. He also got to see all of the best-known hominid skulls. Slowly, he began to get a feel for them as living, breathing beings who actually walked around, ate, had children, and died on the African plains so very, very long ago. He took a similar trip the following year, working at Omo again.

Hominids

Humans are the only surviving species of the hominid (humanlike) family, which split off millions of years ago from ancestors we share with the family of apes. The scientific name for modern humans is *Homo sapiens* (thinking man). Earlier humans, *H. erectus* (upright man), lived as early as 1.5 million years ago. Louis Leakey's announcement in 1964 was of a still older version that he called *H. habilis* (handy man), about two million years old. Other hominid species, which like *H. erectus* and *H. habilis* are now extinct, are not considered human. They are called australopithecines (pronounced "ah-stra-lo-**pith**-ah-sines"; it means southern apes). When Johanson went to Africa, the oldest known hominid was *Australopithecus africanus,* or the southern ape from Africa, first discovered in 1924 by South African anthropologist Raymond Dart. Some australopithecines lived in the time of *H. habilis,* while others lived even earlier, a confusing situation when anthropologists tried to figure out how they were related to humans.

33

Afar region. It was at the end of his second season that Johanson met a young French geologist named Maurice Taieb, who was studying the geology of a region in Ethiopia called the Afar Triangle. As Taieb described his work, it dawned on Johanson that the area sounded like a perfect place to find very old fossils. Layers of rock as old as four million years had been pushed to the surface, where they were being worn away by Ethiopia's seasonal rains. Taieb said that fossil bones were all over the place, simply lying there waiting to be found after heavy rains had washed the surrounding dirt away. Since he was not an anthropologist, Taieb did not care so much about the bones, but he thought somebody ought to look at them in case they were important. It did not take Johanson long to decide that he was going to be the one to study the bones. He arranged to join Taieb there the next spring, before the season's digging at Omo began, to explore the possibilities.

Scrounging expedition equipment. Borrowing camping equipment and two battered Land Rover trucks, Johanson and Taieb headed into the rugged Afar region in early 1972. It was everything Johanson had hoped it would be. The bones he found seemed to be about two to three million years old. There were fossil bones of pigs, elephants, and even the nearly complete skeleton of an ancient monkey. Experts can tell how old animal bones are by their shapes. Pigs, for example, evolved by stages that are well known. A fossilized pig bone or tooth is like a yardstick for measuring the age of a hominid fossil found in the same layer of rock. If hominid fossils are found nearby, the bones of other animals would help date them.

It was unusual for a young student to go off on his own like this, but Johanson was determined to lead a full-scale expedition into the Afar region. By scrounging for money and equipment, he managed to attract the other scientists he would need to make up a team. In the fall of 1973 Johanson and his team set up camp at Hadar, next to the Awash River in the Afar Triangle.

Knee joint. Johanson was staking his whole career on the expedition. He didn't even have his graduate degree yet. If he failed to come through with a worthwhile find, he would be stuck with a reputation for bad judgment. Finding money for future research would be next to impossible. Such were the worries he was pondering one day as he scuffed what looked like a hippo rib with his foot. Then he looked more closely. It was the upper end of a shinbone, and a few yards away he saw its mate, the lower end of a thighbone. From the size, he figured they had belonged to a monkey. He put them together to make a knee joint—and from the way they fit, he suddenly knew that this was no monkey knee. It was the knee joint of a creature that had walked upright on two legs, unlike any ape or monkey. It was the knee joint of a hominid, a hominid who had lived between three and four million years ago.

Lucy. With such a find, Johanson was able to get enough money to continue at Hadar the following year, in the fall of 1974. Before much time had gone by, several hominid jawbones had been turned up. Then one morning Johanson woke up feeling especially lucky. He went out with an assistant, Tom Gray, to examine a nearby gully. Finding nothing, they were about to leave. Johanson, however, remembering his feeling of luck, took one last look around and spotted a small piece of what looked like an arm bone—then a piece of skull—then part of a thighbone, all hominid, and all seemingly belonging to the same creature. Three weeks later, when the whole area had been carefully excavated, the team had nearly half of a complete female skeleton. Nothing like it had ever been found. Other fossil finds had always been limited to just a few pieces. In addition to being more complete, this skeleton was also much older than any found previously. They named her Lucy, after the Beatles' song "Lucy in the Sky with Diamonds," which someone played over and over at the camp celebration.

First Family. Lucy made headlines and secured a place for Johanson at the very top of his field. He was offered a good job at the Cleveland Museum of Natural History. Completing his graduate degree, he began teaching. The following year, 1975, the Hadar expedition found even more spectacular fossils, about 350 pieces of bone from at least thirteen individual hominids, known as the "First Family." The next year's biggest find was a number of primitive stone tools, about 2.5 million years old and probably fashioned by *H. habilis*. After that, war in Ethiopia prevented the team from returning.

35

Australopithecus afarensis. After finding Lucy and the "First Family," Johanson and his coworkers had to figure out exactly what they were. That meant that if Lucy was a previously unknown species they also had to name her. It would take several years of careful measurement, thought, and, as it turned out, argument. They knew she was a hominid, because she clearly walked upright. At first, Johanson thought she was an early human. Soon after finding Lucy, however, he had begun working with a graduate student named Tim White, whose judgment he had come to value highly. White argued that Lucy was not a human at all. In the end White persuaded Johanson that he was right. In 1979 the two published a landmark paper that introduced what they claimed was humanity's oldest ancestor: *Australopithecus afarensis,* the southern ape from Afar.

Another great rift. Hadar, Omo, Olduvai Gorge, and other leading fossil sites in East Africa are part of the geological system known as the Great Rift Valley. Visible from space, the rift (or division) was created by two plates of the earth's crust moving away from each other. Like a giant scar, it runs more than three thousand miles, from central Mozambique to northern Syria. The rift's features make it an ideal place to find old rocks and the fossils they contain.

Johanson's success at Hadar created another rift, one that has scarred the world of anthropology. Before Lucy, anthropology had been dominated by the glamorous Leakey family. Louis and Mary Leakey had worked at Olduvai since the 1930s, making major breakthroughs in our knowledge of human origins. Their brilliant son Richard had carried on the family's work—and its talent for publicity. Leakey announcements always got headlines. And though he had a strong streak of independence, Richard Leakey supported the "Leakey" line when it came to human origins. Louis and Mary had always insisted that humanity was very old, and that the australopithecines were not our ancestors at all, but our cousins. They believed that our real ancestors, creatures that were basically human, had lived just as early as the australopithecines. Their discovery of *H. habilis*—skeletal remains that could be recognized as human—supported this idea. Then along came Donald Johanson. Not only did Johanson match the Leakeys in his fossil-finding ability, he added insult to injury by showing a Leakey-like nose for publicity. And as the final straw, his conclusions went dead against the "Leakey" line.

Ancestors? Lucy and her kind were almost twice as old as *H. habilis,* about 3.5 to 4 million years, compared with 2 million years for the oldest *H. habilis* remains. This age difference in the finds has led most anthropologists to support Johanson's claim that *Australopithecus afarensis* was the ancestor of *H. habilis* and later humans.

Aftermath

Further work. After a confrontation on television in 1981, in which Richard Leakey drew a big *X* through a diagram of Johanson's, the two have not spoken. Since then, Leakey has spent much of his time on interests other than anthropology, such as protecting wildlife in his native Kenya. Johanson, meanwhile, has written several books and hosted a *Nova* series for public television titled *Ancestors: In Search of Human Origins.*

Johanson's first two marriages failed because of the time he had to put into his work, including long field trips. His third wife, Lenora, however, an award-winning documentary filmmaker, has interests that allow them to work together (on the *Nova* series, for example). Since 1981 Johanson has headed the Institute for Human Origins in Berkeley, California, which he founded to pursue his research. In 1992, after years of refusal, the government of Ethiopia that had come to power in the late 1970s allowed him to return to dig at Hadar. He made several important finds, including the nearly complete skull of a male *Australopithecus afarensis.*

For More Information

Johanson, Donald, and others. *Ancestors: In Search of Human Origins.* (Companion volume to the *Nova* series.) New York: Villard, 1994.

Johanson, Donald, and Maitland Edey. *Lucy: The Beginnings of Humankind.* New York: Simon and Schuster, 1981.

Lewin, Roger. *Bones of Contention: Controversies in the Search for Human Origins.* New York: Simon and Schuster, 1987.

McAuliffe, Sharon. "Lucy's Father." *Omni,* May 1994, p. 34.

Edward O. Wilson

1929-

Personal Background

Growing up in the South. Edward Osborne Wilson was
born on June 10, 1929, in Birmingham, Alabama, to a family
whose ancestors had settled in Alabama in the early nineteenth
century. His father, also named Edward Osborne Wilson, was
proud of the family history but had never really settled down himself. Wilson's mother, Inez Freeman, and his father divorced
when he was seven.

Divorce was rare in those days, especially in the South.
While his parents' marriage was breaking up, Wilson was sent to
spend the summer with a family who took in young boarders. The
family lived in Paradise Beach, Florida, within sight of Alabama on
the shores of northwestern Florida. For a young boy curious
about the sea, Paradise Beach was well named. Every morning
Wilson would get up and go off for hours to roam along the beach
in search of whatever he could find. He came back only for meals
and to sleep. Later, when he had grown up, he would have no
memory of the family there, but his memories of combing the
beach that summer stayed strong and fresh. He came across
shimmering jellyfish, caught sea trout and blue crabs, and
glimpsed the dark shadows of flat stingrays cruising along the
bottom in the shallow water. The sea was a dark, deep, and myste-
rious place that summer for the young boy on his own.

▲ Edward O. Wilson

Event: Exploring nature's order and diversity.

Role: Naturalist Edward O. Wilson, a world authority on ants, led the way in creating a new area of biology called sociobiology. Sociobiologists study the way animal societies (such as ant colonies) work and then try to figure out how such societies have come about. Wilson warns that we put our own species in danger when we reduce the world's great variety of other life forms.

Insects. Wilson later wrote that his experiences that summer shaped his life by giving him the sense of wonder about nature that led him into biology. His life was further shaped by a fishing accident that left him almost blind in his right eye. Combined with poor hearing when it came to high sounds like birdcalls, his limited vision left him with a narrow list of choices when it came to pursuing his interest in nature. He "turned to the ground," he says in his autobiography, *Naturalist,* to "the animals that can be picked up between thumb and forefinger and brought close for inspection" (Wilson 1994, p. 15). In other words, he concentrated on insects.

Ants. By the time he was sixteen, Wilson had put in long hours exploring the southern countryside and studying its animals. He had spent one summer collecting water snakes in a swamp. Preparing for college, he decided to train for a professional career in entomology, the study of insects. If he was really serious, he thought, now was the time for him to choose a particular insect to specialize in. And Wilson was serious—he wanted nothing less than to become a world expert. He decided to specialize in ants, which he loved and had spent time studying already. He would prepare for his college studies by conducting a survey of ants in Alabama, attempting to list all of the state's ant species.

Participation:
Exploring Nature's Order and Diversity

New species. It would be a big job. Wilson ordered a copy of the best book on ants, William Morton Wheeler's *Ants: Their Structure, Development, and Behavior.* He bought glass bottles in which to collect ants and built glass-sided cases in which to start colonies of his own to observe. Writing to entomologist Marion Smith in Washington, Wilson asked for advice. Smith sent him an encouraging letter and a key that he could use to classify the ants that he found. He kept up his collecting during his college years at the University of Alabama, where he graduated in 1949. Along the way, he discovered a new species of ant and named it. He also studied the imported fire ant, which was spreading north from the seaport town of Mobile. There it had probably come ashore from a ship. As with other fire ants, its sting felt like a flame held close to the skin.

Dacetines. In 1950 Wilson began graduate work at the University of Tennessee. The following year, however, he decided to transfer to Harvard University in Massachusetts because he had been in touch with a leading myrmecologist (ant expert) there named William Brown. Brown offered him support and advice, and suggested that he give up his survey of Alabama ants, which Wilson was still working on. Instead, Brown said, Wilson should study a single type of ant, but close up, in great detail. That way, he could come up with some new ideas and information that would really add to knowledge of ant behavior. At Brown's suggestion, Wilson began a detailed study of a particular kind of ant, called dacetine, common in the South. There are many species of dacetine ants, but they share the same way of hunting. Dacetines have wide, powerful jaws that can be opened 180 degrees. With their jaws wide open, they slowly sneak up on their prey until they are close enough to snap their jaws shut on their victim. Wilson published several articles on dacetines in academic journals like the *Quarterly Review of Biology.*

Lasius. In 1951 Wilson moved to Boston to finish his graduate degree at Harvard, home of the world's biggest ant collection. At Harvard, he settled on a "sensible" subject to study for his doctoral degree (Wilson 1994, pp. 140-41). He picked a kind of ant called *Lasius,* whose forty or so species are commonly found all over North America. *Lasius* would be cheap, quick, and easy to study. Then, Wilson hoped, he would be free to travel to wild tropical jungles and study the rare species that he hungered for. And that was what happened. He spent the summer of 1952 traveling around the United States with his friend Tom Eisner, living out of Eisner's 1942 Chevy, camping and collecting examples of *Lasius.* (Eisner was also collecting ants for his thesis.) Then, in the spring of 1953, Wilson was elected to the Harvard Society of Fellows. Offered to only a small number of graduate students, this honor gave him three years of financial support to go off and study whatever and wherever he pleased, no strings attached. It was a great opportunity, and Wilson wasted no time in taking advantage of it.

▲ In 1951 Wilson moved to Boston to finish his graduate degree at Harvard, home of the world's biggest ant collection.

Tropics. By June, Wilson was headed for Cuba, where he teamed up with several other Harvard entomologists. Now he would finally get to live the exploring life. In Cuba he fulfilled a dream he had had since the age of ten, when he had read a *National Geographic* article by William Mann. A famous myrmecologist, Mann had collected ants in Cuba forty years earlier and had found a beautiful new species of bright emerald green. Now Wilson went to the same area and himself found the rare green ants. He also picked up a foot-long pet lizard he named Methuselah. From Cuba he flew to Mexico's Yucatán peninsula and then plunged alone for several weeks deep into the rain forests of the Mexican coast. He collected as he went, and among the dozens of species he popped into glass jars were two that turned out to be previously unknown.

Love—and more tropics. Back in Harvard for the school year, Wilson met a pretty young Bostonian named Renee Kelley.

They fell in love and became engaged. In March 1954, though, Wilson made plans for a longer collecting and exploring trip, this time to New Guinea and the South Pacific. That November, he and Renee said goodbye for ten months, and Wilson got on a plane for the long flight across the Pacific. There, too, he followed in William Mann's footsteps, trekking through the rain forests of islands like Fiji, New Guinea, and New Caledonia. He swung south to Australia, where he risked the painful bites of the aptly named bulldog ant and went in search of the fabled *Nothomyrmecia macrops*. This yellow ant—found only once, years before—was known as the "missing link" of ants, an important piece in the puzzle of how ants came to be. Wilson never found it. Not until 1977 did an Australian collector finally come across it, letting out a shout of "I've got the *Notho-* bloody *-myrmecia!*" (Wilson 1994, p. 180).

Thinking about evolution. Wilson returned to Boston in September 1955, and he and Renee got married a few months later. Finishing his doctorate, he began his career by accepting a job offer from Harvard, where he would stay for his entire professional life. But like English naturalist Charles Darwin more than a century before, Wilson found himself filled with scientific ideas that arose from his journeys. (Darwin had come up with his theory of evolution after his famous five-year voyage as naturalist on the H.M.S. *Beagle*.) As Wilson established his reputation in the 1960s and 1970s, these half-formed ideas stayed in the back of his mind, slowly taking shape. Other biologists that he worked with had similar ideas, and slowly a pattern emerged in their work. This pattern, like the one seen earlier by Darwin, also had to do with how life evolved or changed over time and generations. But whereas Darwin had thought mostly about how animals' bodies had changed as they evolved, Wilson and his coworkers began

Natural Selection

Nature "selects" as evolutionary traits certain accidental physical characteristics that best serve an animal population in a specific environment. For example, the evolution of giraffes might have happened like this: some giraffe ancestors millions of years ago happened to be born with longer necks, and they were thus able to eat higher leaves. Their different eating habits might have allowed them to live in places where shorter-necked giraffes could not. Thus a community of long-necked giraffes might have banded together and formed a "pool" that contained more genes for long necks. Only over hundreds of generations did giraffes evolve into their present form. Sociobiology investigates how natural selection may also have shaped animal behavior, including behavior in complex societies.

to think about how animals' *behavior* had evolved. They especially began to study social behavior, which occurs whenever animals (including humans) act together in groups.

Social animals. As an ant expert, Wilson was in a perfect position to think about social behavior, for ants are one of the clearest examples of a social animal. Other examples in the insect world are bees, wasps, and termites. Among mammals, lions and apes are social because they live in groups. One thing all social animals seem to share is the need for rules to govern their behavior. How did these rules arise? Wilson and others began to think that they arose in the same way as physical characteristics, through what Darwin called natural selection.

Hamilton and Altruism

For Wilson a turning point in his life came when he encountered the work of a young biologist named William Hamilton. In the 1960s, Hamilton tackled the problem of altruism, or behavior by which an individual sacrifices himself for others. Such behavior is common among social insects. Altruism seemed to go against traditional ideas of natural selection, which suggested that every individual fights for survival. Hamilton instead showed that altruism serves as a way of helping an individual's *genes* to survive, by improving the chances for his relatives, who share his genes. Sociobiology thus suggests that genes, not individuals, are the driving force behind evolution. The idea is summed up by the title of a popular book by sociobiologist Richard Dawkins, *The Selfish Gene* (1976).

Sociobiology. Biology in the 1950s was dominated by molecular biologists, who had begun their area of study with sensational discoveries about cell structure and DNA. Old-style biologists like Wilson felt left out in the cold. They did not even have a name for what they did, other than plain old biology. Wilson suggested "evolutionary biology," and the name stuck. Instead of thinking about cells and molecules, evolutionary biologists thought about animals and whole populations of animals.

"Evolutionary biology," based on Darwin's ideas, did not seem to cover everything, however. The society of an ant colony, with its workers, its soldiers, and its queen, had always seemed hard to fit in with the idea of natural selection. So had the complicated rules that chimpanzees obey in their societies—or human social rules, for that matter. Yet in founding the new science of sociobiology, as the new field came to be called, that was exactly what Wilson and the others thought they could do. In 1975 Wilson published a lengthy book in which he summed up all the findings and ideas of sociobiology. Called *Sociobiology: The New*

Synthesis, it led to wider acceptance of sociobiology by other scientists, many of whom had earlier doubted the ideas held by its advocates.

Biodiversity. By the 1980s Wilson's sociobiology work on a wide range of animals led him to take a new attitude toward life and nature. He had never been an activist before, but he now began to grow more and more disturbed by accounts he read of the destruction of tropical rain forests. So an activist he became, lecturing and writing about the environment and especially the disappearing rain forests. For it is in the rain forests, with their rich yet fragile ecosystems, that the stunning variety of life is most threatened. Biodiversity, (biological diversity, or the number of species in a given habitat or area) Wilson argues, is valuable not just in itself but also for its potential in medicine and other areas of human life. Although Wilson did not invent the word "biodiversity," in the public mind he, more than any other scientist, is linked to it.

> ## Wilson on Biodiversity
>
> "Biodiversity is our most valuable yet least appreciated resource. Its potential is brilliantly illustrated by the maize species *Zea diploperennis,* a wild relative of corn discovered in the 1970s.... The new species is resistant to diseases and unique among living forms of maize in possessing perennial [year-round] growth. Its genes, if transferred into domestic corn ... could boost corn production around the world by billions of dollars. [*Zea diploperennis*] was found just in time, however. Occupying no more than 10 hectares [25 acres] of mountain land, it was only a week away from extinction by machete and fire" (Wilson 1992, p. 281).

Aftermath

Awards. Wilson has won numerous awards, including the National Medal of Science and the Craaford Prize of the Royal Swedish Academy of Sciences, which is given in fields for which there are no Nobel Prizes. Two of his books, *On Human Nature* (1978) and *The Ants* (1990), have won Pulitzer Prizes, and *Sociobiology* was voted the most influential book of the century by the International Animal Behavior Society.

For More Information

Wilson, Edward O. *The Diversity of Life.* New York: Norton, 1992.
Wilson, Edward O. *Naturalist.* Washington, D. C.: Island, 1994.

Bill Gates

1955-

Personal Background

The Gates family. William Henry Gates III was born on October 28, 1955, in Seattle, Washington. His parents, William Henry Gates, Jr., and Mary Maxwell Gates, were (and are) prominent in Seattle society. Bill Gates, Jr., is a partner in a large Seattle law firm, while Mary Gates takes a leading part in local organizations. Bill Gates III is their only son. He has two sisters, Kristi, a year older, and Libby, nine years younger.

Lakeside. From the start, young Bill (as the third Bill Gates, he is called "Trey" by his family) was an unusual child. It was not just that he was unusually bright. He was also unusually competitive. Whatever he did, he had to do it *better* than anyone else. He had to *win*. Bill's parents found a school that seemed to suit his personality. Called Lakeside, it was a small, private prep school, the most exclusive in Seattle, where competition and independent thinking were the order of the day. Enrolling at the age of eleven, Bill was a Lakeside "lifer," as students who stayed from seventh through twelfth grades were called.

PDP-10. Soon after Gates enrolled, the school bought a teletype machine that, for a fee, could be hooked up to a computer in downtown Seattle. The computer itself, called a PDP-10, was far too expensive for the school to buy. The teletype machine was basically a printer and keyboard through which the user could

▲ **Bill Gates**

Event: Building the Microsoft software empire.

Role: At nineteen, computer expert Bill Gates founded one of the most successful companies in history, the Microsoft Corporation. In creating the computer programs that gave Microsoft dominance in the software industry, Gates helped bring personal computers into wide use among the general public. He has thus been a major figure in the computer revolution of the 1980s and 1990s.

communicate with the PDP-10 over a telephone line. Visiting the computer room with his math class, Gates was immediately fascinated. For Gates and a few others at Lakeside, the new computer room quickly became the focus of life. One of the others was Paul Allen, a quiet boy who was two years older than Gates. The two quickly became friends, spending as much time as possible playing with the computer. "We were off in our own world," he later said. "Nobody quite understood the thing but us. I wanted to figure out exactly what it could do" (Wallace and Erickson, p. 22).

Hacking. A large part of figuring out what a computer could do meant learning to understand programs, the sets of instructions that a computer uses to operate. Gates and Paul both picked up quickly on how programming or "software" works. Soon, Gates was "hacking" or creating game programs of his own. The first was a simple tick-tack-toe game. Then he wrote a lunar lander game, in which the player had to land on the moon before using up the craft's fuel. When Gates was in eighth grade, he and Allen, with others, were hired (in exchange for free computer time) to find "bugs" or problems in the PDP-10 software. Unlike most of his friends, however, Gates was as interested in making money as he was in computer programs. In 1971, as a high school junior at Lakeside, he formed a business with Paul Allen, then a freshman at Washington State University. Called Traf-O-Data, it offered to help cities control traffic by using a computer to analyze traffic patterns. Gates pursued several such business ideas in high school. He could not wait to get out in the real world.

Participation:
Building the Microsoft Software Empire

Harvard. In 1973 Gates headed off to Harvard University in Cambridge, Massachusetts. Paul Allen, who had dropped out of college, was working in nearby Boston for Honeywell, a computer manufacturer. Gates had scored a perfect 800 on his math achievement test and planned to major in math. At Harvard, though, he met students who were as good at math as he was—or better. He changed his major to prelaw. He also took up poker,

▲ Gates on stage at the Gershwin Theatre in New York following a promotional effort introducing a new version of Windows software, October 1992. The hour-long, $1-million effort featured dancers, an original score, and Gates.

winning and losing thousands of dollars over the next few years at Harvard. Ignoring his classes for the most part, he played poker at night and spent the days at the university's Aiken Computer Center. He rarely showered, shaved, or changed his clothes.

Altair. One day in Gates's sophomore year, Allen showed him the latest issue of *Popular Electronics* magazine. The cover photo featured a small metal box with several switches and lights on it. "World's First Microcomputer Kit" ran the headline (Wallace and Erickson, p. 67). Called the Altair, it was the first personal computer. It cost $397, came in kit form, and had to be put together. Allen and Gates saw that, however primitive, the Altair was a huge step forward. It was also, they believed, the beginning of a revolution—one that would end with computers as common in people's homes as televisions. However, its inventor, Ed Roberts, needed a "language" for the Altair, a language that the computer could use to run programs. Without a language, the Altair would be next to useless. A few days later, Gates and Allen called Roberts in Albuquerque, New Mexico, and told him they had the language he needed. They said they had written a version of BASIC, a widely used computer language, that Roberts could use on the Altair. They had done nothing of the sort—but they offered to sell it to him, anyway.

Microsoft. When Roberts accepted, they promised delivery in a few weeks. They now had to keep the promise. Yet they not only did not have a BASIC for the Altair, they did not even have an Altair to work with. Allen had to figure out how to make Harvard's PDP-10 work like an Altair. Gates's job was to write the language itself, to make a BASIC that would fit in the Altair's small memory. It took them eight weeks of nearly constant work (after a month, a friend named Monte Davidoff pitched in), and after seemingly endless all-nighters they were done. In late February, Allen flew to Albuquerque to meet with Roberts and test their version of BASIC. It worked. Roberts now began offering the Altair for sale, and the orders flooded in. Gates and Allen would receive money for each machine sold with their BASIC.

First, though, Gates and Allen had to create a formal business partnership. In the summer of 1975, they did so. They called their company Micro-Soft, short for microcomputer software. Soon they dropped the hyphen, making it just Microsoft.

Ready to rock and roll. Gates and Allen set up Microsoft in Albuquerque, close to Roberts's company, MITS, which produced the Altair. They hired a few employees, young men like themselves who could write fun programs for use on the Altair. Though Microsoft BASIC was a good start, both knew where they wanted

▲ In creating the computer programs that gave Microsoft dominance in the software industry, Gates helped bring personal computers into wide use among the general public.

to go with the company. One of the company's first employees later said that Gates "always had the vision from the time I met him that Microsoft's mission was to provide all the software for microcomputers" (Wallace and Erickson, p. 95). For a year and a half, out of respect for his parents' wishes, Gates stayed in college while helping Allen run the business. By the time he dropped out and moved to Albuquerque to work there full-time, thousands of Altairs had been sold. Microsoft now had several young programmers, a few of them former Lakeside students whom Gates and Allen had recruited. Rock and roll music blared out of their offices as they worked, something that visitors to Microsoft still hear.

Despite the Altair, Roberts's company failed to stay in business. By the time he sold it, however, Microsoft had found other customers for its BASIC, including National Cash Register (NCR) and General Electric. And though MITS had gone under, small new computer companies seemed to be popping up everywhere. Gates's vision was coming true. He was determined that Microsoft would be ready with software to fuel the oncoming computer revolution.

IBM. Gates, Allen, and Microsoft did very well over the next few years. Although Gates's family was very wealthy, he never needed any help from them, even in the company's early days. He spent little money on himself, but he did buy a green Porsche. And in the winter of 1978-79 his rapidly growing company moved to the Seattle area. Home for Gates and Allen, Seattle would remain Microsoft's headquarters, though the company's address would change as it grew.

About a year and a half after the move to Seattle, in July 1980, Gates was approached by computer giant IBM (International Business Machines). Long the leader in the large-computer business, IBM had earlier decided not to get into microcomputers. But IBM had seen the explosive growth of new companies like Apple, which had led the way with small desktop computers. (At the time, in fact, Allen was working on products to sell to the growing number of Apple owners.) Now, IBM leaders had changed their minds and were eager to catch up. They wanted Microsoft to write the operating system, the basic program, for their new, top secret Personal Computer.

Culture clash. Called Big Blue because its employees were known for wearing formal blue suits, IBM was a strange partner for Microsoft. No one at Microsoft—least of all Gates himself—ever wore a suit. It was a case of corporate culture clash. On one of his trips to meet with IBM, Gates was late because he had to stop on the way from the airport to buy a tie. Microsoft, although growing fast, was still a small company, with fewer than twenty-five employees and total income of about $7 million a year. IBM, by contrast, was a worldwide corporation, with thousands of employees and an income counted in the billions of dollars.

MS-DOS. To come up with their Personal Computer (PC) quickly, IBM's team decided to use parts they could buy from other computer companies, rather than starting from scratch (as Apple had, for example). This decision turned out to be a very important one for the computer industry—and for Bill Gates and Microsoft. IBM designed the PC around a computer chip for which an operating system had already been written. Microsoft now simply bought the rights to that operating system and made the changes necessary to suit the needs of the PC. The result was Microsoft's PC-DOS, or PC Disk Operating System. Microsoft made money on each PC that IBM sold with PC-DOS, and IBM sold five hundred thousand PCs within two years.

IBM, however, could not patent its PC. Its decision to use bought parts meant that the PC could be copied by other companies. As these other companies turned out cheaper "IBM-compatible" computers, they too needed operating systems and were forced to turn to Gates and Microsoft. Microsoft had the license for the DOS used on the millions of IBM-compatibles purchased by the mid-1980s. Sales of MS-DOS, or Microsoft Disk Operating System, were soon generating hundreds of millions of dollars a year for Microsoft. MS-DOS became the most widely used operating system in the world. Bill Gates had proved the truth of Microsoft's slogan: "We Set the Standard."

Applications. Despite his huge success with MS-DOS, Gates wanted Microsoft to offer more than just an operating system. He also wanted to offer a wide selection of good programs to run on the operating system. The programs that generally sell best are those designed to help the user do a certain job, such as word processing or accounting. Called applications programs, they had already been introduced by other companies, such as WordPerfect and Lotus. Microsoft introduced such programs (called Word and Excel) in the early 1980s, but

Monopoly?

In entering the market for applications programs, Microsoft has been accused by rival companies of creating a monopoly. Since Microsoft manufactures the standard operating system, when it upgrades MS-DOS its applications programmers will have an unfair advantage, the other companies charge. The Microsoft applications programmers will know what changes are going to be made in MS-DOS and will have a head start when it comes to making their applications work with the new version. The government investigated such charges beginning in the late 1980s but ruled that no monopoly existed.

they did not perform as well as Gates had hoped. With typical determination, he kept his programmers working on them until they had a healthy share of the market.

Windows. The next area Gates focused on was the area dominated by Apple's popular Macintosh computers. Apple took a different approach from that of IBM. Instead of having the user type in special coded commands, Macintosh screens had easy-to-use pictures (called icons) that could be selected to give the commands. The icon then opened a "window" on the screen. This system proved very popular, especially among those who had little or no experience with computers. Apple computers were known for being "user-friendly." When Gates introduced his own version of such user-friendly software for the PC, called Windows, in 1985, it too turned out to be hugely popular. Later versions have "set the standard," as MS-DOS did. In August 1995 computer users lined up at software outlets at midnight eagerly awaiting the release of Windows 95, the biggest unveiling of any computer product ever.

Going Domestic

"Love Bytes: Computer whiz Gates ends his reign as America's richest bachelor" ran the headline in *People* magazine when Gates got married on New Year's Day, 1994. His bride, the former Melinda French, was a Microsoft marketing executive whom Gates had met at a company picnic in 1987. The two will live in the $35 million home Gates is building near Seattle. Constructed partly underground, the house will have wall-size high-resolution computer screens in each public room.

Going Public. In 1986, after successes with Windows and Microsoft applications, Gates and his newly hired president, Jon Shirley, "went public" with the company. That is, they offered Microsoft shares for public sale on the stock market. It took a lot of preparation on Gates's part, but it has paid off. The stock is now worth so much that Gates, who owns nearly half of it, is one of the world's richest men. Other Microsoft employees, not highly paid in cash but given generous stock benefits, have also profited. Several are now millionaires.

Aftermath

Multimedia. The next big thing in computers, Gates believes, is "multimedia," which in the computer world means CD-ROMs. These are compact discs on which all kinds of information is stored—not only text, but sounds, movies, animation, photos, games, and pictures. Multimedia has been around since the early 1990s, and Microsoft has already introduced leading products, like its best-selling interactive encyclopedia, Encarta.

For More Information

Ellis, David. "Love Bytes." *People,* January 17, 1994, pp. 42-44.

Meyer, Michael. "Culture Club." *Newsweek,* July 11, 1994, pp. 38-41.

Wallace, James and Jim Erickson. *Hard Drive: Bill Gates and the Making of the Microsoft Empire.* New York: HarperCollins, 1992.

Zickgraf, Ralph. *William Gates: From Whiz Kid to Software King.* Ada, Oklahoma: Garret Educational Corp., 1992.

Hard Core

Bill Gates is feared throughout his now giant company, but few of his employees would have it any other way. Called Microserfs, they consider themselves the cream of the crop—and they know Bill Gates agrees, or they would not have a job. He keeps on top of everything, despite having thousands of employees. On the college-like Microsoft "campus" at Redmond, near Seattle, a "Gates" meeting is something people rehearse for in fear. Yet those who survive his sharp and often rude questions, his famous shouting fits, or his attempts to get them to back down know that they are "hard core." Being hard core is what it takes to win, and winning is what Microserfs do best.

Literature as a Political Tool

1921

Pablo Neruda wins first recognition for his poetry.

1974

General Kjell Laugerud Garcia becomes president of Chile.

1969

Toni Morrison publishes her first novel, *The Bluest Eye.*

1950

Neruda wins the Soviet International Peace Prize.

1948

Gabriel Gonzales outlaws the Communist Party in Chile; Neruda continues to champion communism through his writing.

1977

Morrison wins the National Book Critics Award for best fiction for *Song of Solomon.*

1978

General Fernando Lucas Garcia becomes president of Guatemala; begins reign of terror against Indians and Ladinos.

1979

Amnesty International estimates number of Guatemalans killed by government forces since 1970 at 50,000 to 60,000.

1980

Rigoberta Menchu helps organize a strike of 80,000 Guatemalan workers.

1993

Morrison becomes the first African American to win the Nobel Prize for literature.

1992

Menchu is awarded the Nobel Peace Prize.

1988

Morrison is awarded the Pulitzer Prize for literature for *Beloved.*

1983

Menchu writes autobiography, *I, Rigoberta Menchu: An Indian Woman in Guatemala.*

LITERATURE AS A POLITICAL TOOL

Writers and history. Throughout history, writers have used their special skills to influence governments and to encourage change, and the twentieth century has offered many opportunities for such activities. World War I upset a longstanding balance among European nations and resulted in the rise of several new nations there. Long before the war, writers such as Karl Marx had been challenging the industrial societies of the West and proposing utopias in which all citizens shared equally in the wealth of the world. Because the war resulted in arbitrary divisions and continued confusion in Europe, within twenty years the experiments in democracy gave way to both fascist and communist dictatorships—and the beginnings of a new war. World War II resulted in a division of powers among the former Allies and continued tensions in Europe and the Americas. The separation of democracy and communism resulted in a cold war that was reflected in Vietnam—a new battle that caused Americans to challenge the methods of their own government and to begin a whole new series of challenges for "rights." While countries and peoples in Latin America and elsewhere continued to look to communism as a sound alternative to capitalism, the capitalist nations, particularly the United States, began to search for improvement through civil rights actions and demands of equality for women. Organizations such as the National Organization for Women began to play a strong role in enacting new laws to strengthen equality.

Neruda. Chile was one of those nations in which communism, whether its advocates were in or out of power, continued to ferment. Raised in view of the poverty of the rain forest region, **Pablo Neruda** became a world-famous poet while championing Marxism. His writing eventually won him several peace awards from the Soviet nations. Poets in Latin America were widely respected and often rewarded with government positions that did not interfere too much with their writing. Thus Neruda became involved in the diplomatic missions of Chile, used these missions to stir up trouble, and found it necessary to exile himself even though he had become a member of the Chilean legislature. A strong supporter of the leftist president Salvador Allende, Neruda was distraught when Allende was overthrown. Some claim that this bitter disappointment led to Neruda's own death.

Menchu. In the Central American country of Guatemala, leftist ideas were also popular and were equally suppressed by a series of military presidents. In Guatemala, however, survival was the main issue among the more than half of the population that was of Indian heritage. The Indians of Guatemala attempted in the 1970s and 1980s to organize and demand land reform and other economic measures that would allow them to rise out of bitter poverty. Their efforts were met with reigns of terror carried out through unions of large landowners and the corrupt governments. One family caught up in the suffering was that of Vicente and Tum Menchu. Fighting for their land, for subsistence, and for the rights of other Indian and Ladino peasants resulted in the deaths—frequently unspeakably violent—of every member of the family except one daughter, **Rigoberta.**

Morrison. In the United States, blacks and other minorities, along with women, were themselves organizing to demand equality. **Toni Morrison,** a university instructor, black woman, and brilliant editor, began to explore the plight of blacks and women from the viewpoint of black society. Beginning with *The Bluest Eye* (1969), her novels explored the experiences, both present and historical, of black Americans and women. For her story

Haunted by Their Nightmares

BELOVED
By Toni Morrison.
275 pp. New York: Alfred A. Knopf. $18.95.

By Margaret Atwood

"**B**ELOVED" is Toni Morrison's fifth novel, and another triumph. Indeed, Ms. Morrison's versatility and technical and emotional range appear to know no bounds. If there were any doubts about her stature as a pre-eminent American novelist, of her own or any other generation, "Beloved" will put them to rest. In three words or less, it's a hair-raiser.

In "Beloved," Ms. Morrison turns away from the contemporary scene that has been her concern of late. This new novel is set after the end of the Civil War, during the period of so-called Reconstruction, when a great deal of random violence was let loose upon blacks, both the slaves freed by Emancipation and others who had been given or had bought their freedom earlier. But there are flashbacks to a more distant period, when slavery was still a going concern in the South and the seeds for the bizarre and calamitous events of the novel were sown. The setting is similarly divided: the countryside near Cincinnati, where the central characters have ended up, and a slave-holding plantation in Kentucky, ironically named Sweet Home, from which they fled 18 years before the novel opens.

There are many stories and voices in this novel, but the central one belongs to Sethe, a woman in her mid-30's, who *Continued on page 49*

Margaret Atwood is the author of "The Handmaid's Tale," "Bluebeard's Egg" and the forthcoming "Selected Poems II."

▲ *New York Times Book Review* **critique of Morrison's** *Beloved;* **in her works Morrison explores the plight of blacks and women from the viewpoint of black society.**

of a black family in *Beloved,* (1987), Morrison was awarded the Pulitzer Prize for literature. In 1993 Morrison became the first African American to win the Nobel Prize for literature.

Pablo Neruda

1904-1973

Personal Background

Early life. José del Carmon Reyes was a railroad man—rough and powerful enough to earn and hold the position of conductor on the repair trains that continually poured fresh rock to anchor the rails over the rugged mountains of the Chilean rain forest. After he courted and wed Rosa de Basoalto, a pretty schoolteacher, the two established a home in Perral, a small farm community in central Chile. It was there that Rosa gave birth to the couple's only son, Pablo, born July 12, 1904. (His real birth name was Ricardo Eliecer Neftali Reyes y Basoalto.) Less than a month after the birth, Rosa lost her long battle with tuberculosis and died.

Three years later, José married again, this time to Trinidad Caudira, whom Pablo would later describe as an angel. It was Trinidad who cared for him while his father was away on the railroad, taught him religion, and encouraged him to explore and to write.

Neruda first attended school at the Liceo de Temuco, where he soon proved to be an avid reader. But much of his early education came at home. The Neruda family lived in a compound with several other families involved with the railroad. Their large, comfortable house and the courtyard around which the homes of the compound were built were popular meeting places for the railroad

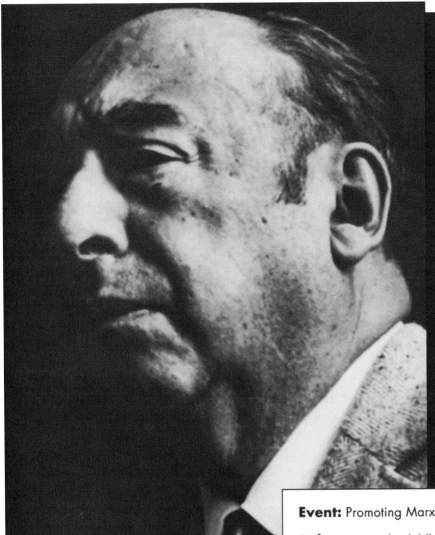

▲ **Pablo Neruda**

Event: Promoting Marxism in Chile.

Role: From early childhood, it seemed that Pablo Neruda was destined to be a poet. Born in the tropical forests of Chile, he championed the cause of the Chilean peasants in his powerful, irreverent, and colorful writing even as a schoolboy. His poetry brought him fame, respect, torment, and positions in the government of Chile.

men and travelers. These visitors soon learned that the young Neruda loved walking in the forests and collecting objects from them. His collection was soon increased by a steady flow of gifts the railroad workers brought him. Later, as an adult with many other adventures filling his memory, Neruda would remember some of these gifts and the wonders of the forests. Throughout his life he would be a keen observer of nature and continue to marvel at the variety of animals and plants in his native land.

But poetry was Neruda's greatest thrill. Even as a child, Neruda would wander off by himself to write bits of poems. At the age of sixteen he moved to a teaching college, the Instituto Peidagogico in Santiago, where he planned to study French, supposedly with a desire to become a teacher. There is little evidence, however, that Neruda ever planned to become anything but a poet. By the time he left for the Instituto, he had already published some verses in the local newspaper in Temuco, and he continued to write. Within a year of his move to Santiago he had entered the poetry competition at the Spring Festival of Santiago. His poem, "Canción de la Fiesta," won first prize, and Neruda began to be recognized as a fine poet.

Participation: Promoting Marxism in Chile

Road map. From his early days at the university, Pablo Neruda was an active Marxist (a follower of the economic and political theories of the German political philosopher Karl Marx), writing poetry and otherwise working to make a socialist state of Chile. His work reflects the political history of his nation.

Poetry and politics. After winning the Santiago poetry prize, Neruda began to divide his time between poetry and his support of leftist Chilean leaders. Even though he used his poetry to expound the basic ideas of Marxism, his growing fame earned the attention of the ruling conservatives. All parties of Chilean politics had carried out a long tradition of honoring native poets by appointing them to diplomatic positions. Neruda was given this recognition in 1927, and in 1933 he was assigned as consul to Buenos Aires, Brazil. The next year he was sent to Spain, where he served as Chilean consul at Barcelona and then at Madrid.

Neruda's major job was to rescue as many Chileans as possible, for Spain was in the midst of a civil war. Neruda began to identify Chilean citizens who wanted to leave the country and to arrange for a ship to take them home. Conditions in Chile were little better than in Spain, however. The Chilean government was weak and indecisive. No sooner had Neruda begun his rescue effort than his own government wired that the mission was to be abandoned. When Neruda called the Chilean leadership and protested, the project was reinstated, only to be abandoned once again a short time later. That was long enough for Neruda to partly accomplish what he had been sent to do. Several hundred Chileans were put aboard a tired and worn ship bound for home.

That achievement was an embarrassment to the Chilean government, but not as touchy an issue as Neruda's other major exploit in Spain. The Chilean government had been careful not to take sides in the Spanish revolution in order to preserve trade relations with Spain. But Neruda was an outspoken Marxist and therefore opposed to any government that did not lean toward "democracy." In 1931 Spain had declared itself a "democratic republic of the workers" governed under a constitution; the republic had the backing of socialists and communists. The various liberal factions in Spain, however, had never been brought together to shape a truly functional government. In 1936 General Francisco Franco, a right-wing commander of rebel troops, flew to Spain from Spanish Morocco, where a Nationalist rebellion against the left-wing government of the young Republic of Spain was already in progress. Franco's arrival on July 17 triggered riots throughout Spain and brought revolution to that country. Although Franco would not win complete victory until 1939, the civil war created a touchy situation, and Chile preferred not to take sides. Without asking for the opinion or consent of his superiors, Neruda announced that the Chilean government stood firmly on

Latin America and Poetry

In the early part of the twentieth century, poets were highly respected in Latin America. They entertained the people and spoke for them. Poets took the lead in movements to improve the lot of the very poor in most Latin American countries. As a poet, one could expect to rise to important positions in the schools and in government. Neruda rose, on the strength of his poetry and the friends it brought him, to positions in the diplomatic departments of Chile and to the national Senate.

How Chilean Politics Informed Neruda's Work

Date	Chilean politics	Neruda activities
1890-1920	Chile enjoys parliamentary government under Jorge Monti.	Neruda writes about nature and the passions of youth.
1920-1925	Arturo Alessandri Palma rules a prospering Chile but usurps Parliament's authority.	
1927-1931	Chile is ruled by a military dictator, Carlos Ibáñez del Campo, who encourages U.S. financial intervention but does not help the peasants of Chile.	Neruda continues to write about nature and love, but he also uses his writing to push for political reform. His writing helps end Ibáñez's rule as a general strike stops most activities.
1933-1938	Arturo Alessandri Palma is returned to power. Though a conservative, he tries to walk a middle path by adding leftists to his government.	Neruda unchangingly writes very personal poetry about his daily experiences, which now include experiences in the Chilean diplomatic corps.
1938-1941	Pedro Aguirre Cerda, a liberal, leads Chilean reforms, but is hampered by a gigantic earthquake.	Neruda returns from Spain to write about nature and to support political reform.
1941-1946	Juan Antonio Rios, a liberal reformer, governs Chile.	In poetry and action, Neruda supports Rios and is elected to the Chilean parliament.
1947-1952	Gabriel Gonzáles Videla becomes president on a coalition platform but soon outlaws the Communist Party.	Now more outspokenly Marxist than ever, Neruda leaves Chile for exile in Mexico.
1952-1958	General Ibáñez is returned to power by popular vote. The Communist Party is again legal.	Neruda returns to Chile to live a quiet life as a poet.
1958-1964	Jorge Alessandri Rodriguez is president of Chile, heading a mixed government (Marxist Salvador Allende wins 29 percent of the popular vote.	Neruda supports Allende, devotes much of his writing to Marxism.
1964-1970	Liberals, but not Marxists, lead Chile under Edward Frei Montalva.	Neruda continues his support of the Marxist Allende.
1970	Salvador Allende leads Marxist reform in Chile.	Neruda writes approvingly of Allende.

the side of the republican regime of Spain and against Franco. The angry Chilean president recalled Neruda to explain his actions.

Neruda returned to Chile and continued to write his autobiographical form of poetry. He included compositions about nearly every event that took place in his life. His poetry, however, unerringly told about the Chilean predicament and drew him to political activity. In 1944 he was elected by a strong majority to serve in the Chilean Senate. There he worked with President Juan Rios to bring reform to Chile, including greater local control of the mostly foreign-held nitrate and copper industries—the mainstays of Chilean wealth.

Exile. President Rios died in 1946 before he could fully carry out his program of reform. His replacement was Gabriel Gonzáles Videla, who was a liberal and had been forced to make an alliance with the communists to win election. He appointed three of them to his cabinet but soon removed them and banned the Communist Party from activity in Chile altogether. Neruda had continually worked for Marxism. In view of the government's action, he decided it best to leave Chile and moved to Mexico. There he continued to write his poetry until 1953, when he returned to Chile.

Peace Prizes. Neruda purchased a home on Isla Negra, one of Chile's small islands, intending to concentrate on his poetry. By that time, he had gained international acclaim for his Marxist political work. In 1950 he had been awarded the Soviet International Peace Prize. The Lenin Peace Prize and the Stalin Peace Prize followed in 1953.

The ban on the Communist Party in Chili was to continue until 1958. During those five years, Neruda had to work underground in support of his ally, Salvador Allende.

Aftermath

Communism in Chile. Slowly the movement lead by Allende and supported by Neruda gained strength. Eleven years after the Communist Party had been banned, it succeeded in being reinstated. In the presidential election of that year (1958), Allende gained a very much improved 29 percent of the vote. Then in 1970, after having lost another election to Edward Frei Montalva six years earlier, Allende became the first Marxist president of Chile. While Neruda lauded his actions in poetry and prose, Allende initiated the most widespread reform ever in Chile. He worked through the Parliament to nationalize (take over by the government) many of the foreign-owned industries in Chile. (Two U.S. mining companies, for example, owned virtually all of Chile's copper industry.) Although Allende's reforms were announced before his election and were at first popular, they soon brought division within the government and among the people. High inflation resulted from the poorly planned takeovers of major industries. Hunger became common among Chileans, and the people began to riot and rebel.

Only three years after he took office, Allende was thrown out of office in another military coup, led by General Augusto Pinochet Ugarte. Pinochet held a tyrannical dictatorship over Chile despite persistent rebellion until 1990. A Chilean government committee continues to investigate Pinochet's inhumane acts.

In the Pinochet takeover of 1973, every active Marxist and many more supposed enemies of the new government were subjected to humiliation, torture, and even death. Allende was killed by the Pinochet forces. Neruda's house was searched, which made him indignant—"Generals, traitors: see my dead house" is how one of the poems he wrote at this time began (Neruda in Poirot, p. 88). Some say that the indignity of having his home disturbed and the fear that Pinochet would soon dispose of him contributed to Neruda's final illness.

In 1973 Neruda was taken to a hospital in Santiago, where he died on September 23. He left a legacy of poems that vividly por-

---

Some Examples of Neruda's Poetry

On Chile's earthquakes and volcanoes:

Who would have said that the earth
with its ancient skin would change so
  much?
It has more volcanoes than yesterday,
the sky has new clouds,
the rivers are flowing differently.

On turtles:

Patriarch, long
hardening
into his time,
he grew
weary of waves
and stiffened himself
like a flatiron.
(Neruda 1969, pp. 7, 99).

tray his own life and those of the people of Chile. His poetry earned him an honorary degree of doctor of literature from Oxford University, bestowed in 1965, just eight years before his death.

The complete works of Pablo Neruda, the prolific poet, fill more than twenty volumes. Toward the end of his life, much of it had been translated into English. Even through the change of language, the dynamic and strident voice of Pablo Neruda sings of the joys of nature—and the miseries of his people.

For More Information

Neruda, Pablo. *The Captain's Verses.* Translated by Donald P. Walsh. New York: New Directions, 1972.

Neruda, Pablo. *A New Decade; Poems: 1958-1967.* Edited by Ben Belitt. Translated by Ben Belitt and Alastair Reid. New York: Grove Press, 1969.

Neruda, Pablo. *Pablo Neruda.* Translated by Hadie St. Martin. New York: Farrar, Strauss and Giroux, 1977.

Neruda, Pablo. *Twenty Love Poems and a Song of Despair.* Translated by W. S. Merwin. London: Cape, 1969.

Poirot, Luis. *Pablo Neruda Absence and Presence.* Translated by Alastair Reid. New York: W. W. Norton, 1990.

Teitelboim, Vlodia. *Neruda: An Intimate Biography.* Translated by Beverly J. DeLong-Tonelli. Austin: University of Texas Press, 1991.

Toni Morrison

1931-

Personal Background

Early life. Toni Morrison was born Chloe Anthony Wofford in the steel production town of Lorain, Ohio, on February 18, 1931. Her father, George Wofford, had grown to be distrustful of most people but particularly those of other races (the Woffords were black). Her mother, Ramah (Willis) Wofford, however, seemed always hopeful in her dealings with others. Toni was born to them in the midst of the Great Depression (a period in the late 1920s and early 1930s of severe economic slowdown and widespread unemployment. From the age of twelve, she worked to help support her financially strapped family.

Morrison proved to be an excellent student in the public schools of Lorain. She graduated from high school there with honors and might have attended any of several universities on a scholarship. She chose to enroll in Howard University in Washington D. C., at that time one of the most respected black schools. Again she excelled in her English classes while taking part in other campus activities. She joined the university theater group, the Howard University Players, and took part in many of their productions.

Morrison graduated from Howard University in 1953 and then enrolled at Cornell University to earn a master's degree. Two years later, having completed the master's program, she

▲ Toni Morrison

Event: Breaking racial barriers in publishing.

Role: Toni Morrison is the first African American to win the Nobel Prize for literature. While an editor for such well-known black personalities as Muhammad Ali and Angela Davis, she honed her craft and built a reputation as an outstanding writer whose works are renowned for their boldness, emotion, and complexity.

moved to Texas to spend the next two years teaching English at Texas Southern University. She then moved back to Washington, D.C., where she took a position on the English faculty at Howard. Morrison remained there until 1964.

Marriage and family. The year Morrison joined the Howard faculty, she married Harold Morrison, an architect. The couple had two sons, Harold Ford and Slade Kevin, before their marriage ended in divorce in 1964. That year, Morrison and her sons moved to Syracuse, New York, where she took a position as a textbook editor with Random House. She had already begun to polish her own writing skills as an author of fictional stories. Soon after joining Random House, her literary skills and her work intensity and dedication earned her an advancement and she became an editor of fiction and nonfiction books. In this position, Morrison was able to guide some of the most famous black personalities in their own writing. Morrison was on her way to helping develop a strong body of black literature.

Participation:
Breaking Racial Barriers in Publishing

Editor. An editor's role in a major publishing house is a difficult responsibility. The editor's job is to help the author express his or her ideas in the clearest manner possible. So the editor consults with the writer, sometimes encourages him or her, sometimes suggests new ways to express an idea, and sometimes nearly rewrites complete passages. At the same time, the editor is an overseer for the publisher, making sure that manuscripts are delivered at the scheduled times. Morrison had to do all this for some of the most famous personalities whose works were published at Random House. Among the black writers whose work she edited were Muhammad Ali and Angela Davis.

Meanwhile, Morrison continued her own writing efforts about black experiences. As she would later explain, she felt an obligation to break with conventional literary "knowledge," because "this knowledge holds that traditional, canonical American literature is free of, uninformed by, and unshaped by the four-

March 30, 1981 / $1.25

Newsweek

Black Magic

Novelist Toni Morrison

▲ Morrison on the cover of *Newsweek;* Morrison's subjects stem from what she believes has been at best neglect and at worst deliberate avoidance of the history of black Americans.

hundred-year-old presence of first Africans and then African-Americans in the United States" (Morrison 1992, pp. 4-5).

The white press. Morrison's subjects stem from what she believes has been at best neglect and at worst deliberate avoidance of the history of black Americans. Her first novel, *The Bluest*

71

Eye (1969), was well received. In the book blue eyes are a symbol of a society that views people with black or brown eyes as inadequate and that confronts black people daily with treatment that leads to their self-hatred. Morrison was widely acclaimed for her exceptional mastery of the language and for her expression of anger at both white and black society for perpetuating racial division. At the same time, she confirmed her skill as a storyteller. Her stories, however, demand close attention: characters come and go, scenes change and reappear, and ideas run as streams of thought through the complex mazes she creates.

Four years later, Morrison added to her continuing story of black anguish with a novel about two black girls with very different personalities growing up together in a poor area of a midwestern town. Once more, Morrison's emotional response to the mistreatment of blacks runs through a story that continuously questions accepted social structure and customs. *Sula,* the life stories of Sula and Nel, received wide recognition, and Morrison was nominated for the National Book Award.

On the move. Morrison's work, even though written for popular reading, began to be taken seriously as statements about the issues of race. She began to receive special attention in the universities. In 1971 she joined the faculty at the State University of New York at Paradise. At the same time she continued to write and publish. In 1974 she selected several of the shorter articles she had previously written for magazines and published them through her old employer, Random House. In 1977 Morrison released *Song of Solomon,* the story of a black man torn between striving for upward mobility, which demanded him to behave differently and his own respect for his elders. *Song of Solomon* won Morrison the National Book Critics Circle Award.

Academic honors. Morrison's recognition in the university world grew with her popularity as a novelist. In 1976 she was

---

Some Books by Morrison

1981   *Tar Baby*
Modern adaptation of the African American folktale of Tar Baby and Brer Rabbit.

1987   *Beloved*
A ghost story focusing on the theme of slavery and its harmful legacy.

1992   *Jazz*
Set in Harlem during the Jazz Age of the 1920s, the novel examines the power the city exerts over its black citizens.

▲ Morrison is the first African American to win the Nobel Prize for
literature.

invited to be a guest lecturer at Yale University. From 1984 to 1989
she occupied the Albert Schweitzer Chair for Humanities at the
State University of New York at Albany. (Universities frequently
persuade wealthy people to endow an honorary position on the
faculty, named a "chair" after them, and then invite especially
deserving scholars to take that position.) Morrison later accepted
the Robert F. Coheen Chair in the Council of Humanities at
Princeton University.

Branching out. At intervals, Morrison continued to publish
novels about blackness and whiteness. These took her on imagi-
nary trips back into history to just after the American Civil War
and to black experiences on a Caribbean island.

Pulitzer Prize. Morrison was awarded the Pulitzer Prize for literature for *Beloved*. By 1987, when the book was published, Morrison was involved not only with issues of racism but also with the women's movement. The book is about the hopeless situation of former slaves following the Civil War. Sethe carries the evidence of her mistreatment as a slave on her back and in her memory of the brutality of her white male oppressors. Most of the book is about Sethe's struggle to deal with a harsh world virtually alone. Morrison disposes of all the male members of the family in the first two or three paragraphs—young male family members run away to escape family responsibility. Sethe struggles through memories and current events that are portrayed so vividly and powerfully that the book has been said to be almost poetic.

After *Beloved* appeared and received international acclaim, Morrison began to write in areas other than fiction. The same year that her next novel was published (*Jazz*, 1992), she wrote lyrics for a musical play, *Honey and Rue*. Lectures she had been invited to deliver at Harvard University in 1990 were published in 1992 in book form under the title *Playing in the Dark*. In this book, Morrison discusses authors ranging from Edgar Allan Poe to Ernest Hemingway in order to illustrate the unspoken influence of blacks on white writers and to present what she believes to be evidence of white ego building at the expense of people of color. Morrison argues that much of American literature is based on black experiences.

In 1992 Morrison turned her attention to sexist behavior in the black experience. She edited pieces about the accusations of Anita Hill regarding sexual misconduct by prospective Supreme Court justice Clarence Thomas. The selections were published as *Race-ing Justice, En-gendering Power: Essays on Anita Hill and Clarence Thomas.*

From *Beloved*

Sethe is distraught over the death of one of her children. Sethe's mother-in-law, Baby Suggs, answers when Sethe suggests that moving is one way to escape the haunting memories:

> "What'd be the point?" asked Baby Suggs. "Not a house in the country ain't packed to its rafters with some dead Negro's grief. We lucky this ghost is a baby.... You lucky. You got three left. Three pulling at your skirts and just one raising hell from the other side. Be thankful, why don't you? I had eight. Every one of them gone away from me. Four taken, four chased, and all, I expect, worrying somebody's house into evil" (p. 5).

Aftermath

In 1993 Morrison was awarded the Nobel Prrize for literature for her body of work. She continues to lecture at Princeton University and has become a trustee of the National Humanities Center. She also continues to work on a new novel, tentatively titled *Paradise*.

For More Information

Evans, Mari, editor. *Black Women Writers, 1950-1980: A Critical Evaluation*. Garden City, New York: Doubleday, 1986.

Morrison, Toni. *Beloved*. New York: Alfred A. Knopf, 1987.

Morrison, Toni. *Playing in the Dark: Whiteness and the Literary Imagination*. Cambridge, Massachusetts: Harvard University Press, 1992.

Ruus, Charles. *Conversations with American Writers*. New York: Alfred A. Knopf, 1985.

Tate, Claudia. *Black Women Writers at Work*. New York: Continuum, 1986.

Rigoberta Menchu

1960-

Personal Background

Guatemala. The central American nation in which Rigoberta Menchu was born lies just south of Mexico. It is a rugged land. A flat coastal plain bordering the Pacific Ocean rises through a transitional hill country to a high plain, the Altiplano, which covers two-thirds of the country. Guatemala's larger cities are located in major valleys in the Altiplano. Most of the land, however, is so rugged that only about half of it has been cleared for agriculture, and much of it is not accessible by road or rail. Most of the native Indian groups live in the Altiplano in small towns and villages, where they farm small plots of land if possible, although most work as farm laborers for large landowners.

Early life. Rigoberta Menchu was born in 1960 in the town of Chimel, Guatemala. Her parents, Vicente and Tum, were among the first to settle in this rugged, hilly area, which is accessible only by foot. As are more than half of all Guatemalans, Menchu is of Indian ancestry. She grew up with the respect for nature that is common among the Indians. She observed native rituals as well as those of the Catholic Church. But mostly, she worked. To survive, nearly everyone in Chimel had to work.

Menchu began working in the fields harvesting coffee beans when she was just eight years old. She was paid twenty centavos a day if she gathered thirty-five pounds of coffee beans. Otherwise,

▲ **Rigoberta Menchu**

Event: Writing about the plight of Guatemalan Indians.

Role: Rigoberta Menchu was awarded the Nobel Peace Prize in 1992 because of her courageous efforts in defense of the rights of the Guatemalan Indians. The detailed and grim accounts of human atrocities depicted in her autobiography, *I, Rigoberta Menchu,* have been judged an accurate representation of the conditions in Guatemala.

she was not paid at all. Even for this small wage, Rigoberta and her family had to travel away from their village to find work in the lower lands. Workers, young and old, walked to the nearest roadway, then rode to the coffee plantation in lorries (horse-drawn wagons without sides) filled with about forty people, along with their animals and personal belongings. Conditions in the lorry, which made no stops for any reason, grew increasingly horrible as the trip progressed. Travelers often vomited from the horrible stench.

Once at the work site, families of workers lived in cramped quarters in a single hut topped with banana or palm leaves, called a *galera*. This house, with sides open to the elements, sheltered four to five hundred people. Worse yet, even though all the workers were Indians, they were from various tribes, each speaking their own dialect. Therefore, little or no communication was possible.

While working in these conditions, two members of the Menchu family died. The first was Menchu's eldest brother, Felipe, who died of exposure to deadly pesticide fumes after being assigned to work a field that had just been sprayed. Her brother Nicolas died from malnutrition when she was eight years old.

Community activity. At age twelve, Menchu began to take more responsibility in the community. She began to get acquainted with other villagers as she harvested maize in the village farm. At this same time, Menchu became involved with the Catholic Church. She took on the responsibility of teaching others and was given materials by priests to spread the message. Rigoberta had not attended school and could not read, so to spread the Catholic message she had to memorize the teachings of the priests. Part of the work of the priests was to organize prayer meetings where they took up

The People of Guatemala

About ten million people live in Guatemala, most of them in the cooler climate of the Altiplano. The official language of the country is Spanish, although the native Indians of Guatemala speak more than twenty different languages. Guatemala is a country of very mixed population. About 60 percent of the people are Indians who speak their own native languages and have traditional and long-standing customs of their own. About 5 percent of the people are Ladinos—mostly poor people who are of mixed Spanish and Indian heritage, speak Spanish, and do not live like the native Indians. Blacks and mulattos live in the hot lowlands that border the Pacific Ocean and the Caribbean Sea. Fewer than 10 percent of Guatemalans are white, but whites control much of the country's wealth.

collections to buy things for the community. The priests taught the Indians that they must unite.

Leaving home. Before Menchu's thirteenth birthday, a landowner offered her a job as a maid in the capital, Guatemala City. Her father did not want her to leave the community. He said, "You'll forget about our common heritage. If you leave, it will be for good. If you leave our community, I will not support you" (Menchu, p. 89). Still, Menchu thought this would be an opportunity to learn Spanish. She could then return home and be of more help to her community since the neighboring Ladinos spoke Spanish.

The life of a maid in Guatemala City was not much better than life on the coffee plantation. In the beginning, the family dog ate better than Menchu—until she learned to eat leftovers with the other servant. Without family support, this was one of the saddest periods of Menchu's life.

Father's arrest. In 1974 General Kjell Laugerud Garcia was elected president of Guatemala. He took office at a time when coffee prices were low, workers' pay was scarce, and the Guatemalan peasants were on the verge of rebellion. To appease the large Indian population, Laugerud decided to enact land reforms. He gave a small plot to each family and formed the Guatemalan Forestry Commission (INAFOR) to look after the forests in Guatemala. Thus when the Indians cut down trees to clear the land, they were arrested. Once the land was cleared and planted, larger landowners appeared. The landowners and the government had made a deal to take the land away from the Indians. Vicente Menchu had long held a small plot of farmland and had struggled to hold it for twenty-two years. The new system threatened to take this land away from him, and Vicente went to the capital to speak with the Guatemalan National Institute for Agrarian Transformation. They asked him to sign a piece of paper. Since he could not read or write and was intimidated by the government surroundings, he signed the paper. It was an agreement that the Indian landowners would give up their lands. When Vicente discovered the trickery, he was willing to fight to keep his land. He first went to the courts, but for his effort was only arrested and taken to the Santa Cruz del Quiche prison.

The entire community worked toward raising money to defend Vicente. Still, he remained in prison for a year and two months and then was out of prison only three months before he was kidnapped. This time, the community prepared to use their everyday tools as weapons to win his release from the government agents who had been responsible for the kidnapping. Within a day, he was found abandoned. Vicente had been severely tortured and was near death. It took over a year for him to recover.

In 1977 Vicente was arrested again. But this time he was considered a political prisoner, a verdict that carried a sentence of life. The unions pressed for his release and the landowners objected. Vicente was finally let out of jail. He then joined the CUC (Comite Unidad Campesina) and went into hiding. The CUC was soon under attack for organizing strikes demanding fair wages.

The Garcia reign of terror. In 1978 General Fernando Lucas Garcia came to power in Guatemala and greater terror began. Military bases were set up in the villages, and rapes and murders of the Indians were widespread. That same year the Menchu family was temporarily reunited. Vicente Menchu returned home and so did Rigoberta from her job in the capital. A great party was held. Following Guatemalan custom, the party began at midnight.

Midnight signifies the ending of the old day and the beginning of the new. Vicente spoke of change that night and the effect he could have on other Indians. He said his farewell to the community and left the next morning. It was also time for Rigoberta Menchu to say good-bye. She had joined her father's CUC and had a specific mission—to use her growing knowledge of Spanish to help organize other Indians and Ladinos.

Union organizer. Menchu traveled from one village to the next organizing the workers to resist government oppression.

Menchu on Land Ownership

"The Government says the land belongs to the nation. It owns the land and gives it to us to cultivate. But when we've cleared and cultivated the land, that's when the landowners appear. However, the landowners don't just appear on their own—they have connections with the different authorities that allow them to maneuver like that. Because of this, we faced the Martinez family, the Garcias, and then the Brols arrived. This meant we could either stay and work as peons or leave our land. There was no other solution. So my father traveled all over the place seeking advice" (from *I, Rigoberta Menchu*, p. 105).

Preparing for resistance was in direct contrast to the teachings of the Catholic Church, which Menchu had begun to lean on. She had learned from the teachings of the priests that it was a sin to kill, and the priests taught the people to be passive. But Menchu was not passive. Her life was about pain and struggle. She believed in organizing her community to fight against the landowners and the soldiers, who were frequent visitors to the village, beating people and stealing.

Preparing for war. The first step was to move the people of the community to a central location where they could more easily defend themselves against their enemies. Next, they set up traps along the main routes to their village. Escape routes were dug. The Indians took turns guarding the village and announcing the approach of the enemy, the soldiers. Dogs were used to signal an attack. The peasants armed themselves with machetes, rocks, and even lime and salt.

One day the villagers captured a soldier and took his guns and grenades. They released the unarmed soldier, but his own people shot him for abandoning his rifle. After this incident, the soldiers stopped coming to the village. Still, the Indians did not leave their village except to go to neighboring villages for salt and other supplies.

Brother murdered. Menchu observed and later wrote about the troubles of her own family with the Guatemalan army and police. Her story was such a grim tale that scholars began immediately to question it. But other observers had seen similar army actions, and her story is decidedly in keeping with other recorded events in Guatemala. On September 9, 1979, Menchu's brother Petrocinio Menchu Tum was kidnapped by Guatemalan soldiers and was severely tortured for sixteen days. On September 23, the military announced that a public display was to be held in Chajul. The commanding officer addressed the audience and shouted that these men before them were commu-

---

Vicente's Lesson to His Daughter

"The rich have become rich because they took what our ancestors had away from them, and now they grow fat on the sweat of our labor. We know this is true because we live it everyday, not because someone else tells us. The rich try to obstruct us. The rich come from over there, where government is. It's the government of the rich, the landowners" (from *I, Rigoberta Menchu*, p. 121).

nists. At the end of the speech, the prisoners were doused with gasoline and set on fire. The Menchu family was present to observe this final treatment. All three, Vicente, Tum, and Rigoberta decided then that they would join more violent protest groups.

Father's death. At the beginning of January 1980, Vicente Menchu was involved in a demonstration against the government in El Quiche. The guerrillas that he had joined took over several radio stations and voiced their protest over the airwaves. They then decided to take over the Spanish embassy to bring international attention to their plight. The government set fire to the building, and all but one of the guerrilla fighters inside were burned alive.

Mother murdered. Just four months later, Tum Manchu was kidnapped by Guatemalan police and taken to a camp named Chajup. Rigoberta Menchu was not an observer of the following events but later reported that her mother had been raped by officers of the camp. They shaved her head, cut off her ears, and left her to die. Her wounds filled with worms, and within a few days she died. The soldiers left her to be eaten by animals.

Strike! The cruel treatment of her parents pushed Menchu to even more action on behalf of the downtrodden Indians and Ladinos. In February 1980 she helped organize a strike of eighty thousand peasants, cotton and sugar workers. The strike lasted for fifteen days and paralyzed the economy. At the beginning of 1981, fearing for her personal safety, Menchu escaped to Mexico City. By 1983 more than one hundred thousand Guatemalans had joined her in exile.

Aftermath

Return to Guatemala. By 1988 international pressure had begun to change the political scene in Guatemala, and Menchu dared to return home. She was greeted at the airport by government police, who planned to detain her. Mobs of people, however, had learned of her arrival and protested the police action, as did members of foreign diplomatic corps. Instead of being detained, she was allowed to speak to a crowd of about 1,500. For the first time in Guatemala, Menchu was able to speak openly about her own experiences as an Indian.

Nobel Peace Prize. In 1992 Menchu, at age thirty-three, was awarded the Nobel Peace Prize. The response to the award has not been completely favorable. Menchu received death threats and bouquets of marigolds—the common funeral flower of Latin America. Today she is under constant protection from bodyguards and does not move about freely. She has gained international fame through the publication of her autobiography *I, Rigoberta Menchu: An Indian Woman in Guatemala* (1983). Venezuelan writer Elisabeth Burgos Debray had worked with Menchu for a week and made tapes of her life story, which she developed into the book. Since its publication, Menchu has gone to the United Nations to lobby for Indian rights.

Menchu has also received $1.2 million from the Nobel Committee, which she plans to use to set up a human rights foundation in her father's name. Still, conditions in Guatemala remain miserable for the Indians. In 1985 the military leaders yielded to free elections, and a nonmilitary president was installed. Despite this change, a United Nations report of 1990 indicated that killings and disappearances of Guatemalans were again on the upswing.

Menchu's Description of Her Brother's Plight

"They cut off his fingernails, they cut off his fingers, they cut off his skin, they burned parts of his skin. Many of the wounds, the first ones, swelled and were infected. He stayed alive. They shaved his head, left just the skin, and also they cut the skin off his head and pulled it down on either side and cut off the fleshy part of his face" (from *I, Rigoberta Menchu*, p. 174).

For More Information

Connors, L. "The Mayan Way." *New Perspectives Quarterly,* vol. 11 (Summer 1994), p. 59.

Jones, Emily. "Rigoberta Menchu." *Texas Observer,* vol. 84 (November 13, 1992), pp. 20-21.

Menchu, Rigoberta, and Elisabeth Burgos Debray. *I, Rigoberta Menchu: An Indian Woman in Guatemala.* Norfolk, Thetford, 1983.

Perera, Victor. *Unfinished Business: The Guatemalan Tragedy.* Berkeley, California: University of California Press, 1993.

Ending the Cold War

1977
Vaclav Havel helps write Charter 77, protesting the lack of civil rights in Czechoslovakia.

1980
Lech Walesa forms Solidarity, the Polish workers' union.

1981
Ronald Reagan announces the beginning of "Star Wars," or the Strategic Defense Initiative.

1983
Reagan orders invasion of Grenada.

1985
Mikhail Gorbachev becomes leader of the Soviet Union.

1987
Reagan calls for removal of the Berlin Wall.

1989
Berlin Wall is torn down.

1989
"Velvet Revolution," a bloodless revolution, frees Czechoslovakia from Soviet domination; Havel becomes Czech president.

1990
Gorbachev wins Nobel Peace Prize for helping arrange arms reductions. Walesa becomes president of Poland.

1991
Boris Yeltsin organizes a new Russian federation with greatly reduced central powers.

ENDING THE COLD WAR

On March 12, 1947, President Harry S Truman, in an address to Congress, described the deepening conflict between the United States and the Union of Soviet Socialist Republics as a conflict between two ways of life. The United States, a democracy, was based on the will of the majority and distinguished by free institutions, representative government, and freedom from political oppression. The Communist Soviet Union was based on the will of a minority forcibly imposed on the majority and relied, according to Truman, on "terror, repression, a controlled press and radio, fixed elections, and the suppression of personal freedoms" (Harry S Truman, "Aid to Greece and Turkey," in *Vital Speeches of the Day*, vol. 13, no. 11 [March 15, 1947], p. 323). Later that year, political commentator Walter Lippmann coined the term "the cold war" to describe this conflict.

Over the next several decades, the cold war continued with varying degrees of intensity. While the Soviets and their allies tried to expand their influence and promote communism around the world, the United States and its allies waged, for the most part, a defensive struggle to prevent the spread of communism and Soviet influence. By the end of the 1970s, the Soviets appeared to be gaining an edge in the struggle. A number of pro-Soviet regimes had been set up in Asia, Africa, and Latin

America, and the Soviets appeared to be gaining military superiority over the West. American leaders, still reeling from the failure of U.S. policy in Vietnam and trying to cope with a sluggish economy at home and terrorism abroad, were hesitant to act against communism.

Soviet successes. By 1979 the Soviets had reached the height of their success. Pro-Soviet governments were established in Grenada and Nicaragua that year; a fundamentalist Islamic regime had ousted the pro-Western shah of Iran; pro-Soviet Vietnam had installed a puppet regime in Cambodia; and the Soviets, later in the year, invaded Afghanistan. That same year, Soviet leader Leonid Brezhnev remarked that events from Vietnam to Iran marked an era in which "the correlation of forces" was "shifting against the capitalists" (Peter Schweitzer, *Victory* [New York: Atlantic Monthly Press, 1994], p. 16).

Western revival. The tide was about to turn, however. American voters elected **Ronald Reagan** president in 1980. Reagan called on the American people to stand firm against the Soviet Union, which he at one point called an "evil empire." He also called on the Soviet leaders to give their people more freedom. His economic policies revitalized the U.S. economy and inspired free market reforms throughout the world. Under the Reagan Doctrine, the United States stepped up aid to groups that were fighting to overthrow pro-Soviet governments. Reagan also began to rebuild the U.S. military and forced the Soviets into an expensive arms race that strained both Soviet and American economies. While Reagan did not hesitate to use military force when necessary, he was willing to negotiate arms reduction agreements with the Soviets.

Reform in the Soviet Union. When **Mikhail Gorbachev** came to power in the Soviet Union in 1985, the Soviets began to withdraw from the cold war. Gorbachev ended military adventuring abroad and negotiated a sweeping arms control agreement with the United States. At the same time, he tried to reform the Communist system, which had resulted in a Soviet economy that was falling further and further behind those in the West. When he tried to export his reform policies to his Communist allies in Eastern Europe and allowed the Berlin Wall and

"Iron Curtain" to be opened, he triggered forces that completely swept away the Communist regimes. Poland, led by **Lech Walesa** and his "Solidarity" labor union, soon announced independence from Soviet domination, while in Czechoslovakia the "Velvet Revolution" swept the Communists from office.

Fallout in Europe. The cold war was coming to an end, but it left many unresolved issues. Lech Walesa was left in charge of an almost bankrupt Poland, with nearly one hundred political parties vying to replace the Communist government. The political maneuvering threatened to break the nation before a new government could get underway. Czechoslovakia, put together arbitrarily after World War I and held together by a common oppressor, now found its Czech and Slovak populations having difficulty finding common ground. Playwright **Vaclav Havel** attempted to lead the nation to unity, but resigned when it became obvious that Czechoslovakia would break into two nations. Havel reappeared as the president of the new Czech Republic and led it through the first phases of change to capitalism.

Halting the cold war. Within the Soviet Union, **Boris Yeltsin** became Gorbachev's strongest rival. Yeltsin frustrated Gorbachev's efforts to keep him out of politics and continually pressed for an acceleration in reforms. He eventually became president of the Russian Federation. In August 1991 Yeltsin climbed onto an armored tank and successfully rallied the people of Moscow to resist an attempt by Communist hard-liners to take over the government. Afterward, he saw to it that the Communist Party was removed from power altogether. By the end of the year, the Soviet Union itself ceased to exist. The cold war had ended.

Mikhail Gorbachev

1931-

Personal Background

Life near Georgia. Mikhail Gorbachev was born March 2, 1931, in Privolnye, a small town near Stavropol near the Caucasus Mountains in southern Russia. Although his mother, a descendant of priests, was deeply religious, both Mikhail's father and grandfather enthusiastically supported communism. In the early 1930s, for example, when Soviet leader Joseph Stalin forced the nation's farmers to move onto *kolkhozes,* or collective farms, the two Gorbachev men organized one of the first kolkhozes in the Stavropol region. The Gorbachevs soon felt the strain of Stalin's policies when Mikhail, then known as Misha, was not yet two years old. In order to crush resistance to his government reorganization of agriculture, Stalin seized food supplies of the farm families. Millions of Soviet peasants (some estimates range as high as twenty million) starved to death as a result, including a third of the population of Privolnye. Although the Gorbachev men remained enthusiastic about communism, they, too, were caught up in Stalin's angry purges; both father and grandfather were arrested in 1937 and jailed for a year and a half.

Against his mother's wishes that Misha have a religious education, his father sent him to the village school, which was run by the state. There he was taught the communist doctrine and eventually joined Komsomol, the Communist Party youth organiza-

▲ **Mikhail Gorbachev**

Event: Turning the Soviet Union toward ending the cold war.

Role: After he became leader of the Soviet Union, Mikhail Gorbachev promoted a series of reforms that led to the collapse of communism in Eastern Europe and eventually to the disbanding of the Soviet Union itself. In 1990 Gorbachev won the Nobel Peace Prize for bringing about arms reduction, and ending the cold war.

tion. Besides the communist ideology, he learned discipline, self-control, respect for authority, and obedience. Misha soon became a Komsomol leader.

Working for the party. In 1941 the Soviet Union became involved in World War II, and Misha's father was soon fighting in the Red Army. Too young for the army, Misha remained at home and took much of the responsibility for his family. He was in Privolnye when, the next year, German troops occupied the town for six months. No longer needed to manage the family affairs after the war, Misha resumed his formal education and worked on the kolkhoz when not in school. The combination of work and school proved effective. In 1949 both Misha and his father were awarded the Order of the Red Banner of Labor for helping their kolkhoz exceed the production quota set by the state agricultural planners. Only three other boys in the Stavropol region were so honored. The award gave Misha the privilege of applying for admission to Moscow State University, an honor normally reserved for children of the party elite.

University student. At Moscow University, Gorbachev eventually studied law. Much of Soviet legal education, however, consisted of memorizing what the government prescribed or prohibited in legal cases. There was much less free questioning, particularly during the Stalin era (he died in 1954), than one would find at law schools in the Western nations. Still, Gorbachev continued his Komsomol activities and then joined the Communist Party in 1952. That year, he married Raisa Titarenko, a university student majoring in Marxist philosophy and a Komsomol organizer.

Gorbachev graduated in 1955 with a degree in law. A graduate of Moscow University could usually find an influential job in

---

Government Spy?

During his university days, Gorbachev was thought by many of his classmates to have been an informer. He is said to have spied on his professors and fellow students, seeking evidence of statements or actions not in keeping with the Communist Party line. One student recalled, "we treated Misha like the devil himself. When he walked by, everyone stopped talking" (Solovyov and Klepikova, p. 145).

Gorbachev showed a different side, however, during the anti-Semitic hysteria whipped up by Stalin in 1953. Stalin suggested a plot by Kremlin doctors, most of whom were Jews, to kill the Soviet leadership. The rumor was without foundation, but university students tried to frame a Jewish classmate by trumping up a false accusation. Gorbachev defended the Jewish student and denounced his primary accuser as a "spineless animal" (Murphy, p. 312).

Moscow. However, Stalin had died two years earlier, and the connections Gorbachev had made during the Stalin era were useless under the new regime. So he returned to Stavropol, where he found a job in the prosecutor's office. By this time, Stalin's victims were returning to Stavropol from the prisons and labor camps to which they had been sent. Gorbachev's office was flooded with complaints of false arrests, an experience that may have dampened his enthusiasm for a legal career. He soon quit this position to accept a job with the Komsomol.

By 1956 Gorbachev had risen high enough in the party ranks to be picked as a delegate to the Twentieth Party Congress in Moscow. Here he heard the new party leader, Nikita Khrushchev, deliver his "secret" speech in which he denounced the crimes of Stalin. Gorbachev viewed this speech as a challenge to reform the system. For the next five years, Gorbachev gradually advanced through the party bureaucracy, moving into posts left vacant by those moving up ahead of him. He learned to dutifully carry out orders and to please his superiors.

Along the way, Gorbachev came to know some of the most powerful party leaders. Fyodor Kulakov, who had been put in charge of the Stavropol area, rewarded Gorbachev by placing him in charge of the agricultural system in 1963. A year later, Yuri Andropov, a frequent visitor to Stavropol resorts, made Gorbachev his protégé. In 1978 Andropov brought Gorbachev to Moscow to head the agricultural department of the Central Committee Secretariat. Three years later, again with the help of Andropov, Gorbachev became the youngest member of the Politburo, the Communist Party's top decision-making body. When Andropov became general secretary on the death of Leonid Brezhnev (1982), Gorbachev became minister of agriculture, then was placed in charge of the economy. This opportunity to view the nation's finances convinced Gorbachev that the Soviet Union must start modernizing. Andropov died in 1984, and Gorbachev continued to quietly build a power base. On March 11, 1985, on the death of Secretary Constantin Chernenko, Gorbachev was easily elected general secretary of the Communist Party and took charge of the government of the Soviet Union.

▲ Once he had the opportunity to view the nation's finances, Gorbachev
was convinced that the Soviet Union must start modernizing.

Participation: Turning the Soviet Union
Toward Ending the Cold War

A troubled nation. When Gorbachev came to power, the
Soviet Union faced a number of formidable problems. Production
was declining, the economy was collapsing, and the Soviets were
falling behind the West in a technology race. Adding to these

problems was the declining market value of Soviet petroleum products and the rise of a strong new competitor for the world markets—China.

Perestroika. It was clear that the Soviet Union would lose its place in the world society if the economy was not immediately improved. Gorbachev initially hardened his successor's cold war policies, but it was soon apparent that he planned to apply new thinking. In 1985 the Soviet leader announced a series of reforms he called *perestroika,* or "restructuring." At the same time, he announced a policy of *glasnost,* "openness." Then, in July 1985 he removed Soviet Foreign Minister Andrei Gromyko and replaced him with reform-minded Eduard Shevardnadze. The next year, a fundamental break with the old foreign policy was announced—and none too soon. The Reagan Doctrine had involved the United States in heavy support of dissidents set on removing the Communist governments of several Soviet satellites, such as Afghanistan, Ethiopia, Nicaragua, Cuba, and Angola. To cut his losses and rebuild Soviet capabilities, Gorbachev began to cut back on efforts in many of these satellite nations. Instead, Gorbachev began to encourage the satellites to give their citizens more liberty, hoping to give the Soviet brand of socialism a better appearance among the world's nations.

Decaying Defenses

In 1982 the Israeli air force shot down eighty Soviet-built Syrian warplanes without losing a single plane of their own. Then in 1986 a West German teenager flew a small private plane through the Soviet air defenses and landed in Red Square in Moscow. NATO, the West's European defense, had positioned superior Pershing II missiles in Europe, and Ronald Reagan had announced the beginning of development of the Strategic Defense Initiative. Gorbachev was faced with a strong need to revitalize the Soviet military.

Breaking out. At first the pace of reform was slow. The Communist satellites were wary of the temperament of leaders in Moscow, who often made 180-degree turns in policy. Besides, hard-line party members had been put in charge of several Eastern European governments and were reluctant to change.

Gradually, though, some governments initiated changes that may have been greater than Gorbachev expected. Janos Kadar, who had been the Communist Party secretary in Hungary for thirty-two years, was thrown out of office in 1988 by the Hungarians. A year later, the Hungarians began dismantling the fences and minefields along the Austrian border. The hard-pressed Soviets approved this first opening in the "Iron Curtain." Poland's military dictator, Wojtech Jaruzelski, under Soviet pressure to reform, began negotiating with the Polish labor union, Solidarity. Jaruzelski agreed with Solidarity demands to hold free elections and in 1989 was defeated by Solidarity, giving way to Poland's first non-Communist government since World War II.

In 1989 Gorbachev urged East German leaders to begin reforms. These reforms led to their choosing a new leader, Egon Krenz (replacing Erich Honecker), and to the opening of the Berlin Wall. A year later Krenz was replaced by a non-Communist Christian Democrat government. The hard-line rulers of Czechoslovakia and Bulgaria soon followed, and in Romania the Communist dictator Nicolae Ceauşescu was thrown out in a violent revolution and then executed.

The Warsaw Pact and the Sinatra Doctrine

The Soviets had forced many Eastern European nations to join them in a mutual defense pact, the Warsaw Pact. Now Gorbachev urged loosening the strings of this pact. The Brezhnev Doctrine enforcing the Warsaw pact had authorized the Soviet military to intervene wherever an ally threatened to leave the pact. This policy was replaced with the "Sinatra Doctrine," allowing each nation to "go its own way" (Gedmin, p. 3).

Inside the Soviet Union. Reforms within the Soviet Union were no less upsetting and were mostly ineffective. The Communist Party remained in control of *perestroika* and inhibited reform, while *glasnost* opened the media to Gorbachev's critics. His rival for power, **Boris Yeltsin** (see entry), articulated the problem: Gorbachev was seeking the unattainable, trying for "communism and a market economy, public property ownership and private property ownership, the multiparty system and the Communist Party with its monopoly of power" (Gedmin, p. 117).

Gorbachev then tried to reform Soviet government by creating a Council of People's Deputies to elect the Supreme Soviet (the legislature) and the Presidium (the executive branch). The council became merely a forum for Gorbachev's critics, among them Boris Yeltsin.

In 1990 Gorbachev won the Nobel Peace Prize for his actions that brought about arms reduction and the termination of the cold war.

▲ Gorbachev and Ronald Reagan in 1985; when Gorbachev came to
power in 1985, the Soviets began to withdraw from the Cold War.

Aftermath

The coup. Despite the award, Gorbachev continued to face economic problems in the Soviet Union, a number of whose member states had begun to separate from Moscow. He came under attack from both sides: hard-liners who wanted to halt *perestroika,* and reformers loudly led by Yeltsin. In December 1990 Shevardnadze resigned from the Soviet leadership, saying, "This reform has gone to hell. Dictatorship is coming" (Solovyov and Klepikova, p. 219).

After Shevardnadze's departure, the hard-liners rose to prominence in Gorbachev's government. Boris Pugo became minister of the interior, and Gennadi Yanaev was made vice-president. Rumors began that the hard-line Communists planned to stage a coup, ousting Gorbachev or encouraging a military takeover.

Amid the rumors, some of the restless non-Russian republics (Lithuania, Latvia, and Estonia, in particular) decided to leave the union altogether. In 1991 Gorbachev proposed a new union treaty that would replace the treaty that had bound the Soviet Union since 1922. The new treaty would give the various states more freedom. That was enough for the old hard-liners. On August 19, the day before the new union treaty was to be signed, Yanaev, Pugo, and others staged their long-rumored coup. They placed Gorbachev under house arrest in the Crimea and tried to force him to declare a state of emergency in which the government would become a dictatorship. When Gorbachev refused, his kidnappers declared him deposed. This gave Yeltsin a new platform from which to act. In Moscow, Yeltsin began to organize resistance to the coup and rapidly gained public support. Three days after it began, the coup collapsed. Pugo committed suicide, and the other plotters were arrested.

Gorbachev resigns. Following the coup, Yeltsin was the most popular leader in the Soviet Union; Gorbachev had lost much of his popularity and power. Many blamed him for having appointed the coup plotters in the first place. Gorbachev made a last effort to conclude a union treaty, but most of the republics were no longer interested in remaining in the Soviet Union. Instead, they chose

Yeltsin's plan for a commonwealth, a loose association of independent states. Gorbachev soon resigned as the Communist Party's first secretary. In December 1991 he announced that the main work of his life was done. On December 25 he made his farewell speech to the Soviet leaders, and on December 31 his job as president—as well as the Soviet Union itself—came to an end. Yeltsin became president of Russia and leader of the commonwealth.

Gorbachev and his wife continued to live in Moscow, and he began a more scholarly life as a public speaker and leader of political seminars throughout the world.

For More Information

Ayer, Eleanor H. *Boris Yeltsin: Man of the People.* New York: Dillon Press, 1992.

Gedmin, Jeffrey. *The Hidden Hand: Gorbachev and the Collapse of East Germany.* Washington, D.C.: AEI Press, 1992.

Murphy, Kenneth. *Retreat from the Finland Station: Moral Odysseys in the Breakdown of Communism.* New York: The Free Press, 1994.

Solovyov, Victor, and Elena Klepikova. *Behind the High Kremlin Walls.* New York: Dodd, Mead, 1986.

Vaclav Havel

1936-

Personal Background

Early life. Vaclav Havel came from an upper-middle-class family. He was born in October 1936, in Prague, to Bozema (Vaumëková) and Vaclav M. Havel. Before the installation of Communist governments in Czechoslovakia after World War II, the elder Vaclav was the wealthy owner of several restaurants. His son was only twelve years old when the family fortune was taken by Communist rulers. The restaurants were seized and Vaclav's father was forced to support the family by working as an office clerk.

Education. The prosperous Havels could afford to give their son a good education. The young Havel was enrolled at St. George's Academy, a boarding school in Podebrady, and was living at the school when the Communists seized power in Czechoslovakia in 1948. In the middle of his third year at the academy, he was forced to leave under a Communist edict that required children from middle- and upper-class families (the "bourgeois") to take manual jobs after completing a minimum education. Havel was assigned to a construction job, but with his mother's help was able to get an apprenticeship as a chemical laboratory technician. The Communist regime that took the Havels' property and caused Havel to leave school disrupted the family in other ways. In 1949 Havel's father was jailed for three months. An uncle,

▲ **Vaclav Havel**

Event: Leading the "Velvet Revolution."

Role: A social reform activist long before the 1968 Soviet suppression of the human rights movement in Czechoslovakia known as the "Prague Spring," Vaclav Havel helped lead the "Charter 77" Czech demands for more civil liberties. In 1989 he led a bloodless revolution that liberated Czechoslovakia from Soviet Communism.

Milos, attempted to escape to Austria but was captured and spent two years in jail. In spite of these setbacks, Havel continued to study at night.

Literary interest. At age fifteen Havel developed a deep interest in poetry. He founded a literary circle (a sort of club) known as the "thirty-sixers," made up of teens who, like him, had become political outcasts under Communism. His interest at this time was to find Czech literary works that had been forbidden by the new government. He began to visit the Cafe Slavia in Prague, a gathering place of older poets and artists who were no longer allowed to publish or exhibit.

Havel became a champion for these people in 1956. In that year, Nikita Khrushchev became leader of the Soviet Union and denounced the old policies of Joseph Stalin. The relaxed atmosphere that followed this announcement allowed Havel to deliver a speech at a meeting of young writers in Dobris. In the course of the speech he attacked the Communist suppression and accused the official Czech Writers' Union of aiding the Communists by blackballing non-Communist writers. Nineteen at the time, Havel had already begun to publish his writings.

Havel Family History

Havel's paternal grandfather was a real estate developer who built, among other structures, the Lucerna Palace, an entertainment complex in Prague that included a cabaret, a cinema, and a concert hall. Vaclav's maternal grandfather was the Czechoslovak ambassador to Vienna during the rule of Tomás Masaryk, the nation's first president.

Playwright. By the late 1950s, Havel had begun to write plays while working as a stagehand at the ABC Theatre in Prague. In 1960, after having written an article about the small-theater scene, he began an eight-year association with the Theater on the Balustrade, where he worked as a stagehand, author, and actor, and where his best-known plays—*The Garden Party, The Memorandum,* and *The Increased Difficulty of Concentration*—were written and produced.

The year 1965 was a memorable one for Havel. In that year he married Olga, who would support his activities throughout her life. By 1965 his fame had spread and Havel, a member of neither the Communist Party nor the Writers' Union, was appointed to the editorial board of the Writers' Union journal, *Tvar.* Planned as a monthly, *Tvar* was published on and off amid constant wrangling with the Writers' Union over its contents. Writers for the magazine frequently criticized the works of writers who were officially recognized and pampered by the state. The bickering gave Havel experience in politics. *Tvar* was finally closed permanently by the government in 1969.

Criticizing the government. In April 1968 Havel published an article in *Literarni Listy* titled "On the Theme of an Opposition." In it he stated the case for a multiparty democracy and argued that if the Communists wanted to retain their leading role in government, they should earn it. That such an article could be openly published suggests a freedom of expression that did not exist before the Prague Spring. After the Soviet invasion, Havel publicly took Alexander Dubcek—who had been replaced by the Soviets with Gustav Husák—to task for failing to resist the invaders. In August 1969 Havel and nine others signed the "Ten Points" petition protesting the undoing of Dubcek's reforms under Husák's process of "normalization," a return to hard-line communism.

As a result of his protests, Havel came under attack from the government-controlled media and his works were removed from libraries and banned. Still, Havel, now working in a brewery, continued his criticism of the rule of fear that he claimed resulted in moral and cultural decay. Copies of a letter to Husák about this fear were printed and spread through theaters. The letter would later be used against Havel as evidence of his disloyalty.

Charter 77. In 1976 Havel met Ivan Martin Jirous ("Magor"), manager of the rock band Plastic People of the Universe. In March of that year, band members and followers, nine-

Communism in Czechoslovakia, 1968

Joseph Stalin had personally appointed Antonin Novotny as first secretary of the Czech Communist Party in 1952. Novotny held the nation so strongly to the Soviet Communist line that he was known as "Little Stalin." Through the next decade and more, Novotny became increasingly unpopular with the Czech and Slovak people, so unpopular that he finally resigned in 1967. He was replaced by another Soviet choice, Alexander Dubcek. But Dubcek had ideas about shaping a more humane communism. He began making reforms immediately, and the people of Czechoslovakia were so relieved and hopeful over the relative freedom of speech and action that a blissful period known as the "Prague Spring" filled the first part of 1968. The Soviets, however, found Dubcek's changes intolerable and invaded Czechoslovakia with armed forces in August 1968. Dubcek was replaced by a more hard-line Communist, Gustav Husák. The Prague Spring was officially over.

teen people altogether, were arrested by the Czech government and accused of subversive activities. Havel came to their defense. The publicity of their trial brought together many people who united with Havel to create "Charter 77," a manifesto issued in January 1977. Written by Vaclav Havel and Jan Patocka, a professor of philosophy who had been banned from teaching, Charter 77 protested the loss of human rights in Czechoslovakia. It was signed by 242 people. Publication of the charter resulted in Havel's spending a few months in jail. He was released after he agreed to give up being spokesman for the Charter 77 group.

Imprisonment. Ashamed of having compromised himself, Havel plunged back into underground activities after his release and was soon in trouble again. In November 1978 Havel was placed under house arrest. Less than a year later, in May 1979, he and fifteen other members of the underground Committee for the Defense of the Unjustly Prosecuted were charged with undermining the republic. Havel was convicted and given a four-and-a-half-year sentence. This time he welcomed his imprisonment as an opportunity to redeem himself for his earlier weakness in abandoning leadership of Charter 77. While he was in prison, Charter 77 expanded its efforts beyond civil rights to problems of the economy and politics. Meanwhile, Havel left a record of his prison experiences through letters to his wife Olga. Upon his release, Havel again took up his protest. Four years later, his work and that of others had prepared Czechoslovakia for revolution.

"The Power of the Powerless"

In October 1978 Havel wrote an essay that was widely distributed in Czechoslovakia, titled "The Power of the Powerless." The essay suggested that the first step in resistance to oppressive government was to stop making excuses for conforming to that government's regulations. Such conformity, Havel argued, was destructive since it meant denying one's innermost identity.

Participation:
Leading the "Velvet Revolution"

November 17, 1989. In 1989 the Soviet satellite system in Eastern Europe collapsed. (The satellites were countries that had been united with the Soviet Union for military and economic rea-

▲ **Havel reads out the names of Czechoslovakia's first noncommunist government officials since 1948 from a balcony overlooking Prague's Wenceslas Square. Thousands gathered to bear witness to the success of the peaceful revolution, December 10, 1989.**

sons.) The Communist regimes in Hungary and Poland were the first to go. By the fall of the year, the Communist governments in East Germany and Czechoslovakia were in trouble. On November 17, fifteen thousand people gathered in Prague to remember the funeral, fifty years earlier, of Jan Opletal, a student killed by the Nazis. Some younger members of the gathering used this occasion to raise banners calling for democratic freedom. These young people broke away from the ceremony for Opletal and set out to demonstrate in Wenceslas Square in the center of Prague's "New Town." Fifty thousand people were soon gathered to hear the protesters. The demonstrators were attacked by riot police. A hundred people were arrested and more than five hundred were injured.

The next day, students from the drama section of the Prague Academy of Performing Arts set up the first student strike committee. Prague theaters canceled their performances and overnight became meeting places for the government's opposition.

A loosely knit group that would lead the revolution, Civic Forum, represented a merger of Havel's old Charter 77 group with the Independent Students' Organization. It took its first action on November 19, calling for the resignation of the Prague Communist Party leader, Miroslav Stepan, and of the interior minister. Civic Forum also demanded an investigation of the police action of November 17 and the release of prisoners held as protesters. In addition the forum called for the resignation of Czech leaders who had supported the 1968 Soviet invasion, starting with President Husák and Communist Party leader Milos Jakes. To back its demands, Civic Forum called for a general strike on November 27.

First rally. By the time Civic Forum held its first mass rally in Wenceslas Square on November 21, student delegations had already fanned out across the country to build support for the upcoming strike. Havel addressed the crowd from the balcony of the Socialist Party's publishing house. The next day, leaders of Civic Forum's Slovak counterpart, Public Against Violence, addressed a crowd of one hundred thousand in the Slovak capital of Bratislava. Two days after Havel's speech in Wenceslas Square, three hundred thousand people gathered there to hear Civic Forum's new demands: free elections and the removal from the constitution of the clause giving a leading role to the Communist Party. Alexander Dubcek, who had been watched closely under near house arrest for almost twenty years, addressed a mass meeting in Bratislava. Czech television began to broadcast limited reports of the meeting in Wenceslas Square. The rapid pace continued when, the next day, the Communist Party's Central Committee met to replace Jakes with Karel Urbanek and remove Husák and two others from the Presidium, the Communist top-ranked advisory group. On that same day, Dubcek received an emotional welcome when he addressed the crowd in Wenceslas Square.

Negotiations. On November 25, more than half a million people gathered on Letna Field, a bluff above the river where, in the 1950s, a giant statue of Joseph Stalin had stood. They listened

▲ Havel walks past an honor guard at Prague castle after the National
Assembly elected him president of Czechoslovakia, December 1989.

to Havel as he declared that the general strike two days later
would be a sort of vote as to whether the Communist Party had
the right to retain its leading role in the government.

The following day, Havel met face-to-face with Prime Minister Ladislav Adamec. Later that day, Adamec spoke to the crowd
at Letna Field, and Civic Forum increased its pressure on the government by demanding an end to Communism and the restora-
tion of political democracy and a market economy. This demand
was followed by a very successful nationwide strike the next day,
and on November 28, Havel and Adamec met again. The following
day, the Federal Assembly voted to remove the leading role of the
Communist Party from the Czech constitution, and Adamec

announced on television that the government would reassess the Soviet invasion of 1968. This was followed on November 30 by the Presidium's admission that the invasion had been in error.

Completing the Velvet Revolution. After a promised reshuffling of the government failed to yield a government not dominated by Communists, massive demonstrations forced Adamec to resign. His replacement, Marian Calfa, organized a government dominated by Civic Forum and its allies. On December 9, the hated Husák, architect of the post-Soviet invasion "normalization" of Communist Czechoslovakia, resigned from the presidency. Vaclav Havel became president of Czechoslovakia on December 29, 1989, after a unanimous vote in the Federal Assembly. A bloodless revolution that became known as the "Velvet Revolution" had been completed.

Aftermath

Havel remarked that his abrupt elevation from leader of the opposition to the presidency made him feel like a literary critic who had to write a novel. Nevertheless, in June 1990 he was reelected president of the Czechoslovak Federal Republic.

The Czech government had tried to keep a careful balance between the Czechs and Slovaks according to their numbers. For example, one of the two houses of Parliament, the House of the People, represented membership by population; the other, the House of Nations, had equal representation of Czechs and Slovaks. Nevertheless, Slovaks were rumbling for independence even as the Communists were evicted. Havel, therefore, rather than being elected for the established five-year term, was elected for two years while the new government resolved the Czech-Slovak (and other) issues. In 1992, however, an election in Slovakia gave power there to a separatist party. This party wanted not only an

Czechs and Slovaks

Czechoslovakia had been formed after World War I as the best arrangement that could be made at that time. It was an uneasy union of Czechs, who were part of the highly industrialized West, and Slovaks, who had long led mostly agricultural lives under Hungarian influence. Widely different in their economies and with different languages, the union of Czechs and Slovaks was always uncomfortable. Some Slovaks had long yearned for independence.

independent Slovakia but also a slowing of free-market reforms. Havel had been careful not to dismiss all Communist activities entirely. A practical leader, he had preferred to move toward a market economy slowly while preserving gains made under the Soviet management and to bring those who had grown accustomed to Communist rule slowly toward a free market. Nevertheless, Czechs and Slovaks proceeded to divide the nation. In 1992 Havel resigned the presidency in protest over the split.

In 1993, the separation of the Czech Republic and Slovakia completed, Havel was elected president of the new Czech Republic.

For More Information

Ash, Timothy Garton. *The Magic Lantern: The Revolution of '89 Witnessed in Warsaw, Budapest, Berlin, and Prague.* New York: Random House, 1990.

Frankland, Mark. *The Patriot's Revolution: How Eastern Europe Toppled Communism and Won Its Freedom.* Chicago: Ivan R. Dee, 1990.

Kriseova, Eda. *Vaclav Havel: The Authorized Biography.* Translated by Caleb Grain. New York: St. Martin's Press, 1993.

Lech Walesa

1943-

Personal Background

Walesa's early years. Lech Walesa, the fourth child of Boleslaw and Feliksa Walesa, was born on September 29, 1943, in Popow, a hamlet in central Poland. Lech's father was a carpenter, but at the time of Lech's birth he was in a Nazi concentration camp. Boleslaw died shortly after his release from the prison, leaving his family in the care of his brother Stanislaw. Feliksa had a strong influence on her son and instilled in him both her religious faith and her patriotism. Unable to study engineering because of the family's poverty, in 1959 Walesa began attending vocational school in Lipno, and in 1961 he took a job as an electrician. Two years later he was drafted into the Polish army, grew his famous mustache, and reached the rank of corporal. He refused an offer to proceed to officers' school and returned to his electrician's job.

Gdansk. In 1966, while en route to the Baltic port of Gdynia, Walesa got off at Gdansk for a beer, missed the train, and decided to stay behind. He found work laying cables on fishing boats at the huge Lenin Shipyard. In May 1968 he met Danuta Golos, and the couple married the following November. The Walesas would eventually have eight children.

1970-80. Walesa took an active part in the general turmoil arising from price hikes and protests in 1970 by helping to orga-

▲ Lech Walesa

Event: Freeing Poland from Soviet domination.

Role: Lech Walesa was a founder and leader of the Polish general labor union, Solidarity. Although the union was banned and Walesa imprisoned in 1981, Solidarity continued as an underground movement and in June 1989 achieved a landslide parliamentary victory that ended Communist rule in Poland.

nize and lead strikes in Gdansk, a great port city. After that, he took up the call for erection of a shipyard memorial to workers killed by the Communist security forces. He would continue this agitation for ten years. Meanwhile, like many Polish workers, he welcomed Edward Gierek's rise to power as the promise of a better future, but he was soon disappointed. Early in 1976, after he had criticized Gierek during a union meeting for failing to live up to his promises, Walesa was fired from his shipyard job. Over the next four years the authorities would punish him for his activism on behalf of worker's rights by having him fired from one job after another.

The Polish Situation, 1968-70

After World War II, during which Poland had been occupied by Germany, the Soviet Union took control and established a Communist government, which by the late 1960s was led by the moderate Communist Waldyslaw Gomulka. Popular at first, Gomulka boldly declared that Poland would follow its own path to socialism, but he soon lost his courage to confront the Soviets and also lost the trust of the Polish people. His pledge that Poland would adhere to the Warsaw Pact (an agreement of mutual support by the Soviet Union and its satellites) led to a particularly trying year in 1968. Polish students demanding an end to censorship were beaten up and arrested. Polish troops joined the Soviet Union in ending the "Prague Spring" period of liberalism in Czechoslovakia. The troubles continued in 1970 when the government announced food price hikes just before Christmas. Violent riots occurred, and Gomulka resigned under great pressure, to be replaced by another Communist leader, Edward Gierek.

Participation: Freeing Poland From Soviet Domination

Events leading up to 1980. In April 1978 Walesa was one of a small group of activists at Gdansk who announced the formation of the Baltic Committee for Free and Independent Trade Unions. Under Communist rule, the so-called unions had always functioned as Party bodies for keeping workers under control. The demand for independent, self-governing trade unions was therefore a revolutionary one.

Crisis. At the end of the 1970s, with Poland near bankruptcy and Western banks unwilling to advance any more loans, there were severe and chronic shortages of food and other essential items. The Gierek regime's response was to deny the problem and strengthen the repression of the Polish people. Then in July 1980, the government, having finally acknowledged the economic crisis, warned the public that things were going to get worse and proceeded to raise the price of meat.

Amid the turmoil of this announcement, much-loved shipyard activist Anna Walentynowicz was fired, five months before her retirement was to have become effective. She had worked at the Lenin Shipyard for thirty years. Her dismissal and the government's action over meat prices touched off the strike that gave birth to the Solidarity workers' movement.

Strike. The wave of strikes that swept Poland started on July 1, 1980, in Lubin where railwaymen welded an engine to the rails of the Moscow line in protest of the exporting of scarce meat to the Soviet Union. In Gdansk, Walesa and his Free Trade Union associates called for an occupation strike to begin at the shipyard on August 14. Walesa had been fired from the shipyard four years earlier and had to be smuggled in to lead the strike. The strike committee's first demands were deliberately limited in scope in order to attract as broad a base of support as possible. They called for the reinstatement of Walentynowicz and Walesa, a pay raise, and an increase in the family allowance, along with immunity for striking workers and permission to erect the memorial to the December 1970 victims.

The strike spreads. Three days later, having won most of their demands, the strikers prepared to leave the shipyard they had occupied. By this time, however, the strike had spread to several other businesses in the area, and the end of the strike at the Lenin Shipyard was greeted by other strikers as a betrayal. Quickly summing up the situation, Walesa took it upon himself to rally the shipyard workers to resume the strike. A new, more militant Inter-enterprise Strike Committee, with Walesa as chairman, was hastily put together. This strike committee scrapped the old list of demands and presented a new set of twenty-one. Foremost on the new list was the demand for the recognition of free and independent trade unions. As Walesa would later state, Solidarity was born at the moment the shipyard strike expanded from the local shipyard to support demands of other factory workers.

Solidarity. At first the government refused to negotiate with the Inter-enterprise Strike Committee, but on August 23 Gierek sent Mieczslaw Jagielski, deputy prime minister for economic affairs, to hold talks with the Gdansk strikers. The workers were aided in their negotiations by other activist advisers, and the

▲ A Solidarity demonstration in Warsaw in May 1985; by 1980, when the union was formed, Solidarity drew strength and support from workers, intellectuals, and the Catholic clergy.

release of jailed activists was one of the demands on which Walesa and his group would not budge. Negotiations between the strikers and the government were broadcast over loudspeakers to all the workers in the shipyard and to crowds that kept watch outside.

Agreement was finally reached at the end of August. Similar agreements were reached between strikers and the government in the cities of Szczechin and Jastrzebie. By the middle of September 1980, Solidarity could boast of three million members, almost a third of them Communists who had broken ranks with the party. In November, with the union threatening a nationwide strike if the government blocked its registration, Solidarity was recognized as the first legal, independent trade union in the Soviet bloc. At the first National Congress of Solidarity in October 1981, Walesa was elected president of the union. By this time Solidarity's membership had grown to ten million.

Imprisonment and honors. Solidarity lasted as a legal trade union until December 13, 1981, when the prime minister and first secretary of the Polish Communist Party, General Wojciech Jaruzelski, announced a "state of war" and imposed martial law. Thousands of Solidarity activists, including Walesa, were rounded up and jailed.

Unable to operate legally, Solidarity became an underground opposition movement. Walesa, held in solitary confinement throughout his stay in prison, was released November 12, 1982. Throughout the period that Solidarity was banned, Walesa remained a powerful symbol of the Polish people's struggle for human rights. A year after his release from prison, Walesa was awarded the Nobel Peace Prize. The award was roundly protested by the Polish government.

The end of Polish Communism. The Nobel Prize winner spent the next five years working again as an electrician at the Lenin Shipyard, meeting a steady stream of journalists and struggling to keep Solidarity alive in the face of government opposition. **Mikhail Gorbachev's** (see entry) rise to power in the Soviet Union and the reforms he set in motion there gave the Polish people cause for hope, but even in 1988 it was impossible to foresee that the Communist regimes of Eastern Europe would all crumble within a year, or that their removal would be achieved—except in Romania—without bloodshed.

Solidarity triumphs. By 1988 the economic situation in Poland had worsened to the point that workers began to strike without encouragement from Solidarity. In August the government invited opposing organizations to join a "round table" to reach an accord that would unify the nation. Solidarity's condition for participating in the round table was the re-legalization of the union. Reluctantly the

Forerunner of the Solidarity Movement

In 1976 the Polish economy had again tumbled. As prices rose, riots broke out and protesters were brutally dispersed by government forces. The savagery of the government response led to the formation of the Committee for Workers Defense (KOR), an organization dedicated to helping victims of the crackdown. KOR and other opposition to the government received a boost in 1978 when the cardinal of Cracow, Karol Wojtila, became Pope John Paul II, the first Slavic pope in church history. By 1980, when Solidarity was formed, it could draw strength and support from workers, intellectuals (who had organized KOR), and the Catholic clergy.

▲ Walesa greets a crowd gathered at Daley Center Plaza in Chicago, November 1989; two months later the Polish Communist Party would dissolve itself, and in December 1990 Walesa would be elected president of Poland.

government agreed, and talks were held throughout February and resumed in the first week of April. An agreement was reached that called for free elections to select 35 percent of the representatives in the Sejm, Poland's lower house of parliament, with the rest reserved for the Communist Party and its allies. All seats in the Senate were to be freely elected. In June 1989, barely two months after being legalized, Solidarity won 99 of 100 Senate seats and all the "free" seats in the Sejm. The following January the Communist Party dissolved itself, and in December 1990 Lech Walesa was elected president of Poland.

Aftermath

Walesa's presidency was not an easy one. His first choice for prime minister, Jan Olszewiski, could not organize a government and was replaced by a more radical politician-economist, Jan Krzysztof Bielecki. The new government was fragmented from the start with non-Solidarity representatives joining union members on the Council of Ministers, the prime minister's cabinet. Progress under Walesa's five-year term was slowed by the new political fervor that swept the nation, resulting in the formation of more than one hundred political parties. At first, because of opposition in Germany, Poland was not even allowed to enter discussions about establishing its borders firmly. In 1989 Poland's average income had risen to only $1,760 per person.

For More Information

Craig, Mary. *The Crystal Spirit: Lech Walesa and His Poland.* New York: Crossroad, 1986.

Eringer, Robert. *Strike for Freedom: The Story of Lech Walesa and Polish Solidarity.* New York: Dodd, Mead, 1982.

Frankland, Mark. *The Patriots' Revolution: How Eastern Europe Toppled Communism and Won Its Freedom.* Chicago: Ivan R. Dee, 1990.

Walesa, Lech. *The Struggle and the Triumph: An Autobiography.* New York: Arcade, 1992.

Walesa, Lech. *A Way of Hope: An Autobiography.* New York: Henry Holt, 1987.

Ronald Reagan

1911-

Personal Background

Youth. Ronald Reagan was born on February 6, 1911, in Tampico, Illinois, the son of a shoe salesman. When he was nine, the family moved to Dixon, Illinois, where he completed elementary school and high school. A hard worker, Reagan became a star football player in high school while earning good grades. During the summers he worked as a construction worker and a lifeguard. His hard work earned him a college scholarship, with which he attended Eureka College near Peoria, Illinois. Again he combined study and work, supporting himself while in college with jobs as a waiter, dishwasher, and lawn raker.

At Eureka, Reagan majored in economics. His studies included the works of classical economists such as Adam Smith and David Ricardo. Reagan would continue to read the works of classical economists even after he left college. Working and carrying a heavy economics study program, Reagan still found time to act in college plays and to be on the football and swim teams. Before he graduated in 1932, he had been selected captain of the swim team and president of a fraternity.

Acting. His college degree was in economics, but Reagan had found a special interest in theater. Upon graduation he looked for a job in radio and was hired by station WOC, in Davenport, Iowa, to announce University of Iowa football games. When WOC

▲ **Ronald Reagan**

Event: Engineering the end of the cold war.

Role: As president of the United States, Ronald Reagan rallied the American spirit of democracy, revitalized the U.S. military, and promoted innovative programs such as the one popularly known as "Star Wars." His assertive policy toward the Soviet Union helped bring about the termination of the cold war.

merged with station WHO of Des Moines, he became a sports-caster and, later, sports editor for WHO.

In 1937 Joy Hodges, a former associate of Reagan's who had become a lounge singer at the Biltmore Bowl in Los Angeles, introduced Reagan to some movie industry executives. They soon discovered his acting talent, and he was placed under contract with Warner Brothers, a major Hollywood studio. Reagan was soon appearing in movies. Perhaps his best known role was that of George Gipp, a football player, in the 1940 motion picture *Knute Rockne: All American*. The role earned him the nickname "the Gipper," which he would carry throughout life. By 1941 Reagan was one of the top stars in Hollywood, his fan mail second only to that of Errol Flynn.

Reagan's acting career was interrupted when he was drafted at the start of World War II. He spent much of the war making films for the air force. After the war, Reagan returned to Hollywood, but his acting career never again reached its prewar heights. Still, he became active in the Screen Actors' Guild, and eventually became its president. Concerned about the influence of Communists in an industry that could affect public opinion, Reagan expelled Communists from the union and required members to swear an oath of loyalty to the United States.

The Reagan Family

In 1940 Reagan married actress Jane Wyman. The couple had two children, Maureen and Michael. Maureen would later enter politics in California, and Michael would become a radio talk show host.

Reagan's marriage to Jane Wyman ended in 1948. Four years later he married Nancy Davis, an actress who was the daughter of a neurosurgeon. This marriage would produce two more children, Ronald Jr. and Patty. Ronald Jr. would become a ballet dancer and television personality, and Patty would become an author.

Television and politics. In 1954 Reagan launched a television career when he became host of the series *General Electric Theater*. The job included making off-screen appearances at General Electric plants to give speeches and sign autographs. Another part of the job was to make community relations speeches. These positions fostered his growing interest in politics.

In 1948 Democrats had tried to persuade Reagan to run for Congress, but he refused. Then in 1950 he actively campaigned for Helen Gahagan Douglas, a Democratic candidate for Congress who eventually lost to her Republican opponent, Richard Nixon. Soon after this election, Reagan switched parties and supported Republican politicians.

The speech. On October 27, 1964, Reagan delivered a televised speech in support of presidential candidate Barry Goldwater. He had written the speech himself, mixing facts, anecdotes, dire warnings, and humor. Reagan supported Goldwater's campaign to cut government in Washington. He cautioned that continued growth of centralized government in Washington would eventually erode individual freedom and self-reliance. "The Speech," as this address became known, generated thousands of favorable letters and telegrams and persuaded thousands of people to vote for Goldwater, who, nonetheless, lost the election. Reagan, who was then hosting the television series *Death Valley Days,* found himself a political star pursued by the Republicans to challenge Democratic incumbent Edmund G. "Pat" Brown for the governorship of California.

Some Candidates for Whom Reagan Campaigned	
1952	Dwight Eisenhower, presidential candidate
1960	Richard Nixon, presidential candidate
1962	Richard Nixon, California gubernatorial candidate
1964	Barry Goldwater, presidential candidate

Governor. Reagan campaigned on a platform calling for welfare and tax reform and for downsizing California government. In 1966 he defeated Brown by more than a million votes and, in 1970, was reelected governor by almost half a million votes.

Buoyed by his supporters, Reagan even made an unsuccessful run for the White House in 1968. He was only partially successful, however, in his efforts to cut taxes, spending, and government growth. Faced with a massive budget deficit, he authorized the largest tax increase in the state's history. In 1973 he sponsored a ballot initiative to cut taxes, but that bill failed.

Reagan left the governorship when his second term ran out in 1975. The next year, he ran for the presidential nomination against Republican incumbent Gerald Ford. The campaign was hotly contested all the way to the Republican National Convention, where Ford defeated Reagan by a close margin. Ford lost the

▲ Reagan shortly after he won his third bid for the presidency, 1980. This time the voters elected him, responding to his call for reducing government, increasing defense, and pursuing a firmer policy toward the Soviet Union.

general election to Jimmy Carter. Reagan then became an outspoken critic of the Carter administration. In 1980 he made his third bid for the presidency. This time the voters elected him, responding to his call for reducing government, increasing defense, and pursuing a firmer policy toward the Soviet Union.

Participation:
Engineering the End of the Cold War

The cold war. At the time Reagan took office, the Soviets appeared to be winning the so-called cold war. Over the previous decade, several pro-Soviet and anti-United States governments had come to power in Asia, Africa, and Latin America. The Soviets were making greater efforts to develop more nuclear weapons than the Americans. Soviet leaders even boasted that world forces were shifting in their favor. American policymakers seemed to be in the grip of uncertainty and guilt resulting from policy failures in Vietnam. As leaders wavered, the economy stagnated, with high unemployment, high interest rates, and double-digit inflation.

Reagan set out to raise the nation's spirits. In his speeches, he "succeeded in getting across at the popular level the notion that America was a dynamic, resourceful nation again, after the doubts of the 1970s" (Johnson, pp. 749-50). His ability to hold the attention of a popular audience won him the nickname "the Great Communicator." In his speeches, he took a firm stand against Communism. At one point, he referred to the Soviet Union as an "evil empire" and the "focus of evil in the world" (Muir, p. 75). The president told students at Notre Dame University that the final pages in the history of Communism were being written as he spoke in 1981. However, to successfully confront the "evil empire," Reagan set out to rebuild the nation's military and economic strength.

Defenses. Soon after taking office, Reagan began to overhaul the nation's defenses, which he believed had been neglected and underfunded since the Vietnam War. A program to build a supersonic bomber, the B-1, was revived, and a campaign was

begun to add nearly 150 ships to the navy. Spending on military research was doubled.

"Star Wars." Perhaps the most technologically advanced—and controversial—of Reagan's defense programs was the Strategic Defense Initiative (SDI), known as "Star Wars," a program designed to protect the United States from missiles. A White House committee had been studying ballistic (skyborne) missile defense (BMD) since Reagan took office, and in early 1983 the Joint Chiefs of Staff recommended proceeding with BMD research. Reagan launched the SDI program in a televised speech on March 23, 1983. He told listeners that the United States would try to build a defense by which "we could intercept and destroy missiles before they reached our soil or that of our allies" (Johnson, pp. 389-90). However, critics of the plan pointed out that it was technologically unrealistic, that it would not defend against certain missiles and aircraft, and that it would lead to further militarization—not exploration—of space.

At arms control negotiations, shocked Soviet leaders tried to persuade Reagan to scrap the SDI program, to which they had responded with large and expensive research and development programs of their own. Reagan refused. But due to the high cost of developing the SDI program, progress on it moved very slowly or not at all. Still it accomplished the goal the president had described to British prime minister Margaret Thatcher in 1984: it was a useful means of applying economic pressure on the Soviet Union.

Active resistance. Reagan's overhaul of the military was matched by his willingness to use this force when necessary. Wherever the Soviets or their allies challenged militarily, Reagan responded with force. He ordered navy pilots to shoot down Libyan planes on two occasions (1981 and 1989) when they chal-

◀

The assassination attempt on Reagan: he waves and then looks up before being shoved into the presidential limousine by secret service agents after being shot outside a Washington hotel, March 30, 1981. Reagan recovered completely and quickly; the would-be assassin, John Hinckley, Jr., was sentenced to life in a psychiatric prison.

The Reagan Doctrine and Iran-Contra

The Reagan administration searched for ways to roll back Soviet gains by supporting resistance groups and providing economic aid all over the world: providing missiles to the rebellious Mujahideen in Afghanistan, supporting rebel groups in Nicaragua and Angola, giving money and other supplies to Solidarity in Poland. In his 1985 State of the Union Address, Reagan defined this action: "On every continent from Afghanistan to Nicaragua support for freedom fighters is self-defense" (Edwards, p. 261). The policy thus defined what became known as the Reagan Doctrine.

Sometimes, however, in its zeal to fund these groups, the Reagan administration disobeyed the wishes of Congress. In 1983 Congress passed legislation forbidding any government agency from providing aid to the Nicaraguan rebels (known as contras). The Reagan administration, in response, used the National Security Council to direct the selling of weapons to Iran and then to use the money collected to fund the contras. This secret arrangement was soon discovered, and it became known as the Iran-contra affair. Special charges were brought against most of the major players in the scandal, but the roles of Reagan and Vice President George Bush were never made clear.

lenged U.S. Navy positions. The invasion of the small island nation of Grenada, which had been taken over by Marxists (1983), and the bombing of Libya in response to Libyan terrorist bombings in Berlin (1986) were other demonstrations of U.S. military aggressiveness under Reagan.

Reagan and Gorbachev. The strained Soviet-American relations eased gradually after **Mikhail Gorbachev** (see entry) took over the leadership of the Soviet Union in 1985. Reagan soon came to realize that Gorbachev was a man who could—and would—effect change in the Soviet Union. In 1987, after two summit meetings, the two world leaders were ready to make a deal. Gorbachev agreed to dismantle a number of Soviet missiles if NATO would do the same. For the first time in history, both sides actually agreed to reduce their nuclear arsenals.

Aftermath

Visit to Russia. Gorbachev and Reagan continued to have cordial, even friendly, relations. Reagan softened his descriptions of the Soviet Union, but continued to prod Gorbachev on the issue of human rights and urged him to tear down the Berlin Wall. Gorbachev's series of reforms, called *perestroika* ("restructuring") and *glasnost* ("openness"), soon led to the weakening of the rigid Communist structure in Russia. In 1988 Reagan visited Moscow and was even permitted to explain to Moscow University students the advantages of American-style freedom and constitutionalism.

Out of office. In the same year, Reagan's vice-president, George Bush, was elected president. Reagan, seventy-eight years old, went into retirement. He had seen improvements in the military and a reduction in inflation. However, his sharp increase in military spending, the largest ever in peacetime America, resulted in budget deficits. Under Reagan's administration, the national debt more than doubled in size. His actions in office consequently encouraged the Soviet Union to withdraw troops from Afghanistan, to loosen its influence on Poland and Nicaragua, and to arrange a temporary truce in another trouble spot, Angola.

After his retirement, Reagan oversaw the establishment of his presidential library in Simi Valley. In November 1994 he announced that he had contracted Alzheimer's disease, a degenerative illness of old age.

For More Information

Edwards, Lee. *Reagan: A Political Biography.* San Diego, California: Viewpoint, 1967.

Johnson, Paul. *Modern Times: The World from the Twenties to the Nineties.* New York: Harper Perennial, 1991.

Muir, William Ker, Jr. *The Bully Pulpit: The Presidential Leadership of Ronald Reagan.* San Francisco: Institute for Contemporary Studies, 1992.

Weinberger, Caspar W. *Fighting for Peace.* New York: Warner Books, 1993.

Boris Yeltsin

1931-

Personal Background

Difficult start. Yeltsin almost did not survive his baptism because a drunken priest forgot to take him out of the baptismal font. Noting that the baby had survived the ordeal, the unruffled priest named him Boris, meaning "fighter."

Boris Nikolayevich Yeltsin was born February 1, 1931, in Butko, a village near Sverdlovsk (now Yekaterinburg) in western Russia. There, despite his near fatal beginning, Boris lived in a communal barracks with about one hundred other people. The Yeltsin family was extremely poor and caught up in Soviet leader Joseph Stalin's abrupt move to bring all Soviet agriculture under national control. Peasant farm families such as the Yeltsins were forced to give up the land they had worked and move to collective farms, *kolkhozes*.

As he was growing up on a kolkhoz, Yeltsin learned of the inequalities of life in the Soviet Union. At food stores, he would sometimes sneak into the section were the Communist Party leaders were allowed to shop and noticed the cheese, white bread, and canned beef for sale there. Ordinary citizens like himself were only allowed to purchase coarse flour, rancid butter, and occasionally fish. At one point, the young Yeltsin told his mother that he wanted to be a party boss so that he could enjoy their shopping privileges.

▲ **Boris Yeltsin**

Event: Restructuring the former Soviet Union.

Role: As president of the Russian Republic, Boris Yeltsin reluctantly accepted the breakup of the Union of Soviet Socialist Republics and began to replace it with a confederation of more independent states.

Yeltsin had a tendency to be bold to the point of recklessness. At his junior high school graduation, he presented a speech denouncing a teacher he believed to be unworthy. (The teacher was eventually dismissed.) As a teenager, he talked some friends into taking a long hike into the Ural Mountains. The boys got lost and contracted typhoid fever after drinking swamp water. They were at the point of death when they were finally rescued.

Engineer. When he was eighteen years old, Yeltsin decided that he wanted to study civil engineering at the Ural Polytechnic Institute in Sverdlovsk. In the Russian tradition, he would need his family to agree. To earn his grandfather's approval, he spent the summer building him a *banya,* or Russian sauna. Boris cut trees from a nearby forest, dragged the logs to the site alone, and cut them into boards. He completed the structure and won his grandfather's blessing in time to start school.

Boris Yeltsin, Athlete

Yeltsin was fond of sports. He belonged to skiing, boxing, wrestling, and decathlon teams, but he was especially fond of volleyball. Although he lost his left thumb in an explosion while playing with a hand grenade during World War II, he overcame this handicap to become an accomplished volleyball player.

At Ural Polytechnic Institute, Yeltsin was a successful and popular student. He excelled in sports and won many fans around the campus. Upon earning his degree in civil engineering, he was considered qualified to supervise construction work. He believed, however, that to successfully manage a construction site one must know all the trades involved. Therefore, Yeltsin imposed on himself another year of training to learn twelve trades of construction. One month, he would learn to be a carpenter, the next a concrete mixer, and so on for the whole year. Yeltsin "worked until he dropped with fatigue," but he eventually learned all the trades (Solovyov and Klepikova, p. 133).

Working and raising a family. When he landed a job supervising construction, Yeltsin worked up to sixteen hours a day and drove his crews almost as hard. His workers, however, considered him fair and honest. Yeltsin refused special privileges and would not give friends or relatives unfair advantages in the work force. While still a beginning construction boss, he married Naya Girina, whom he had met in college. The Yeltsins would eventually have two daughters.

By the 1960s Yeltsin was supervising thousands of workers and had developed a reputation for high-quality work and for completing projects on time. He joined the Communist Party in 1961 and, by the end of the decade, had become chairman of the party's construction committee in Sverdlovsk. In 1976 General Secretary Leonid Brezhnev made him first secretary of the Sverdlovsk region. Even in this position as regional political leader, Yeltsin refused the privileges normally given party bosses and lived modestly. He believed that those who worked with him should share his love of labor and drove them ruthlessly to complete projects on time. During his rule, the Sverdlovsk area was relatively free of the bribery and corruption that was rampant elsewhere in the Soviet Union.

No matter how hard Yeltsin worked, however, his region was frequently unable to meet the industrial production goals set unrealistically high by planners in Moscow. Yeltsin was not willing to bribe or arrange other intrigues with government auditors, so he was frequently reprimanded by his superiors in Moscow for failing to meet the goals. Sometimes he earned this rebuke by defying Moscow, as when, in the late 1970s, he defied directions to concentrate on industrial construction. Instead Yeltsin ordered old communal barracks, like the ones in

> ## Yeltsin, the Adventurer
>
> In 1952, while still at the Polytechnic Institute, Yeltsin took a tour around the Soviet Union to satisfy his desire to see the country and, especially, the ocean. He traveled in freight cars and slept in railroad stations and parks—a dangerous way to take a tour during the Stalin era.

which he grew up, to be razed. Modern apartments were built to house the residents. Such actions made him popular with the people of Sverdlovsk.

Meeting Gorbachev. During his years as party boss in Sverdlovsk, Yeltsin got to know **Mikhail Gorbachev** (see entry), the boss of the Stavropol region. The two often negotiated trade agreements between their regions. Gorbachev became the Soviet Union's leader in 1985 and apparently saw Yeltsin as a potential supporter for his ideas of *glasnost* ("openness") and *perestroika* ("reconstruction")—reform movements that Gorbachev deemed necessary. He appointed Yeltsin head of the construction section of the Central Committee a few weeks after coming to power.

▲ Yeltsin talks to a shopkeeper in the Volga region at Saratov, January 1992; when Yeltsin was growing up, Communist Party leaders could buy cheese, white bread, and canned beef while ordinary citizens like himself were only allowed to purchase coarse flour, rancid butter, and occasionally fish.

Later that year, he made the reluctant Yeltsin Moscow's party boss. In early 1986 Gorbachev made Yeltsin a candidate (nonvoting member) of the Politburo, the Communist Party's highest decision-making body.

Participation:
Restructuring the Former Soviet Union

***Glasnost* and *perestroika*.** Yeltsin was an enthusiastic supporter of the Gorbachev reforms. He often traveled around Moscow in disguise and even stood in food lines with ordinary citizens in his zeal to uncover corruption. His crusade for reform and openness resulted in the firing and prosecution of a number of party bureaucrats and officials. Yeltsin himself continued to live modestly and refused to ride in party limousines, preferring public transportation.

Break with Gorbachev. Never a patient follower, by 1987 Yeltsin had become impatient with the slow pace of Gorbachev's reforms. On September 12 he sent the party leader a letter listing his grievances and resigning from the Politburo. When Gorbachev failed to respond, Yeltsin delivered a speech at a meeting of party leaders criticizing the sluggish pace of reform. When he finished, several of those in the audience denounced him.

A few days later, while Yeltsin was in a hospital with a heart condition, Gorbachev personally ordered that he be brought to the Politburo. Although the doctors said he should not be moved, Yeltsin was filled with tranquilizers and taken to the meeting. In a scene that reminded some of the Stalin-era atrocities, the drugged Yeltsin was forced to confess his misdeeds, subjected to further denunciations, and then fired. Gorbachev may have taken this action to appease the Communist hard-liners. Yeltsin's enthusiasm for *perestroika* and his anticorruption campaign had made some members of the party elite nervous.

After he ousted Yeltsin, Gorbachev told him, "I'll never let you back into politics" (Solovyov and Klepikova, p. 107). Gorbachev was, however, sensitive to publicity. To limit negative public reactions to the firing, he appointed Yeltsin to the State Committee for Construction (Gostroi), which he hoped would distance him from the center of Communist politics and keep him out of trouble. Yeltsin, however, began almost immediately to plan a comeback.

Reappearance. It soon became apparent that Gorbachev would not find it easy to keep Yeltsin out of politics. The position at Gostroi allowed Yeltsin to attend the June 1988 Communist Party Conference along with five thousand delegates from across the Soviet Union. Blocked from being a delegate from Moscow or his home region, Sverdlovsk, he maneuvered a last appointment to represent Karelia, a region on the Finnish border. He eventually won the right to speak to the conference and used this opportunity to deny the confession he had been forced to make. He also

▲ Yeltsin makes his first address as President of the Russian Federation Parliament in May 1990; never a patient follower, by 1987 Yeltsin had become impatient with the slow pace of Gorbachev's reforms.

took party leaders to task for their exploitation of special privileges and demanded that *perestroika* be speeded up. He called for quick action on free elections. The speech brought him loads of supporting mail. By the end of the year, he was seen as a major rival to Gorbachev.

Completing the break. Less than two years after he was purged, Yeltsin became the recognized leader of the reform opposition movement to Gorbachev. Then in July 1990, the rebellious leader made his first bold move to break up the Communist domination of the Soviet Union. The party was holding its twenty-eighth congress (and, as it turned out, its last), and Yeltsin chose this forum to announce his resignation from the Communist Party. The next year, he ran for president of the Russian Republic, which was holding its first elections. Although the media was still controlled by the Communist Party and conducted a mudslinging campaign, Yeltsin decisively defeated his Communist opponent.

> ## Taking Advantage of *Perestroika*
>
> Part of the Gorbachev reform called for establishing a Congress of People's Deputies, a smaller, more action-oriented group whose main job would be to select the Supreme Soviet (Soviet legislature) and the Presidium (executive leaders). Yeltsin decided to run for a spot in the Congress and, despite a vicious campaign against him, was elected with nearly 90 percent of the votes. Soon afterward, a deputy from Siberia serving in the Supreme Soviet resigned, giving his seat to Yeltsin. He had made good personal use of *perestroika*.

Heroism: The Gorbachev kidnapping. The Soviet Union had been held together, sometimes ruthlessly, under a treaty of 1922 that placed all the states under strict domination of the Communist Party at Moscow. In 1991 Gorbachev prepared to present a new treaty. At the insistence of Yeltsin and others, he had decided that it was time to greatly reduce the role of the central Soviet government. The new treaty was threatening to the Communist Party hard-liners. On August 19, the day before the new Union Treaty was to be signed, a group of these hard-line leaders, some of whom had been put into office by Gorbachev, placed him under arrest at his vacation home in the Crimea.

From his home outside Moscow, Yeltsin and his staff rushed to the Soviet "White House" and began to organize resistance to the coup. He realized that he would have to restore his old enemy to power or face the probability of reversion to old-line Communism and even military government. Yeltsin began by asking the Soviet people to stage a general strike and demand to see Gorbachev on television. Yeltsin himself climbed atop an armored tank and began addressing the Moscow crowd, which soon grew to tens of thousands. Troops sent by the kidnappers to put down his resistance turned around and joined Yeltsin's protest.

The next day, 150,000 people demonstrated in front of the seat of government. Yeltsin told them he intended to hold out as long as he and his supporters needed to remove the newly organized junta (group controlling the government) from power. Citizens began building barricades in the streets. Yeltsin declared all army units in the Russian Republic to be under his command and soon pro-Yeltsin army units were joining the Yeltsin demonstration. The coup, which had been poorly planned from the outset, now began to unravel. Much of the military, including the air force commander in chief, and probably elements of the KGB, the Soviet secret police, were apparently opposed to the kidnapping. Although elite KGB troops might have crushed the resistance, none appeared.

Within seventy-two hours the coup had collapsed and Gorbachev had flown back to Moscow. Yeltsin, however, now held the real power in the Soviet Union; Gorbachev was reduced to a figurehead. The Communist Party was soon outlawed altogether, and Yeltsin ordered its property seized by the Russian government. After one last attempt to conclude the new treaty in late 1991, the Soviet Union was dissolved and replaced by a loose association known as the Commonwealth of Independent States. In agreeing to this dissolution, Yeltsin gave up all of Russia's conquests from the reign of Peter the Great in the late seventeenth century through that of Alexander II. in the late nineteenth century

Aftermath

The years following the breakup of the Soviet Union were difficult for Russia. The Communist government apparatus had not been entirely dismantled. Communists retained a power base in the army, police, and the kolkhozes. Yeltsin nevertheless continued to follow his commitment to change. In 1993 he withdrew the last Russian troops from Poland, the Baltic states, and Cuba. That same year, he ordered troops to fire on the Parliament building to put down an uprising of Communist members of Parliament. After Communists and extremists made strong gains in the elections, however, he was forced to slow the pace of reforms toward a free-market economy.

Russia also continues to suffer from ethnic violence. In December 1994 Yeltsin sent troops to Chechnya, a region in the Caucasus Mountains, to suppress a rebellion of Chechen people. Russian troops and aircraft killed tens of thousands of Chechen civilians in bloody campaigns. Guerrilla resistance by the Chechens continued into the summer of 1995, costing Yeltsin much popular support in Russia. Amid rumors of ill health, Yeltsin faces a tough challenge as he prepares to run for reelection as president of the Russian Republic in 1996.

For More Information

Ayer, Eleanor H. *Boris Yeltsin: Man of the People.* New York: Dillon, 1992.

Malia, Martin. "Apocalypse Not." *New Republic,* vol. 208, no. 8 (February 22, 1993), pp. 21-27.

Malia, Martin. *The Soviet Tragedy: A History of Socialism in Russia, 1917-1991.* New York: The Free Press, 1994.

Solovyov, Victor, and Elena Klepikova. *Boris Yeltsin: A Political Biography.* New York: G. P. Putnam's Sons, 1992.

Winning African Independence

1956
France yields to independence movement for Morocco and Tunisia.

1960
Italy yields independence to Somalia. Belgium leaves an independent Congo.

1960-70
1.5 million black South Africans are forcibly moved from their homes and collected in "homelands."

1963
Robert Mugabe organizes the Zimbabwe African National Union (ZANU).

1964
Jomo Kenyatta becomes the first elected president of Kenya.

1974
After eleven years in detention, Mugabe becomes leader of Zanu.

1975
Portugal abandons claims to Mozambique and Angola.

1979
Rhodesians win universal right to vote.

1980
Zimbabwe wins independence; Mugabe elected first president.

1989
F. W. de Klerk becomes president of South Africa.

1990
African National Congress (ANC) is legally recognized in South Africa. ANC leader **Nelson Mandela** is freed from prison.

1994
Nelson Mandela becomes first black president of South Africa.

WINNING AFRICAN INDEPENDENCE

Except for Egypt and Ethiopia, which won independent status in 1922 and 1928, respectively, and the small nations of Liberia and Réunion, no modern African nation existed before 1955. Most current nations in Africa are less than forty years old.

The nineteenth century saw a scramble among European nations to carve great territories from Africa and to settle African colonies with Europeans who would control them. Resistance of blacks and other native Africans to this colonization effort existed from the beginning and finally became organized in 1912. That year, the African National Congress began to unite Africans to press for their own independence. The wealth of some regions of Africa, however, was cause enough for European nations to hold on to their African claims.

World War II left European countries weakened and short of the manpower needed to control their African colonies. One after another, European nations abandoned Africa. Some, such as Belgium and Britain, yielded parts of their colonial possessions to independence without a quarrel; others, including France and, in the south of Africa, Britain, yielded to native African self-rule only after prolonged guerrilla warfare.

The Birth of African Nations

Year Gained Independence	Nation	Former colony of
1847	Liberia	United States*
1934	South Africa	Great Britain
1946	Réunion	France
1956	Morocco	France
1957	Ghana	Great Britain
1960	Benin	France
1960	Burkina Faso	France
1960	Cameroon	France
1960	Central African Republic	France
1960	Chad	France
1960	Congo	France
1960	Côte d'Ivoire (Ivory Coast)	France
1960	Gabon	France
1960	Guinea	France
1960	Madagascar	France
1960	Mali	France
1960	Mauritania	France
1960	Niger	France
1960	Nigeria	Great Britain
1960	Senegal	France
1960	Somalia	Italy
1960	Togo	France
1960	Zaire	Belgium
1961	Sierra Leone	Great Britain
1961	Tanzania	Great Britain
1962	Algeria	France

The ANC. In 1912 the African National Congress (ANC) was formed to seek civil rights for blacks. The white governments responded by enacting laws that gave them absolute power over blacks. With small minorities in Kenya, South Africa, Mozambique, Zimbabwe, and other regions of Africa, whites controlled

The Birth of African Nations

Year Gained Independence	Nation	Former colony of
1962	Burundi	Belgium
1962	Rwanda	Belgium
1962	Gambia	Great Britain
1962	Uganda	Great Britain
1963	Kenya	Great Britain
1964	Zambia	Great Britain
1966	Botswana	Great Britain
1966	Lesotho	Great Britain
1966	Malawi	Great Britain
1968	Mauritius	Great Britain
1968	Swaziland	Great Britain
1974	Cape Verde	Portugal
1974	Guinea-Bissau	Portugal
1975	Angola	Portugal
1975	Comoros	France
1975	Mozambique	Portugal
1975	São Tomé and Príncipe Island	Portugal
1975	Sudan	Great Britain; Egypt
1977	Djibouti	France
1980	Zimbabwe	Great Britain
1989	Namibia	South Africa; Great Britain
1993	Eritrea	Ethiopia; Italy

* The colonization and organization of Liberia was aided by the United States, but Liberia was never an official U.S. colony.

the economies and governments. The first strong resistance to white control came in 1944, when a coalition of black groups in Kenya formed the Kenya African Union (KAU). Out of this union arose **Jomo Kenyatta,** a strong leader adept at guerrilla warfare and political intrigue. In 1954 he was imprisoned for his

▲ **F. W. de Klerk and Nelson Mandela shared the Nobel Peace Prize of 1993; they negotiated an agreement on a new constitution that gives all South Africans the right to vote.**

work within the banned KAU and with a radical group known as the Mau Mau. Released ten years later, Kenyatta became the first president of the independent, black-dominated socialist Republic of Kenya. Years later a Zimbabwe African National Union would produce another black leader, **Robert Mugabe,** who would lead the black majority in Zimbabwe to independence in 1980.

The end of apartheid. In South Africa, it soon became evident that *apartheid* (the racial segregation policy) was not working. As unemployment increased, blacks drifted into the cities despite the laws requiring passes. By the late 1970s, employers were illegally hiring blacks to fill "whites only" jobs, and blacks were moving into whites-only neighborhoods. Several countries, including the United States, imposed economic sanctions on South Africa because of its racist policies. Inside the country, black anti-apartheid groups such as the ANC waged a terrorist campaign against the government.

The thinking of Afrikaner leaders (the controlling group of the white government) was also changing, and many were coming to the realization that apartheid was not working. The Dutch Reformed Church, to which most Afrikaners belonged, had once supported apartheid but similarly turned against it.

The government began to relax its policies. In the 1970s sports teams and theaters were integrated. State president Pieter W. Botha announced in 1986 that he was making a complete break with apartheid. By 1989 nearly all apartheid legislation had been repealed. Outside support of the ANC by such nations as the Soviet Union and Cuba was withdrawn, and the ANC was weakened militarily. That quieted white South African fears of the ANC.

Botha's successor, **F. W. de Klerk,** began the process that led to the final demise of apartheid when he removed the ban on the ANC and other rebel groups. The new president also began freeing political prisoners. In 1990 he freed **Nelson Mandela,** an ANC official and leading anti-apartheid spokesman who had served more than twenty-seven years in prison. His wife, Winnie Mandela, had popularized his cause while he was in prison.

Nelson Mandela and de Klerk eventually negotiated an agreement on a new constitution that gives all South Africans the right to vote. For this achievement, the two shared the Nobel Peace Prize of 1993. In 1994 Mandela became South Africa's first black president and de Klerk became deputy president and a prominent leader of the opposition to the ANC.

Robert Mugabe

1924-

Personal Background

Rhodesia. In 1888 a British capitalist, Cecil Rhodes, reached an agreement with Logenbula, chief of the Ndbele people, giving Rhodes mineral rights on Ndbele land. The founder of the De Beers Mining Company, Rhodes believed Britain should rule all of Africa, "from the Cape to Cairo." Although he had promised to send only ten whites into the region, within two years Rhodes had begun large-scale settlement in the land he named Rhodesia. The native black people were the victims of this movement, losing their land, being herded onto tribal reserves, being forced to work in the mines and factories of the whites, and receiving no political rights in the new British colony.

The Mugabe family. It was into these circumstances that Robert Mugabe was born, on February 21, 1924, to a peasant family in Kutama, a village fifty miles from Cecil Rhodes's capital, Salisbury. Kutama was known as a center of learning for Africans. Catholic Jesuit priests had established a mission there and begun schools for the blacks. By the time Mugabe was born, most of the blacks of Zimbabwe had blended their old religions with Christianity.

Teacher. Mugabe's father was a traveling carpenter who, when Mugabe was about ten years old, abandoned the family altogether and moved to South Africa to work in the mines there. But

▲ **Robert Mugabe**

Event: Leading the African independence movement in Zimbabwe.

Role: A rural schoolteacher turned revolutionary, Robert Mugabe united and led black nationalists in guerrilla warfare against the white minority government of former Southern Rhodesia. Fighting for black majority rule, Mugabe eventually became the president of the nation of Zimbabwe, one of Africa's most successful new nations of the postindependence era.

Mugabe's mother, Bona, was a strong woman with high standards for her children. As a child, Mugabe did his part to support the family by caring for the family cattle. Bona saw that her son attended school when he was old enough.

Mugabe attended the Jesuit elementary school and later entered the teachers' training college; teaching was one of the few occupations open to blacks. In 1943 Mugabe left Kutama to teach at mission schools throughout the country. It was at a mission school that he first met Ndabaningi Sithole, who was to become a leader in the Zimbabwean struggle for independence.

Great Zimbabwe

In precolonial times, the land that is now Zimbabwe was the home of peoples from the Shona nation. One thousand years ago, they settled throughout southern Africa, in lands they called "Great Zimbabwe." In the early nineteenth century, the Shona were defeated by the Ndbele tribe, thus losing their domination over the region. It was the Ndbele leadership that began the dealings with British businessmen that turned Ndbele and Shona land into a British colony. After the British defeated the Ndebele in 1893, both the Ndebele and the Shona fought unsuccessfully against the new, commercially motivated rulers of their land.

After winning a scholarship, Mugabe left teaching and Southern Rhodesia to pursue further studies at Fort Hare University College, an all-black college in South Africa. There Mugabe earned a degree in English and history in 1951. At the college, Mugabe was exposed to different modes of political thought and action, including black nationalism and communism. He learned of **Nelson Mandela** (see entry), the leader of the African National Congress, who was leading a political struggle against the apartheid regime of South Africa, and Mohandas Gandhi, a prominent spokesman against discrimination in South Africa and the leader of India's independence movement.

Participation: Leading the African Independence Movement in Zimbabwe

Early revolutionary politics. Black citizens of Zimbabwe knew that they wanted and needed reform, but they differed widely in their goals. Some worked for black majority rule; some only wanted a sort of power sharing with whites. In 1955

Mugabe's childhood friend, James Chikerema, founded the Southern Rhodesia African National Congress, an organization aimed at removing whites from power. At the other end of the spectrum was Joshua Nkomo, who advocated sharing power with whites and was already involved in negotiating with the white minority government for more rights for blacks.

Mugabe had little interest in the two black movements. He was concerned with the salaries of teachers like himself. His only early political encounter was with the Rhodesian prime minister with whom he pleaded unsuccessfully not to lower teachers' salaries. He would later claim that he threatened to fight the prime minister if the salary cuts were made.

Mugabe left Southern Rhodesia again in 1958, this time for Ghana, which, led by black revolutionary Kwame Nkrumah, had gained independence from England. Ghana was the model for an independent, black-controlled African nation, and Mugabe returned to Rhodesia inspired to recreate that model in his homeland.

> ### Marriage
> Mugabe found time for social affairs while in Ghana. There he met an attractive young Ghanian woman who was, like him, a teacher. A year after his return to Rhodesia, Sally Hayfron joined him, and the two were married.

The National Democratic Party. The only black nationalist organization in the colony, the Southern Rhodesia African National Congress, was banned by the government in 1959. The next year, Mugabe joined the newly formed National Democratic Party (NDP), an organization founded by nationalists Michael Mawema and Leopold Takuwera, whose goals were to attain black majority rule in Southern Rhodesia without sharing power. When the two leaders were arrested in 1960, Mugabe joined in forming a protest march. It was the beginning of a long political career marked by struggles to destroy white supremacy.

Constructing a revolutionary platform. From the day of that march, Mugabe was a leader in a growing rebellion to give blacks control over their own nation. In 1961 Mugabe's followers refused to accept any compromise short of rule by a black majority. Pressure to meet black demands was growing, however, and

145

▲ Mugabe at a press conference in 1984; when Mugabe joined in forming a protest march in 1960, it was the beginning of a long political career marked by struggles to destroy white supremacy.

the government sought to ease the tension by striking a deal with the NDP's moderate leader, Joshua Nkomo. Blacks would be guaranteed fifteen parliamentary seats under this bargain, a guarantee to be backed up by a new Rhodesian constitution. Recognizing that fifteen of sixty-five seats left the white minority with complete political power, Mugabe and the NDP convinced Nkomo to reject the proposal and held protest marches against the new constitution.

ZAPU/ZANU politics and the beginning of the guerrilla struggle. In 1961, after the banning of the NDP, the Zimbabwe African People's Union (ZAPU) was formed, electing the moderate Nkomo as its leader. The organization was promptly banned in 1962 and its leaders arrested. Mugabe was confined to a tribal reserve for several months. He fled to Tanzania to direct ZAPU operations, but the plans broke down and Mugabe and the others formed the Zimbabwe African National Union (ZANU) in 1963.

That same year, a more conservative white government took control of Rhodesia.

The new colonial government decided to become independent from Britain and began a military crackdown on the African nationalist movement. Once again, in 1963, Mugabe, Nkomo, and other nationalist leaders were arrested. Mugabe was to spend the next eleven years in prison.

Rebellion. In 1964, while Mugabe languished in prison, ZANU commenced guerrilla operations against the Rhodesian regime, starting with attacks against white settlers. At first the black efforts were mostly unsuccessful, but intensive training with the help of Chinese advisers soon made the ZANU army a formidable force. It began to gain support from the African villages, and leaders were able to convince the tribal chiefs to allow them to hide their arms there, a crucial psychological as well as military gain.

Release of Mugabe and the intensification of the guerrilla war. In 1974 the fall of Mozambique to black nationalists and the release of Robert Mugabe from prison, along with support from the newly formed Marxist state of Mozambique, helped turn the course of the war. Fearing economic strangulation by the surrounding, now black-ruled, nations, Rhodesian president John Vorster attempted to negotiate a solution with the black nationalists. Nevertheless, discussions with Prime Minister Ian Smith always ended in a stalemate because of his refusal to concede to black majority rule.

Head of the Zimbabwe African National Union. After his release from prison, Mugabe became the recognized leader of ZANU and continued to organize raids against white farmers and white towns.

The war intensified in 1976; guerrillas began destroying bridges, blowing up mills and water-pumping stations, and terror-

---

Rhodesia

Ian Smith, a leader stubbornly committed to Rhodesian nationalism and white rule, made the Rhodesian declaration of independence from Britain official in 1964. Britain and the United Nations responded by refusing to recognize the outcast nation and forcing international trade sanctions. Though hurt by the economic sanctions, the government was supported economically and militarily by the white minority regimes in South Africa and Portuguese Mozambique.

---

izing white mines and farms. The Mugabe-led warfare forced thousands of whites to abandon their property.

No negotiations: The guerrilla war continues. Yielding to the economic and military pressures imposed by thirteen years of guerrilla war, Rhodesian president Vorster, Great Britain, and the United States, represented by Henry Kissinger, joined in negotiations with Prime Minister Smith for a peaceful settlement with the black nationalists. Smith finally agreed to black majority rule. It was to be achieved within two years, with whites maintaining control during the interim. Mugabe refused to negotiate with the Rhodesian government, calling instead for the destruction of Smith's army and total political control by ZANU. The war continued into 1978, with no end to the atrocities or terrorist attacks.

Smith finally agreed to negotiate with black moderates, forming a new nation, Zimbabwe-Rhodesia, and appointing the African bishop Abel Muzorewa as the new prime minister. The agreement resulted in a puppet government, however; whites still retained political power. Smith had hoped that the appointment of a black prime minister would encourage black moderates to end the guerrilla war, but his maneuvering only brought more criticism of the government.

British backing. In 1979 British commonwealth nations met to discuss a settlement to the Rhodesian conflict. British prime minister Margaret Thatcher had refused to recognize the Smith-Muzorewa government and called for black majority rule. Negotiations began again in London, bringing together all of the major participants in the conflict: Mugabe, Nkomo, Smith, Muzorewa, and the British foreign secretary, Lord Carrington. After discussions that lasted throughout the fall, it was agreed that a new Zimbabwean constitution would be drafted, with eighty seats allocated to blacks and twenty to whites. The land settlement was less favorable to blacks and against the wishes of Mugabe. He had advocated land redistribution to blacks, but the finalized agreement declared that whites were to be paid for any lands that would be reallocated to blacks. Finally, new elections were to be held in 1980.

▲ South African president F. W. de Klerk and Mugabe meet for the first time as heads of state, January 1994. Mugabe maintains a one-party state in Zimbabwe, arguing that it is important for the country's unity.

ZANU claimed fifty-seven seats in the Parliament and elected Mugabe prime minister. On April 18, 1980, the new, black-ruled nation of Zimbabwe was formed, and Robert Mugabe became its first—and as of 1995 its only—president.

Aftermath

Continued capitalism. Mugabe realized that immediate removal of all white structures would bring economic disaster to the nation. He had seen the disaster that resulted when Mozambique won independence and turned suddenly to socialism. So, although a Marxist, Mugabe did not implement socialist economic principles in the governing of Zimbabwe. There was no nationalization of industries, but rather a continuation of capitalism and the free market. He continued the agricultural policies that had been developed by whites; 80 percent of Zimbabwe's crops still came from white estates. Whites could sell their land to the government for redistribution, but only 25 percent of the white farmers chose to do so. This made it nearly impossible for the new government to redistribute lands to needy Zimbabwean farmers, and the majority of black farmers continued to work on the tribal reserves established during colonization. Whites also retained power in industry, controlling the factories and mines; they were slow in promoting blacks to positions of power.

Political improvements. Despite these setbacks, Mugabe was able to make strides in providing blacks with health services and education. From his election in 1980 through the first half of the 1990s, the Zimbabwe government built two hundred rural health centers, increasing the access of Zimbabweans to health care (in 1976, for example, there had been one doctor for every 410,000 Zimbabweans in some areas). Mugabe made elementary education free and completely nonracial and began a massive recruiting effort to bring more teachers to Zimbabwe's schools. He also recognized the achievements of women—many of whom had fought alongside men in the guerrilla war and in the process changed many of the traditional gender roles—by granting them equal rights.

Staying in power. Mugabe maintains a one-party state in Zimbabwe, arguing that it is important for the country's unity, and has severely restricted and even repressed the opposition politics of groups such as Nkomo's ZAPU. After seven years of the expulsion, imprisonment, and execution of ZAPU members, Nkomo and Mugabe reached a settlement to unite the parties in 1987. At that time, Mugabe formed a new government with himself as president and Nkomo as vice-president. However, Mugabe's policies are sure to continue; he was successful again in the 1990 elections, winning 80 percent of the vote and a ZANU majority in the Parliament.

For More Information

Eide, Lorraine. *Robert Mugabe.* New York: Chelsea House, 1989.

Mugabe, Robert. *Our Way of Liberation.* Gweru, Zimbabwe: Mambo, 1983.

Smith, David, and others. *Mugabe.* Harare, Zimbabwe: Pioneer Head, 1981.

Jomo Kenyatta

c. 1890-1978

Personal Background

Early childhood with the Kikuyu. Jomo Kenyatta was born between 1890 and 1895 in the village of Ngenda. He was of Kikuyu origin, thus a member of one of the largest tribes in Kenya; his people lived in and cultivated a region known as Kikuyuland.

Kenyatta's father, Muiga, died when he was young, and his mother was inherited by Muiga's brother, Ngengi. His mother eventually returned to her people with the son that she had borne Ngengi, and Kenyatta was sent to live with his grandfather, a local magician named Konyo. There he assumed the traditional role of Kikuyu children: shepherding the family goats and sheep.

In 1904 Scottish missionaries first traveled to the village, settling in nearby Thogoto. Kenyatta was attracted to the new ways of the missionaries, particularly their method of communication using the Morse code. He left the village and went to the mission in 1905, wearing a loincloth and looking for a new life. Shortly afterward, he began to work in Thogoto as a servant, staying with relatives who lived in the surrounding areas.

Kenyatta began to live the life of a mission child. He became accustomed to the regimens of school, hard work, and discipline, and was baptized in 1914.

▲ **Jomo Kenyatta**

Event: Winning independence for Kenya.

Role: Jomo Kenyatta rose from a Kikuyu shepherd boy to become the popular leader of the independent Republic of Kenya. His politics of liberation played an influential role in guiding the African independence movements of the day.

Colonization. Kenya's future as a colony was decided in 1905 when Britain appointed a governor and established a legislature for the new possession. The new colonial policies were harsh to the native population. The British installed a native tax, which forced the Africans to work for Europeans occupying the lands they had once inhabited and from which they were often removed by violent threat. For the Kikuyu, who for centuries had been farmers, being forced onto greatly reduced land areas represented a severe alteration in their native way of life.

World War I and colonial Nairobi. When World War I broke out in 1914, the British enlisted Indian colonists who had settled in Kenya and made sweeps of the countryside, forcing Africans to join the army. Kenyatta, who had left the mission in 1916 after refusing to take an apprenticeship course as was expected of mission students, fled to Nairobi. Because Kenyatta had ties with the Masai tribe, despite their being traditional enemies of the Kikuyu, he was able to stay with them during the later years of the war in order to avoid being captured.

Exceptional Missionaries

Though many of the missionaries regarded Africans as savages who needed to be "civilized" through the adaptation of European lifestyles, Kenyatta did meet two men who had more sympathetic, understanding views of African and Kikuyu culture: Arthur Barlow, the nephew of one of the founding missionaries, and John Arthur, one of the mission doctors. Both became important influences in Kenyatta's life.

Returning to Kenya in 1918 after his brief stay with the Masai, Kenyatta worked with a local British engineer and began to accept European language and dress. Life as a European colonial was in striking contrast to the tribal life of his youth; Kenyatta enjoyed a much more free and easy lifestyle. He was, however, subject to the daily indignities suffered by Africans under colonial rule, forcibly registered, and made to wear an identification tag with the name of his employer at all times.

Participation:
Winning Independence for Kenya

Early Kenyan independence politics. In 1920 a young Kenyan named Harry Thuku founded the Kikuyu Association, an organization aimed at addressing African grievances with the

▲ Kenyatta, wearing ceremonial robes, waves his fly whisk as he watches a military parade in Nairobi, December 1965; Kenyatta has developed near-cult status in Kenya and is continually characterized as the "Father of the Kenyan nation."

colonial system. Thuku boldly began to lobby the government even though the right to intercede with the authorities was traditionally reserved for tribal chiefs. James Beauttah, another Kenyan angry at the oppression suffered by his people under colonial rule, organized the Central Kikuyu Association (CKA). The lobbying of the government by both parties led to the establishment of local native councils, whose leadership was composed of government-appointed chiefs.

Kenyatta, who had been working as a clerk and was well known by the locals, began to do work for the CKA—writing letters to missions requesting a decrease in school fees for African children. In 1929 he was sent to London as the CKA representative to present the organization's complaint that the new leader of the Kenyan colonial administration, Sir Edward Grigg, was a racist.

African politics in London. It was in London that Kenyatta was first exposed to the broader African nationalist movement by other Africans, particularly West Africans. These nationalists encouraged their peers to rediscover their history and traditional institutions, and spoke of the day when Africans would be running their own affairs in their countries. As a part of this re-education process, Kenyatta became involved with the local Marxist organization and the League Against Imperialism. Through his Marxist connections, he was able to make a trip to Moscow, where he was influenced by Russian anti-imperialist ideas.

Kenyatta eventually attended to his business in London: dealing with the issue of Kikuyu land rights and the release of Harry Thuku. He met with Governor Grigg in London later that year but found the governor totally unresponsive and unwilling to negotiate the issues.

As a result of these meetings, Kenyatta began to criticize the colonial regime, first in an article titled "Give Back Our Land," which discussed African opposition to colonization. He later explained his ideas in an article in the influential newspaper *Manchester Guardian* that summarized the political, economic, and social aspirations of Kenyans.

Upon his return to London in 1930, Kenyatta focused on revolutionary training while working at the job he had been sent to do—represent native issues for the CKA before a parliamentary panel. He began a course of self-education at a Quaker college in

The Colonial Land Grab

In 1929 the major issue in Kenya was the loss of Kikuyu land rights. These had been increasingly eroded by the colonial administration. The tribes were protesting the Grigg Bill, which called for settlers to take and hold the native lands in a trust for later use. It was a land-grab bill in disguise. Settlers could use the land they were supposedly holding until the Africans were "civilized." Kenyatta's opposition had led to the setting up of CKA branches throughout Kikuyuland. The colonial government became increasingly hostile toward the expanding CKA. It was unrepresentative of the Kikuyu people, the government claimed, as it began to work to diffuse CKA power by arresting its leader, Harry Thuku.

▲ It was in London that Kenyatta was first exposed to the broader African nationalist movement by other Africans, particularly West Africans.

Woodbrook, where he studied English and drew up and submitted a plan on native land rights to the colonial office.

Communist training in Moscow. Kenyatta visited Moscow for the second time in 1932, where he became involved with a Trinidadian revolutionary named Gregory Padmore, whom he met at an institute for colonized races. At the institute, Kenyatta received paramilitary training and was educated in Marxist literature. The young activist began to see the revolutionary potential for Africa, but he also was critical of the Marxist ideology that argued that class, not race, was important. To Kenyatta, that idea seemed to impose another white vision of reality that ignored the daily indignities suffered by Africans because of race.

Involvement in the Pan-African cause. Kenyatta began a series of writings in 1933 on the issue of African liberation. "An African Looks at British Imperialism" addressed the issues of land rights and missionaries. In his *Negro Anthology,* he discussed the British strategy of divide and rule, comparing the luxury of European life with the misery suffered by Africans living under colonial rule. Kenyatta's main theme was that black revolutionaries were the soul of Africa.

Kenyatta's views on African liberation were radical compared to those of Kenyan moderates such as Harry Thuku, who wanted to continue to improve black rights under British rule. The moderates said that the government had helped the natives and that the natives should pledge their allegiance to the king of Britain. These moderates saw their future within the British colonial system, whereas Kenyatta advocated African self-rule.

Rallying Blacks for Independence

The takeover of Abyssinia (modern Ethiopia) in 1935 and the Italian atrocities committed in the capital city of Addis Ababa two years later rallied black intellectuals in London to the cause of Pan-Africanism. Two committees were formed to gather international support for the peoples of Abyssinia and Ethiopia—the International Friends of Abyssinia and the International Friends of Ethiopia. A group formed to deal with the advancement of African interests was the International African Service Bureau. During 1943 and 1944, the group was joined by Kwame Nkrumah, who was to be the future president of an independent Ghana. He convened the Fifth Pan-African Congress under the slogan "Africa for Africans," a testament to the strength of the African peoples and their struggles for liberation.

In 1938, as a part of an anthropology program he had initiated at the University of London, Kenyatta published *Facing Mount Kenya,* aimed at challenging colonialist views on history. The book was an autobiographical collection of studies of Kikuyu life and customs. In it Kenyatta detailed the complex nature of Kikuyu society, showing the establishment of political, social, and economic institutions that would have provided natives with a better life than that afforded under colonial rule. The book demonstrated that the Kikuyus were self-sufficient and orderly before the arrival of the whites.

Effects of World War II. The movement for African rights intensified in Kenya as the Pan-Africanist message spread. The idea of independent schools became more popular, an important step in the nationalist struggle. As a result, Kenyans gained increased political awareness.

World War II radicalized Kenyans. While abroad, many came into contact with African Americans as well as Africans and Indians living under other colonial rules. Following the war, Kenyans began to build a grassroots resistance to the policies of the colonial regime. It was a radically different Kenya that Kenyatta returned to in 1946.

Kenyan politics and the rise of the Mau Mau. Kenyatta had strained relations with the political elite of his country by his long stay in England. The Kenyan African Union (KAU) had been formed in 1944. Uniting the several tribes, it had replaced the former CKA, which had been banned by the colonial regime. Nevertheless, Kenyatta was appointed to the African land settlement board in 1947. Through it he worked to unite the different tribes under a more political organization.

The Mau Mau. In 1948 an organization known as the Mau Mau began guerrilla warfare aimed at driving Europeans from Kenya. Its objectives were even more militant than those of the KAU, which had gone so far as to call for full independence from the colonial government within three years.

Kenyatta worked to build support for the KAU, denouncing the violent objectives of the Mau Mau. He began to assert a model of self-rule to African leaders, in contrast to European indirect rule and African acceptance of colonial policies. However, his plans were thwarted after the government implicated him in the murder of sixty settlers by Mau Mau militants. Kenyatta was sentenced to seven years' hard labor.

The Mau Mau quickly took control of the population of Kikuyuland, enforcing bans on smoking and operating secret courts. Thousands of Africans died under the terror imposed by the Mau Mau.

Toward independence. Following the end of World War II, Britain granted independence to several of its colonies. India gained its independence in 1947, and 1957 marked the liberation of Ghana. The turning point in the independence period, however,

> ### Britain Begins Decolonization
>
> In 1944 the Atlantic Charter, signed by President Roosevelt and Britain's prime minister Churchill, declared universal human rights. At first these rights were not extended to the British colonies, but as the war dragged on, armies began to include colonized peoples. In recognition of their efforts during the war, Britain offered independence to India and its West African colonies.

was the Sharpesville murders in South Africa in 1960. The South African government killed seventy children involved in an anti-apartheid demonstration, resulting in worldwide condemnation. Such brutality hit home in Kenya when eleven African prisoners were killed by security guards in a counterterrorism rehabilitation prison.

In January 1960 the British colonial secretary, Iain McLeod, made it known that he soon planned to grant independence to Kenya. Realizing that elections for self-rule were quickly approaching, Kenyan politicians went into action. Two political parties were quickly formed: Kenyan African National Union (KANU), of which Kenyatta was elected president, and the Kenyan African Democratic Union (KADU). Because of his alleged complicity with the Mau Mau, the colonial government was opposed to Kenyatta and threw their support behind other African leaders. Among the leading candidates was Tom Mboya, who had been trained in Britain and was backed by the United States, and Oginga Odinga, who was supported by the Soviet bloc and was a well-regarded intellectual. In 1963 the elections for a new government were held, and Kenyatta, whom Kenyans linked with the struggle for independence, swept the elections and was named the first prime minister of an independent Kenya; he assumed the presidency in 1964.

Aftermath

Kenyatta governed Kenya for fourteen years. As a president, he was conservative. Though Africans had taken over, he still maintained the colonial structure, and many whites continued to operate in the judicial, civil, and parliamentary posts that they had held before independence. The Kenyatta cabinet abided by the economic policies of the World Bank and the Commonwealth Development Corporation, rather than by the experiments in African socialism that many other countries were following.

Politically Kenya developed into a one-party state; opposition groups were banned, such as Oginga Odinga's Kenyan Peoples Union. Kenyatta developed near-cult status in Kenya and has been continually characterized as the "Father of the Kenyan nation." He died in Mombasa in 1978.

For More Information

Arnold, Guy. *Kenyatta and the Politics of Kenya.* London: J. M. Dent and Sons, 1974.

Howarth, A. *Kenyatta: A Photographic Biography.* Nairobi: East African Publishing House, 1967.

Murray-Brown, Jeremy. *Kenyatta.* New York: E. P. Dutton, 1973.

F. W. de Klerk

1936-

Personal Background

Early life. Frederik Willem de Klerk was born on March 18, 1936, in Mayfair, a working class district of Johannesburg, South Africa. He was one of two sons of Jan de Klerk, a schoolteacher. The de Klerks were considered *volksleiers,* or people's leaders, and were a politically prominent family.

The de Klerks belonged to the Christelijk Gereformeerde Kerk (Christian Reformed Church), also known as the "Dopper-kerk" (from the Afrikaans word *doppen,* which means to extinguish, as one would a candle). The Doppers denied all reforming influences, which they considered corrupt. Unlike the larger Dutch Reformed Church, though, they did not use church doctrine to justify apartheid, the South African policy of separation of the races.

De Klerk's involvement in politics began at an early age. In May 1948, when he was twelve, he counted returns in the election that brought the National Party to power.

As a teenager, de Klerk attended Monument High School, a boarding school in Krugersdorp, in western Transvaal, one of the best schools in South Africa. There he distinguished himself as a debater and Latin scholar. He also became active in the Jeugbond, the National Party's youth organization.

▲ **F. W. de Klerk**

Event: Leading white South Africans toward a break with apartheid.

Role: As South Africa's president, F.W. de Klerk oversaw the removal of the last vestiges of apartheid and negotiated an arrangement by which all South Africans gained the right to vote.

After graduating, de Klerk attended Potchefstroom University for Christian Higher Education, the most prestigious college run by the Dopperkerk. There he continued his political activities and became an executive member of the Afrikaner Student Union, vice-chairman of the Student's Representative Council, and editor of a student newspaper. He also met Marike Willemse, a professor's daughter, whom he later married. In 1958 he graduated cum laude (with honors) with a law degree. After a three-year trip to England, de Klerk began law practice in Vereeniging, a city south of Johannesburg.

Politics. In 1972 de Klerk was appointed to the Chair of Administrative Law at Potchefstroom University. Before he assumed this post, however, he ran for a vacant seat in Parliament and won. He was reelected in 1974, and the next year he became information director for the National Party in the Transvaal.

Four years later, de Klerk was appointed minister of posts and telecommunications, a cabinet position. In this capacity, he was able to arrange for the purchase of South Africa's first digital telephone system despite international economic sanctions against the country for its apartheid policies. De Klerk would hold other cabinet positions over the next eleven years. In 1982 he became the leader of the National Party in the Transvaal.

Alternatives to apartheid. As minister of posts and telecommunications, de Klerk had to deal largely with technical issues, but as a National Party leader, he had to confront the issue of South Africa's racial policies for the first time. He became involved in a National Party think tank whose members sought to solve the race problem through the apartheid structure by concocting schemes such as setting up a black parliament or a "council of states" consisting of black "homelands" that would help run the country. De Klerk's involvement in the think tank exposed him to

The de Klerk Family

De Klerk's grandfather was a friend of Paul Kruger. Kruger was president of the South African Republic and had fought the British in the Boer War of 1899-1902. His uncle by marriage, Johannes G. Strijdom, served as premier from 1954 to 1958. His father was also active in politics and was secretary general of the National Party in the Transvaal from 1948 to 1954 and later served in the Senate and the Cabinet. In the 1960s and 1970s, Jan de Klerk was president of the Senate.

reformist thinking on race issues that was beginning to take hold in the National Party (Sparks, p. 97).

De Klerk's thinking may also have been influenced by a number of trips he made abroad as a National Party leader. He met with political leaders in several European and African countries who emphasized the need for South Africa to change and warned of dire consequences if reforms were not made. They also promised to welcome South Africa back into the community of nations if it scrapped apartheid.

Participation: Leading White South Africans Toward a Break With Apartheid

Party leader. By 1989 de Klerk was one of the National Party's top leaders. In January Premier Pieter W. Botha suffered a stroke. He resigned as National Party leader on February 2 but retained the presidency. De Klerk was one of four candidates to replace him as party leader. Although Botha favored his finance minister, the National Party's parliamentary caucus chose de Klerk by eight votes. Upon assuming the party's leadership, de Klerk made a speech in which he promised to work for a "totally changed South Africa free of domination or oppression in whatever form" (Ottaway, p. 55).

de Klerk's Changing Position on Apartheid

De Klerk initially supported the government's apartheid policies, but his views began to change in the mid-1980s. He claims that his outlook changed along with that of the National Party. In 1986 President Pieter W. Botha announced that the government wanted to "break with apartheid" and that it would stop trying to turn black "homelands" into mini-states and commit itself to one citizenship for all South Africans in an undivided country. Willem "Wimpie" de Klerk, Frederik's brother, said he believes that this event started an "evolutionary conversion" in Frederik's thinking and that "imperceptibly, incrementally, de Klerk shifted one hundred and eighty degrees." Wimpie added that Frederik may have been alienated by the racist views of right-wingers in the National Party (Sparks, p. 95).

At a cabinet meeting on August 14, 1989, which Botha himself had called, the members all urged him to step down. Botha reluctantly yielded and in a bitter and blustering speech announced his resignation on national television. The next day, de Klerk was appointed acting state president. At fifty-three, he was the youngest chief executive in the nation's history.

Erasing apartheid. A few days later, it became apparent that the government's attitude was changing when de Klerk allowed a protest march to take place in Capetown. Previous administrations had usually banned such demonstrations. Permission for other demonstrations was soon given.

On October 15, 1989, de Klerk ordered several African National Congress (ANC) members released from prison, including Walter Sisulu. The ANC was allowed to hold a rally to welcome them home. The government also suspended the death penalty for several convicted terrorists and abolished the use of whips by police to control riots. In November the government scrapped the Separate Amenities Act, which segregated public facilities, and opened public beaches to all races.

On February 2, 1990, de Klerk made a thirty-five minute speech in Parliament in which he "crossed the Rubicon and committed his government to negotiated change" (Norval, p. 221). He announced a series of reforms that included incorporating the black "homelands" back into South Africa, suspension of the death penalty, lifting the state of emergency that had been imposed to combat violence during the mid-1980s, and reducing the size of government and privatizing state companies. Most important, he announced that he was releasing **Nelson Mandela** (see entry), the ANC leader who had been in prison since 1962, and lifting the ban on the ANC, which had been outlawed since 1960. On February 11 Mandela walked out of prison.

All that remained to do away with the apartheid system was to set up a government that would represent all South Africans. In March 1990 the government began negotiating with the ANC to form a united government, but the two sides had different ideas as to how such a government should be set up. Mandela and the ANC wanted a strong central government that would be popularly elected on the principle of "one man, one vote." It would be a "winner take all" system in which the winning party would form a government excluding all others. De Klerk wanted a federal system with a weak central government. He envisioned an Assembly, to be elected at large, and a Senate, composed of representatives from states or regions. In addition, three racial groups—the

Asians, the English, and the Afrikaners (which included Coloreds, or people of mixed blood)—would be represented in the Senate.

Meanwhile, the dismantling of apartheid continued. In 1991 the Parliament, by an overwhelming majority, voted to scrap the Population Registration Act, in which every South African was classified according to race.

In early 1992 de Klerk called a whites-only referendum on the negotiating process. Mandela urged the ANC not to take actions to disrupt the voting. Voters endorsed the negotiations by a two-thirds majority and rejected the right-wing Afrikaner groups who opposed the negotiations altogether.

In June 1992, after Zulu tribesmen attacked a migrant workers' hostel in Boipantong, a township near Johannesburg, and killed thirty-eight people, Mandela broke off negotiations. The ANC then organized a series of strikes and demonstrations. On September 7 a communist-led mob crossed the border into the "independent homeland" of Ciskei in an attempt to occupy its capital, Bisho, and overthrow its ruler, Oupa Gqozo. Ciskei troops fired on the mob, killing twenty-eight.

Soon afterward, Mandela and de Klerk, both expressing concern over the increasing violence, unrest, and economic disruption, resumed negotiations. Meanwhile, the violence continued.

> ### De Klerk's Inaugural Address
>
> In his inaugural address, de Klerk stated, "Our goal is a new South Africa, a totally changed South Africa, a South Africa free of domination and oppression in whatever form." He also pledged to "handle violence and terrorism with a firm hand."

Despite the distractions, the talks continued, with rapid progress. By December 1993 the two sides decided on a compromise that finally broke the impasse.

De Klerk and Mandela agreed that a "government of national unity," including all parties receiving 5 percent or more of the vote, would rule until 1999. All South Africans would be allowed to vote. The leader of the party receiving the most votes would become president, and the leader of the runner-up party would become deputy president. After 1999 this system would be replaced by a winner-take-all system, a major concession by de Klerk. The ANC made a concession when it agreed to a somewhat weaker central

▲ De Klerk and Nelson Mandela shake hands after receiving Freedom Medals from U.S. president Bill Clinton, July 4, 1993.

government than it wanted. For reaching this agreement, de Klerk and Mandela were awarded the Nobel Peace Prize.

Aftermath

Mandela won the presidency in the 1994 elections, and the ANC swept most of the country. However, de Klerk and the National Party won decisively in the Western Cape, with its predominantly Colored population. Many Coloreds resent the ANC for its alliance with the South African Communist Party, its socialist orientation, and its reputation for violence. On the other hand, many of de Klerk's former white supporters defected to the right-wing parties.

De Klerk now serves as one of South Africa's main opposition leaders. He remains sharply critical of the ANC. In March 1995 he warned, "If this country were to be governed by the ANC alone, we will face a very dark future." He vowed, "We will not allow the ANC's troublemakers to push this country into an abyss" ("De Klerk Addresses Crowds in Western Cape," Johannesburg SAPA broadcast, FBIS SA [8 March 1995], p. 11).

De Klerk, however, has said he has no regrets for the actions he took that brought the ANC to power. In April 1991 he told an interviewer for *US News and World Report,* "If we hadn't done what we'd done, then I'm convinced that maybe before the end of 1990s, South Africa would have been in flames."

For More Information

Finnegan, William. "The Election Mandela Lost." *New York Review of Books,* vol. 41, no. 17 (October 20, 1994), pp. 33-43.

Gastrow, Shelagh. *Who's Who in South African Politics.* 3rd ed. Sevenoaks, England: Hans Zell, 1990.

Norval, Morgan. *Politics by Other Means: The ANC's War on South Africa.* Washington, D.C.: Selous Foundation, 1993.

Ottaway, David. *Chained Together: Mandela, de Klerk, and the Struggle to Remake South Africa.* New York: Times Books, 1993.

"President De Klerk's Inaugural Address," Johannesburg Domestic Service broadcast, United States Foreign Broadcast Information Service Daily Report—Sub-Saharan Africa (21 September, 1989), p. 4.

Sparks, Alister. *Tomorrow Is Another Country: The Inside Story of South Africa's Road to Change.* New York: Hill and Wang, 1995.

"The White Man Who Jumped," *US News and World Report,* vol. 116, no. 16 (April 25, 1994), p. 59.

Nelson Mandela

1918-

Personal Background

Early life. Nelson Rolihlahla Mandela was born on July 18, 1918, in Muezo, a village near Umtata, the capital of the Transkei, an area on the Indian Ocean coast. His father was a chief of the Tembu, a subtribe of the Xhosa, who calculated their wealth in sheep and cattle. Another indication of his father's position and wealth was that he had five wives.

Mandela grew up in Qunu, a village of small mud-and-thatch huts about eighteen miles south of Umtata. While Mandela was a small child, his father began grooming him to become a chief. In 1930, however, his father died, and the twelve-year-old Mandela was sent to live with a cousin, David Dalindyebo, the acting paramount chief of the Tembu.

Soon afterward, Mandela enrolled in a Methodist missionary boarding school in Healdtown. When he graduated, he attended Fort Hare University College, one of the few colleges in South Africa open to blacks at the time.

Fort Hare was a hotbed of political activity. Its alumni include **Robert Mugabe** (see entry), president of Zimbabwe, and Mangosuthu Gatsha Buthulezi, the leader of South Africa's Inkatha Freedom Party, who remains one of Mandela's chief antagonists. It was while attending Fort Hare that Mandela started his political

▲ **Nelson Mandela**

Event: Leading blacks of South Africa to victory over apartheid.

Role: Nelson Mandela became one of the leaders of the African National Congress in its fight against apartheid. Mandela and F. W. de Klerk won the Nobel Peace Prize for their roles in setting up a government that represents all South Africans.

activity. In 1940 he was expelled, along with Oliver Tambo, another student activist, for leading a student strike.

It was at about this time that Mandela met Walter Sisulu, a political activist who was also a Xhosa. Sisulu helped him to find employment with a legal firm. In 1941 Mandela completed his bachelor's degree by correspondence and then was admitted to the University of Witwatersrand, where he earned a law degree. In 1952 Mandela and Tambo opened a law partnership in Johannesburg—the first black-owned law firm in South Africa. Although black enterprise was severely restricted by the government's apartheid laws, they were able to set up business in a building owned by a sympathetic Indian, and they resisted government efforts to move them out to the black townships.

Participation: Leading Blacks of South Africa to Victory Over Apartheid

The ANC. Besides helping Mandela to start his legal career, Walter Sisulu introduced him to the African National Congress (ANC). The ANC had been organized in 1912 by a group of black lawyers for the purpose of promoting the interests of blacks in the newly created Union of South Africa. In 1944 an ANC Youth League was formed that came to be dominated by young militants who resented the ANC's rather conservative leadership. The militants, including Mandela, opposed cooperating with other racial groups and called for strikes, boycotts, and civil disobedience to promote the cause of black South Africans.

Since the 1920s the South African Communist Party (SACP) had been trying to penetrate the ANC. Mandela and Tambo were, in the 1940s, militantly anticommunist. Mandela and others broke up communist meetings and disrupted SACP recruiting campaigns. In 1946 Mandela tried to persuade the ANC to exclude SACP members.

A more militant ANC. By 1949 Mandela and the militants had ousted the ANC's conservative leadership, and Mandela became president of the Youth League in 1950. That same year, following a series of strikes, the South African government passed the Suppression of Communism Act, which outlawed the SACP. After their party was banned, communists began to join the ANC, which was still a legal organization, and moved into positions of leadership.

In 1951 Moses Katane, who headed the SACP, became secretary of the ANC. Katane and Mandela soon became friends. Katane was instrumental in forging an alliance between the ANC and the SACP. Mandela was soon defending this move as a tactical alliance against apartheid. The ANC/SACP alliance is still in effect.

In 1952 the ANC leadership appointed Mandela "volunteer-in-chief" of a "defiance campaign," by which the ANC hoped to combat apartheid through strikes and massive civil disobedience. Mandela traveled around the country recruiting volunteers to break apartheid laws through such acts as passing through "whites only" entrances to railroad stations, defying curfews, and burning passes. On June 26 he and fifty-one others started the campaign by breaking a curfew.

Mandela's actions quickly got him into trouble with the government. In December 1952 he, Sisulu, and other ANC leaders were arrested under the Suppression of Communism Act. Mandela was given a suspended sentence of nine months and was then served with an order prohibiting him from attending meetings or leaving the Johannesburg area. The banning order would be continually renewed.

By now Mandela was deputy national president of the ANC. He developed a scheme known as the "M Plan" (M for Mandela) to set up ANC cells throughout the black townships. In September 1953 he resigned from the ANC because of the banning orders, but he continued to exercise his leadership secretly.

In addition to being "banned," Mandela and 155 others were charged with treason in December 1956. The trial did not begin for three years. Meanwhile, Mandela's home in Soweto, near Johannesburg, was frequently raided by police. In the midst of this turmoil, Mandela met Winnie Madizekela, a medical social worker. The couple met in Johannesburg in 1957 and were married the next year.

The Sharpesville massacre. In March 1960 the Pan-African-ist Congress (PAC), a black nationalist group that had broken away from the ANC, staged a series of protests against the pass laws (laws requiring all nonwhites to carry identification passes). In Sharpesville, a black township near Vereeniging, one such protest resulted in a confrontation with police in which sixty-nine protest-ers were killed. The Sharpesville massacre led to worldwide con-demnation of South Africa and was followed by strikes and riots.

The government responded by declaring a state of emergency—under which Mandela and hundreds of others were arrested—and by outlawing the ANC and PAC. Man-dela was released a few months later, but the ANC remained banned until 1990.

During this time the treason trial was proceeding. Mandela helped to conduct the defense, and it was largely through his efforts that he and all of his co-defendants were acquitted.

Independent South Africa. In May 1961 South Africa formally left the British Empire and proclaimed itself a republic. Mandela organized a campaign of strikes and civil disobedience and demanded a convention to set up a nonracial government. When it became clear that the civil disobedience campaign would not succeed, Mandela called it off.

Sentiment was growing within the ANC to begin an armed struggle. A military wing, the *Umkhoto we Sizwe* (MK), or "Spear of the Nation," was organized within the ANC to conduct sabotage and guerrilla warfare. Mandela was made commander of the MK.

Immediately after he was acquitted on charges of treason, Mandela went underground (disappeared to avoid police). For seventeen months, he evaded police. During this time he is believed by some to have aided an armed struggle that began in December 1961 with a series of sabotages across South Africa.

A month later Mandela slipped out of the country on a false Ethiopian passport and traveled to several African countries. He

> ## The ANC and Communism
>
> As the ANC came under the influence of the SACP, it abandoned black national-ism, which could not be reconciled with the Marxist view of class warfare, and began to push for a multiracial socialist state. In 1955 it adopted a "Freedom Charter," which called for turning the country's wealth over to "the people" (Ott-away, p. 43). Three years later, the Free-dom Charter was incorporated into the ANC's constitution.

attended the Pan-African Freedom Conference in Addis Ababa, Ethiopia, as part of an ANC delegation and visited a camp run by Algerian guerrillas in Tunisia to study their tactics. He also visited London.

On August 5, 1962, shortly after Mandela returned, South African police, acting on a tip from an agent of the U.S. Central Intelligence Agency, arrested him as he was posing as a chauffeur. He was convicted of leaving the country illegally and of incitement to riot and was sentenced to five years in prison.

The next year police raided the ANC's secret headquarters at a farm at Rivonia, a town near Johannesburg, at which they found a large cache of explosives and weapons. They arrested several ANC leaders, including Sisulu. Among the documents recovered was a plan drawn up by Mandela for a campaign of guerrilla warfare and terrorism. The "Rivonia Trial" of Mandela and others began in October 1963. Eleven months later, Mandela, Sisulu, and five others were convicted of sabotage and sedition.

Because of protests and pressure from abroad, Mandela and the others were spared the death penalty. Instead they were sentenced to life in prison. Mandela was eventually sent to Robben Island, South Africa's "Alcatraz," near Capetown. There he was assigned tasks such as gathering seaweed and breaking rocks. At the same time, he "painstakingly, and very successfully taught himself to speak Afrikaans" (Carlin, p. 17).

Mandela soon became a leader among the prisoners. He mediated disputes and ran a political education campaign. During the 1970s he converted many black nationalist prisoners to the nonracial philosophy of the ANC. Robben Island soon became known as "Mandela University."

Despite his imprisonment, Mandela remained the most popular opponent of apartheid within South Africa and abroad. International sentiment for his release began to rise. A movement to free Mandela was launched in 1982 and rapidly gathered steam.

Negotiating with the government. Meanwhile the government had entered into secret negotiations with Mandela. Beginning in 1968, Mandela had called for opening a dialogue with the government, which some of his more militant colleagues opposed. In 1973 he turned down an offer of freedom if he would agree to live in the Transkei or go into exile abroad. Nevertheless, negotiations resumed in the mid-1980s. In 1985 Mandela's wife, Winnie, had a chance encounter with South Africa's justice minister, Hendrik J. Coetsee, and convinced him to visit Mandela, who was, at the time, hospitalized. Coetsee and Mandela soon began to meet periodically. Against Coetsee's advice, the government offered to free Mandela if he would renounce violence and call off the ANC's armed struggle. He refused, as Coetsee had predicted.

The Mandela Position

At his trial Mandela defended his actions with eloquence. He pleaded for racial tolerance, declaring, "I have fought against white domination. I have fought against black domination. I have cherished the ideal of a democratic and free society in which all people live together in harmony and with equal opportunities." In 1994 he would repeat these remarks during his presidential campaign (Ransdall and Eddings, p. 35).

Mandela was eventually moved to a prison on the mainland. An upsurge in violence across South Africa, much of it instigated by the ANC, began in September 1984 and took hundreds of lives. The government responded by declaring a state of emergency and making thousands of arrests. In 1988 the ANC conducted a bombing campaign against mainly civilian targets.

By the end of the 1980s, however, tension seemed to be lessening. The bombing campaign, which caused a number of civilian casualties, generated a backlash in public opinion against the ANC. Angola and Mozambique began closing down the ANC and MK guerrilla sanctuaries after signing peace agreements with South Africa, and the ANC's Cuban and Soviet advisers in Angola went home.

Botha's actions. The government, under the leadership of Pieter W. Botha, was busily scrapping apartheid laws. Botha apparently decided that the time was right to meet with Mandela. On July 5, 1989, the two met in Pretoria. Although nothing came of the discussion, the meeting served to legitimize the ANC, which remained outlawed.

F. W. de Klerk. A few weeks later, Botha was replaced by F. W. de Klerk. In late 1989 de Klerk released all of the Rivonia defendants except for Mandela, who was now being held in relatively comfortable quarters at a prison near Capetown and being allowed to make regular excursions—under escort—around the countryside. On February 2, 1990, de Klerk ordered Mandela released without any preconditions. A week later, on February 11, he finally walked out of prison.

Mandela and de Klerk differed widely on ideas for a new form of government for South Africa. Mandela wanted a one-man, one-vote system in which the party that won a simple majority would take power. De Klerk held out for some form of power sharing, commenting that "a party that wins 51 percent of the vote should not have 100 percent of the power" (Ottaway, p. 171). Each man accused the other of negotiating in bad faith.

The end of apartheid. Constitutional talks finally collapsed in 1992. ANC and SACP radicals then began a campaign of strikes and demonstrations that caused massive disruption but failed to shake the government. The campaign was called off after twenty-eight demonstrators were killed in a clash with troops from the "independent homeland" of Ciskei, and both Mandela and de Klerk returned to the negotiating table.

Both sides were now willing to compromise, and by December 1993 an agreement on a new constitution was reached. In April 1994 South Africans of all races elected a new government. For their accomplishment, Mandela and de Klerk were awarded the Nobel Peace Prize.

International Concern

In 1986 the U.S. Congress made Mandela's release one of the conditions for lifting the economic sanctions it had imposed on South Africa. In July 1988 a twelve-hour rock concert, the Freedom Fest, was held in London to celebrate his seventieth birthday. The concert was broadcast to more than fifty countries.

Aftermath

In the election campaign, Mandela, at 75, worked vigorously for the ANC. He hired two of American president Bill Clinton's advisers, Stan Greenberg and Frank Greer, as aides and conducted a "meet the people" style of campaign, visiting townships and squatter camps. When the voting finally took place, nineteen parties

competed. Several right-wing Afrikaner groups refused to participate, and the Inkatha Freedom Party chose to take part only at the last moment. The ANC won an overwhelming victory, taking 252 of 400 available seats in the legislature, and Mandela became president. The "Government of National Unity" also included de Klerk as deputy president and Inkatha leader Buthulezi as home affairs minister. The SACP, which won about sixty seats in the legislature, was awarded several ministries, including the justice ministry.

Now 78, Mandela is said to be in less-than-robust health, and he is said to have problems with his vision. In 1995 he announced that he would step down when his term ends in 1999.

For More Information

Carlin, John. "Mandela Unbound." *New Republic,* vol. 202, no. 11 (March 12, 1990), pp. 14-20.

Norval, Morgan. *Politics by Other Means: The ANC's War on South Africa.* Washington, D.C.: Selous Foundation, 1993.

Ottaway, David. *Chained Together: Mandela, de Klerk, and the Struggle to Remake South Africa.* New York: Times Books, 1993.

Ransdall, Eric, and Eddings, Jerelyn. "Man of the Moment," *U.S. News and World Report,* vol. 116, no. 18 (May 9, 1994), pp. 34-35.

Sparks, Alister. *Tomorrow Is Another Country: The Inside Story of South Africa's Road to Change.* New York: Hill and Wang, 1995.

Welcome to Freedom

Following his release, 120,000 people welcomed Mandela home at a rally in a Soweto soccer stadium. When Mandela addressed the crowd, he took a moderate line. Among other things, Mandela urged that school boycotts as a means of resisting apartheid be called off and rejected the view of some militants that "liberation must come before education." He called for demonstrating "goodwill to our white compatriots" in order to "convince them by our conduct and arguments that a South Africa without apartheid will be a better home for all" (Carlin, p. 16).

◄
Mandela casts his vote in South Africa's first all-race election, held on April 27, 1994; in negotiations with de Klerk, Mandela wanted a one-man, one-vote system in which the party that won a simple majority would take power.

Middle East Peace Process

1959
▼
Shimon Peres becomes Israel's deputy minister of defense.

1965
▼
Yasir Arafat organizes El Fatah.

1978
▼
Camp David Agreement. Israel agrees to transfer the West Bank and Gaza to Palestinians over five years.

1977
▼
Anwar Sadat of Egypt officially recognizes Israel.

1974
▼
The United Nations accepts the PLO as voice of the Palestinians.

1973
▼
Yom Kippur War.

1967
▼
Six-Day War.

1979
▼
Arab League expels Egypt and rejects Camp David plan.

1982
▼
Israel invades PLO-dominated Lebanon.

1984
▼
King **Hussein I** of Jordan admits Palestinians into Jordan government.

1985
▼
Hussein and Arafat propose confederation of Jordan and occupied territories into a nation of Palestine.

1994
▼
Arafat, Peres, and Israeli prime minister Yitzhak Rabin are awarded the Nobel Peace Prize for their drafting and signing of a peace accord.

1993
▼
Israel agrees to transfer Gaza and the West Bank to Palestinian self-government. Hussein begins negotiations with Peres.

1990
▼
Gulf War.

1987
▼
Peres becomes Israel's foreign minister.

MIDDLE EAST PEACE PROCESS

The unyielding positions in the Middle East during the twentieth century—often leading to turbulence in the area—are exemplified by the following statement by an adviser of Palestinian leader Yasir Arafat:

> There will be no existence for either the Palestinian people or for Israel unless one of them disappears. The Arabs must deal with the Palestinian problem from the vantage point that there will be no peaceful coexistence with Israel. The PLO has no right to discuss recognition of the enemy Zionist state. The final goal of the PLO is to restore the Palestinian people sovereignty over its lands, and there to establish the independent state (Khaled al-Hassan in an interview published by the United Arab Emirates News Agency, January 12, 1982).

The determination to return to Arabs the Palestinian lands they held for fourteen centuries is matched by the determination of Israelis to establish and hold a homeland in Palestine, an old section of the Ottoman Empire included in the Ottoman state of Syria. Israelis claimed the right to establish a homeland where their ancestors ruled nearly two thousand years ago.

Jews began to return to Palestine early in the twentieth century, buying land and establishing cooperative farms. They built a Jewish seaport, Tel Aviv, next to the old Arab port of Haifa. By the beginning of World War I, fewer than twenty-five thousand Jews had bought land and settled among the more than one million Arabs. The number of immigrants would grow dramatically after a 1917 proclamation by British foreign minister Lord Balfour establishing support for a Jewish homeland. The statement contradicted British policy at the time because the British, seeking allies to upset the Ottomans, who had joined Germany in the war, had promised to reestablish independent Arab states in the area.

Thus, when Jewish leaders declared the establishment of an independent nation, Israel, that country was instantly attacked by its neighboring Arab states. Already concerned by the rapid migration of Jews into the area (by 1948, when Israel was formed, Jews constituted 40 percent of the population), Egypt, Syria, Jordan, and Iraq massed their armies against the new nation. That Israel was able to survive and continue to grow is attributed largely to two men, David Ben-Gurion and his protégé, **Shimon Peres.** Ben-Gurion, the inspiration behind Israel's founding, became the nation's first prime minister and minister of defense. Peres was his deputy. Together they raised support from other nations and created the most powerful military in the Middle East. They were so effective that when, in 1967, Egypt and Syria, armed with weapons from the Soviet Union, invaded Israel, it took only six days to drive them away. Since the beginning of Israel, Shimon Peres has worked steadfastly to defend his nation.

Caught up in the turmoil, not unwillingly, has been King **Hussein I** of Jordan. Hussein has managed, through military discipline and great expertise in international politics, to gain recogni-

▶

An Israeli soldier wearing a prayer shawl over his combat uniform and with a assault rifle between his knees prays at the Western Wall in Jerusalem on the eve of Yom Kippur, 1979. The determination to return to Arabs the Palestinian lands they held for fourteen centuries is matched by the determination of Israelis to establish and hold a homeland in Palestine, where their ancestors ruled nearly two thousand years ago.

tion as one of the world's greatest statesmen. He is committed to Arab unity, but also to peace and prosperity in the area. His small nation borders Israel and is surrounded by more powerful Arab states. Nevertheless, Hussein has managed to maintain friendly relations with nearly everyone, to build his own nation despite the influx of hundreds of thousands of Arab refugees from Israel, and to serve with the Egyptian government as a valuable intermediary in the long and difficult peace negotiations. His position has often placed him in opposition to the spokesman for Palestinians, **Yasir Arafat.**

Born in Cairo, indoctrinated with the philosophy of the Arab League, and exposed to Marxism, Arafat organized a military unit called El Fatah to fight for Arab control of the Middle East. His organization was soon taken in as a fighting unit of the Palestine Liberation Organization (PLO). Eventually, Arafat became the dominant leader of the PLO—an organization whose objective is made clear in articles of its covenant:

Article 19: The partition of Palestine in 1947 and the establishment of the State of Israel are entirely illegal.

Article 20: The Balfour Declaration, the Mandate for Palestine and everything that has been based upon them are deemed null and void.

Article 21: The Arab Palestinian people, expressing themselves by the armed Palestinian Revolution, reject all solutions which are substitutes for the total liberation of Palestine.

For more than twenty-five years, both Arabs and Jews held stubbornly to their positions—the Jews committed to the preservation of their state, the Arabs equally committed to the destruction of Israel. At about the twenty-year mark of this stalemate, the United States succeeded in bringing the two sides to a bargaining table. In a momentous agreement at Camp David, the Israelis tried to break ground for peace by agreeing to a five-year timetable for returning Arab lands taken in the Six-Day War. Although the Arabs rejected this offer, negotiations continued—pushed by Presidents Anwar Sadat and Muhammad Hosni Mubarak of Egypt and King Hussein, and directed by Arafat and Peres.

The stimulus to resolve differences may have come from a rebel Arab state. When, in 1990, Iraq invaded Kuwait and brought on the Gulf War, it became obvious to most of the leaders that wars were no longer acceptable methods for protecting or changing borders. Soon after the war, Yasir Arafat initiated direct talks with Shimon Peres. Peres had recognized the need for such negotiations but was forbidden by Israeli law from initiating them with Arafat.

Egypt, Norway, and the United States supported this dialogue. The result was an agreement in 1993 by both sides to the plan laid eight years earlier. Israel would return the occupied Arab lands of the Gaza Strip and West Bank to Arab rule—Arafat rule, since he had been elected president of a country without land. The transition would be spread over five years in order to give the Palestinian Arabs opportunity to create the necessary governmental structures. The delay has proved necessary because some Arab nations, particularly Iran, still do not approve of a Jewish state. Nevertheless, the Arafat-Peres agreement has provided the opportunity for a Middle East peace that has been centuries in coming.

Hussein I

1935-

Personal Background

Creation of Jordan. In 1908 Sharif Hussein ben Ali, the great-grandfather of the future King Hussein I, began what was to become a successful Arab revolt against Ottoman Turks, who had ruled the Arab provinces for four hundred years. He was greatly respected throughout the region, a member of the noble Hashimite house and a direct descendant of the Islamic prophet Muhammad. Needing help in World War I, Britain stepped in to offer Sharif Hussein liberation from Turkish rule and Arab self-rule thereafter in exchange for his continued rebellion against the Turks.

Unknown to Sharif Hussein, however, Britain had secretly negotiated a settlement with France that divided the Arab lands between the two European nations. The Sykes-Picot agreement, as it was called, divided the former Ottoman province of Syria into three parts, with the French receiving Syria and Lebanon, and Britain receiving Palestine and Iraq. In the agreement the British had excluded the desert and mountainous region east of the river Jordan from the rest of the province of Syria. They named this area Transjordan. The son of Sharif Hussein, Abdullah, was granted control of Transjordan in 1921 by a British mandate. In 1946, the year that marked Jordanian independence from Britain, the tiny country was renamed the Hashimite Kingdom of Jordan.

▲ Hussein I

Event: The Middle East peace process.

Role: Since assuming the throne at age eighteen, King Hussein I has thrust Jordan into the role of peacemaker in Middle East politics, working tirelessly in the name of Arab nationalism to maintain peace in the Middle East and to reach a settlement resolving the issue of the Palestinian state.

Early years and the assumption of the throne. Hussein was born in Amman, Jordan, in November 1935. His father, the crown prince Talal, was looked upon with contempt by *his* father, King Abdullah, for his gentle, nonaggressive nature, and thus was accorded a lower status, both financially and socially, in the family. King Abdullah, however, dearly loved his grandson, and they spent a great deal of time together in the royal palace in Amman. The young Hussein loved and admired his grandfather. Although he was a bright and quick youngster, Hussein liked bicycles more than books and enjoyed walks in the desert setting of Amman more than sitting at home.

Hussein's fondness for his grandfather nearly cost the future king his life in 1951. Abdullah worshipped in the mosque at Jerusalem, access to which he had retained in fighting against the Israelis. On one visit to the mosque, Hussein accompanied his grandfather to worship. Although they were so closely guarded that Abdullah protested, a gunman managed to approach within a few feet and shoot the king. The fifteen-year-old Hussein watched as his grandfather was killed and the gunman turned on him. He was also shot at, but the bullet was miraculously deflected by a badge that he was wearing on his uniform. It was the first of many assassination attempts that Hussein was to survive.

Talal, despite his lower status, immediately inherited the throne. He proved to be a liberal-minded ruler, introducing a new constitution in 1952 that reduced his own powers and made the cabinet responsible to Parliament. However, his rule was to be short-lived; his health began to deteriorate within the first year, and in 1952 a panel of royal doctors declared that he was unfit to rule. After parliamentary debate, it was agreed that he should turnover the throne to the young Hussein, who at the time was attending private school in London. Talal stepped down, and at age sixteen, Hussein was named king of Jordan. He was officially installed as king when he was eighteen, following an intensive military training course at the prestigious Sandhurst Institute in London. He had earlier been educated at a British public school, Harrow, and at Victoria College in Alexandria, Egypt.

Issues facing the young king. The Jordan Hussein had inherited was much different from the one his grandfather Abdullah had ruled. The pressures of Arab nationalism and the plight of Palestinians and the Palestinian state dominated the Arab political agenda. Egypt and Iraq were vying for control of the Arab world, and Iraq pressured Hussein to join its newly established Baghdad Pact, an accord with Britain that would provide military support to Jordan's army, the Arab Legion, which was key to Jordan's defense and stability. Hussein accepted British help, making Sir John Glubb head of the legion. Glubb built it into a modern army, even though it was limited to twenty thousand men. The move strongly angered Egypt, which began to encourage plots against the young Hussein and withdrew from the pact in 1955. Amid riots among his people, the next year Hussein separated from Britain, firing his friend and supporter John Glubb.

> ## Hussein's Family Life
>
> King Hussein has been married five times. In 1955 he married Dina Abdel Hamid. The couple had one daughter, Alia, before divorcing in 1957. Four years later he married Toni Gardiner (Princess Muna). They had two sons, Abdullah and Feisal, and two daughters, Zein and Aisha, before divorcing in 1972. In that same year he married Alia Toukan. The couple had a son, Ali, and a daughter, Haya, before Alia was killed in a helicopter accident in 1977. The next year, Hussein married his current wife, Lisa Hallaby (Queen Noor). They have two sons, Hashim and Hamzeh, and two daughters, Iman and Raiyah.

Palestine. When Israel was established as an independent nation in 1948, hundreds of thousands of Palestinians chose to leave the country. Most of these found their way to Jordan, doubling that nation's population and greatly adding to the economic problems that Hussein would inherit. These refugees in Jordan soon began raids into Israel, making Jordan the target of retaliation from Israeli defense forces, heightening the tension along the border.

Hussein as proponent of Arab nationalism. From the beginning of his rule, Hussein has steadfastly held to his principles: belief in Islam, commitment to Arab unity, belief that his family was chosen by God to rule, and commitment to independence for the Palestinian people. He has opposed communism in the Middle East as counter to religious beliefs.

▲ **Actor Anthony Quinn and Hussein during the filming of the 1962 motion picture *Lawrence of Arabia***

Arab peacemaker. The rift between Egypt and Iraq heated the tense relations among the Arab nations, and Hussein, acting for the first time as peacemaker, set out to solidify his alliances in the Arab world, visiting every Arab capital. He informed his colleagues that his commitment to Arab nationalism was symbolized by the cutting of ties with the region's still-influential colonial power, Britain. Hussein later guided the country into a military pact with Egypt and Syria, preferring the support of his Arab cousins.

Crumbling Arab nationalism. Jordan entered a pact with Iraq in 1958 to counter the newly formed, socialist-bent United Arab Republic, a union of Egypt and Syria. The Jordan-Iraqi pact united the two countries—whose leaders, incidentally, were cousins—in foreign policy, finance, education, and diplomacy. King Faisal of Iraq was to be the head of the new state, with Hussein as his deputy. The plan proved to be ill-fated, however. Shortly after the agreement, Faisal was deposed in a coup d'etat (overthrow of the government) and assassinated. Hussein's power on the throne was again threatened, and the British army came to his aid to protect the kingdom, following an attack by Egypt and Syria. During the next two years, several assassination attempts were made against King Hussein and his ministers. In 1960 Hussein put his reputation and that of his country on the line in an address to the United Nations, stating his opposition to communism and his strength as a leader despite the attacks of Egypt and Syria. The address won him allies from around the world. He reconciled with Egypt a year later, only to have the relations sour over his new military pact with Saudi Arabia and Egypt's union with Syria and Iraq. Hussein's optimism regarding Arab nationalism had faded; he saw the danger of Jordan, as a small country, joining an Arab union, and began to think of a union where each Arab country would keep its own identity within a united whole.

The Palestinian issue. For Hussein, the resolution of the Palestinian issue began to take precedence over the politics of Arab nationalism. The highly skilled Palestinians had put much effort toward building a strong Jordan, yet the flood of refugees, which had nearly doubled the country's population, increased its social, economic, and military problems. The uneasy

Short-Lived Representative Government

In 1958 Hussein began a short-lived experiment with representative democracy, approving the liberalized constitution that had been introduced during the reign of his father, Talal. Elections were held later that year, and the winner, a West Bank lawyer named Suleiman Naboulsi, was allowed to form a government and choose cabinet ministers.

From the beginning, however, there existed a conflict of authority: it was uneasily exercised by both the new president and the king. For example, after an attack on the Sinai Peninsula by the British and the French—with Israel's aid—Hussein, still pressing his agenda of Arab nationalism, invited Syria, Saudi Arabia, and Iraq to enter Jordan in defense of Egypt, against the wishes of the newly formed government.

The relationship between the government and the king quickly deteriorated. Hussein dissolved the government and formed a new one that would accommodate his views. The United States and Saudi Arabia rewarded his maintenance of stability by increasing economic support, solidifying the end of the country's experiment with representative democracy.

peace between Jordan and Israel was frequently broken by attacks—supported by the Palestine Liberation Organization (PLO)—against Israel, which were met with swift retaliations by the Israeli defense forces. The continued shelling of Jordan by Israel began to wear on the Jordanian people, who believed the king was not responding and pressed for his overthrow. Hussein again pushed Arab nationalism by joining an Islamic pact among Arab countries against communism. Jordan finally took action against Israel by becoming involved in the 1967 war against Israel.

The 1967 War against Israel. Fearing the loss of the West Bank to increasing Israeli attacks, Jordan joined Egypt and Syria as they launched their second attack against Israel. The military superiority of Israel, however, led to the sound defeat of the Arab nations within six days. Jordan suffered both militarily and geographically. Not only was the royal palace bombed and the Jordanian air force destroyed, but Israel captured the holy city of Jerusalem and the West Bank (area west of the Jordan River), causing an exodus of two hundred thousand Palestinian refugees.

Seeking a resolution to the Palestinian conflict, which continued to dominate Arab politics and the affairs of his own country, Hussein aided in drafting United Nations Resolution 242, aimed at establishing peace between the Palestinians and the Israelis. The resolution would create a Palestinian and a Jewish state, relying on the borders established in 1948. Hussein was able to convince President Nasser of Egypt to accept the agreement, but he could not convince the PLO.

Disputes with the PLO. In 1970 Jordanian clashes with the PLO *feyadeen,* the foot soldiers of the PLO military wing, El Fatah, increased inside the country. The hostilities culminated in a siege on Amman, the Jordanian capital. A peace agreement was signed by both parties, only to be broken shortly afterward, and battles erupted all over the country, most fiercely in Amman. A cease-fire was finally reached in 1970; heavy control of the feyadeen was one of the criteria for peace. Nearly two thousand Palestinians were massacred by the Jordanian army during the short war. At peace talks begun by Egypt, restrictions were put upon the feyadeen and the Jordanian army. Hussein, however, was condemned, thus again occupying an uneasy position with his Arab brethren.

▲ From the beginning of his rule, Hussein has steadfastly held to his principles: belief in Islam, commitment to Arab unity, belief that his family was chosen by God to rule, and commitment to independence for the Palestinian people.

A world advocate for the Palestinian cause. In 1972 Hussein made a proposal to the PLO and Israel calling for a united East and West Bank, of which he would be the president and Jerusalem would be the capital. The proposal was rejected by

193

both Israel and the PLO. Hussein's disfavor continued at the 1973 meeting of the Arab Summit, where it was resolved that the West Bank was to be handed over to the PLO if Jordan managed to recover it. However, despite the passage of the resolution and the tarnished images of the Arab nations following their third resounding defeat by the Israelis in the 1973 Yom Kippur War, Hussein continued to speak around the world on the plight of the Palestinians. He made a second proposal for Jordanian-Israeli peace; the proposal was again rejected by Israel's prime minister Golda Meir. From 1977 to 1978, Hussein found a sympathetic ear in U.S. president Jimmy Carter, who was working to forge a Middle East peace and was already holding intensive negotiations with Egypt and Israel. Hussein discussed the return of the West Bank and Jerusalem and insisted on a role for the PLO in any peace talks that were to be held.

Reconciliation with the PLO. In 1982 Hussein attempted to reconcile with the PLO in the midst of peace talks initiated by U.S. president Ronald Reagan and the Arab Summit. A year later, Jordan recognized the PLO as the sole representative of the Palestinian people. PLO chairman **Yasir Arafat** (see entry) held talks with Jordan in 1985, and it was decided that they would form a joint Jordanian-Palestinian delegation to negotiate with Israel. Despite this positive step toward reconciliation, Arafat continued to refuse to accept United Nations Resolutions 242 and 338 regarding Palestinian rule. Hussein's plans fell apart without Arafat's PLO support, and he again broke off relations with the PLO. The PLO was expelled from its bases in Jordan. Hussein and the PLO would not reconcile again with Jordan until 1988. In 1993 the agreement long fought for by Hussein and other world leaders finally resulted in an Israeli-PLO agreement for Palestinian independence in Gaza and the West Bank.

Aftermath

Hussein has transformed Jordan from a largely rural desert region to an urban, modernized nation and has placed it among the distinguished countries of the world. He continues to be a strong voice for peace in the Middle East, working tirelessly to unite his fellow Arab countries and supporting a peaceful resolution of the Palestinian conflict, using his position as a national leader to help in the struggle.

For More Information

Carr, Winifred. *Hussein's Kingdom.* London: Leslie Frewin, 1966.

Lunt, James. *Hussein of Jordan: Searching for a Just and Lasting Peace.* New York: William Morrow, 1989.

Snow, Peter. *Hussein.* London: Barrie and Jenkins, 1972.

Yasir Arafat

1929-

Personal Background

Childhood. Yasir Arafat was born on November 24, 1929, in Cairo, Egypt, during the struggle against British colonialism in the Middle East. His parents were actively involved in those efforts. His father was a businessman, and his mother came from a prominent Jerusalem family that descended from Muhammad, the Islamic prophet. Yasir's mother died when he was still a child, and his father remarried three times. The boy received little attention during his early years.

In 1939 Arafat's family moved to Gaza. There he was influenced by a young Lebanese math teacher, Majid Halaby, who was training young male guerrilla fighters to work for the Arab nationalist cause. After the death of Halaby in a guerrilla raid, Arafat carried on his work, recruiting more than three hundred sympathizers to form an organization in his honor, the Martyr Abu Khalid Society.

World War II and Arafat's development. While still a teenager, Arafat returned to Cairo, where he continued to encourage young Arabs to become soldiers and fight for Arab nationalism. He was influenced by his parents' earlier struggles. His relatives plotted strikes against British occupation and protested the dramatic increase of Jewish settlers in Palestine. Among those most distressed by this influx was the mufti (mayor of Muslim

▲ **Yasir Arafat**

Event: Creating a Palestinian homeland.

Role: As a leader and spokesman of the Palestine Liberation Organization (PLO), Yasir Arafat has brought the PLO cause to the attention of the world. His twenty-five-year campaign resulted in a 1993 agreement for Palestinian self-government on land in the Middle East.

Jerusalem), whose family had ties with Arafat's mother. The mufti and his followers led a series of anti-Jewish attacks. The Israelis' repeated defeat of the Arabs further heightened Arab fears of being displaced by Jews and promoted a growing nationalist sentiment. During this period, the Muslim Brotherhood, an organization in which Arafat's father was involved, won over many recruits that sought a return to a simpler Islam in Arab countries.

Israel. In 1948 Britain became weary of its involvement in the Middle East and withdrew its forces. The Jews who had settled in Palestine immediately declared the independence of a new nation, Israel. Neighboring Arab nations refused to recognize the Jewish claims and immediately began a war immediately to destroy Israel. They had, however, miscalculated Jewish resolve and were beaten. In the process Israelis won 72 percent of Palestine. Although there was no indication that they would be forced out of the new nation, as many as 700,000 Arabs fled Palestine to become worldwide refugees. Another 160,000 became Israeli citizens.

Jews and Arabs in Palestine

Before World War I the land that is now mostly Israel was a section of the Ottoman Empire known historically as Palestine. It was inhabited by Arabs. In 1917, when the Ottomans were being defeated and the land was about to be taken under British protection, British foreign minister Lord Arthur Balfour was persuaded to declare British intent to establish a Jewish homeland. Encouraged by this declaration, Jews began to return to the land they had occupied centuries earlier. They bought land from the Arab owners on which to build a new city, Tel Aviv, and establish cooperative farms, *kibbutzim*. The Jewish population grew rapidly until in the mid-1940s the Jewish settlers made up nearly 40 percent of the area's population.

In 1948, as a college student in Cairo, Arafat became involved in the Muslim Brotherhood, which had been formed to unite the Arabs after the initial Israeli victory. Four years later, Arafat urged President Nasser of the new revolutionary government of Egypt not to forget Palestine, handing him a petition signed in blood.

Gaza. Arafat began work in Gaza with the mufti, who was trying to form a Palestinian government in the region. Gaza was full of Egyptian radicals trying to overthrow the government. Arafat made friends with key officers in the group that won power in 1952.

Arafat later returned to Cairo, where he resumed his studies and was elected president of the Palestinian Student Federation at

▲ Although Arafat did not found the PLO, he was one of those who began El Fatah, a military organization dedicated to the same goals as the PLO.

the University of Fuad. His active involvement convinced Egyptian leadership to establish camps to train students to battle the British for control of the Suez Canal. In his role as president, he also convinced the Arab League to grant scholarships to Palestinian students. He and his followers later founded a newspaper called *Voice of Palestine,* which circulated in other Arab nations. From this publication grew a vast number of underground contacts that distributed information to help Arab groups organize.

Participation:
Creating a Palestinian Homeland

Early roots of PLO and El Fatah. In 1956 Arafat attended a conference on Palestine in Prague, Czechoslovakia, sponsored by the Soviet Union. At that time, Arab interests in Palestine were represented by the Arab Higher Committee. This committee stood for complete elimination of a Jewish state in the Middle East. By 1964 the committee had given way to a new organization, the Palestine Liberation Organization (PLO), with the same purpose. Although Arafat did not found the PLO, he was one of those who began El Fatah, a military organization dedicated to the same goals as the PLO. The idea of a military unit grew out of discussions begun at the Prague conference and moved ahead with the help of the Palestinian intellectual Khalad al-Hassan. Arafat was the chief fund-raiser for the organization, investing much of his own fortune.

The Gaza Strip

Gaza is a narrow strip of land along the Mediterranean Sea abutting the Egyptian land called the Sinai Peninsula. Although it is less than thirty miles long and only five or six miles wide, this area is home to nearly one million Arabs and Jews. Since Arafat's work there, this strip has taken on world significance far beyond its real size and economic importance.

The PLO soon began publishing its own magazine, *Our Palestine,* devoted to winning people over to the Palestinian cause. Egypt and Syria labeled the publication subversive, but the effort won many recruits for El Fatah.

The Six-Day War and the near end of El Fatah. In May 1967 Egypt, Syria, Jordan, and Iraq gathered to declare war on Israel. Observing the military buildup on its borders, Israel struck first and quickly destroyed the effort. Israel emerged with four times the land it had prior to the combat, taking Sinai from Egypt, the Golan Heights region of Syria, and the West Bank from Jordan. An additional two hundred Arabs in these regions became refugees. During the negotiations to end the Six-

Day War, Israel offered to return the West Bank and Gaza in return for the official recognition of the Israeli state by Arab nations. This proposition was refused.

El Fatah, whose attacks on the Israelis in the Golan Heights region had backfired, suffered a tremendous loss of momentum and nearly disbanded. The leadership of the group, however, soon allied with Palestinian students training in Algeria. The focus of El Fatah changed from direct confrontation to setting up centers of continuous resistance in the occupied territories. These centers of resistance, organized under the direction of Arafat, brought him to prominence within the struggle for Palestinian liberation. One center established in the West Bank village of Karameh ("Dignity") was particularly effective. As a result of successful attacks from Karameh on Israeli troops, Arafat became an instant hero. Karameh became a catalyst for the establishment of El Fatah headquarters at the town of Salt.

The merging of El Fatah and the PLO. Following the 1968 successful military campaign, Arafat accepted an invitation by Nasser of Egypt to visit the Soviet Union, whose leadership was offering support to the Arabs in the war against Israel. Nasser then encouraged Arafat to merge the revived El Fatah with the PLO. By this time, various leaders had taken different approaches to a Palestine Arab solution and the PLO had become a combination of diverse groups. El Fatah now became the most powerful splinter group. As the leader of El Fatah, Arafat's position as the head of the Palestinian struggle was secured. Under his guidance, the PLO continued its harassment of Israel but also became highly involved in offering a variety of services to Palestinian refugees, including health and education assistance.

> ### El Fatah
>
> *El Fatah* means "victory." Among the founding principles of El Fatah were 1) the goal of Palestine liberation, 2) armed struggle to reach that goal, 3) cooperation with international allies, and 4) collective leadership.

Challenges to PLO. For more than twenty-five years Arafat has used his organizing ability, his steadfastness of purpose, and his diplomatic skills to keep the various factions of the PLO moving toward its central purposes. In spite of the PLO's successes, there was significant opposition. The larger obstacles were presented by others in the Arab world. There was a substantial Jor-

▲ For more than twenty-five years Arafat has used his organizing ability, his steadfastness of purpose, and his diplomatic skills to keep the various factions of the PLO moving toward its central purposes.

danian crackdown on the PLO in 1970 after it challenged King **Hussein I**'s authority (see entry). The PLO was officially expelled from Jordan. Also, the PFLP, a Marxist Palestinian liberation group, emerged as a strong rival of the PLO. Their terrorist acts, several of which were aimed at King Hussein, further complicated efforts by the PLO. This set of circumstances once again brought Arafat to the fore as he set out to mediate between the groups. His efforts, however, were soon undermined by the killing of Palestinian refugees, organized by Hussein in retaliation. Five thousand were killed. Many El Fatah members were arrested; Arafat managed to escape.

Black September. El Fatah leadership immediately regrouped after the 1970 massacre with plans to form Black September, a group aimed at overthrowing Hussein. Black September was responsible for the death of nine Israelis at the 1972 Olympic Games in Munich. Following that event, El Fatah separated from the Black September organization.

During the 1970s, as other terrorist organizations arose, the PLO was forced to maneuver carefully in order to separate its image from those groups. Arafat and his allies in the PLO were successful. He led a national organization without a nation so skillfully that he was eventually invited to speak for Palestinians before the United Nations General Assembly in 1974.

PLO and United Nations talks. After Arafat's appearance, United Nations Resolution 3236 officially recognized the right of the Palestinian people to self-determination and sovereignty (freedom from outside control). The PLO was granted observer status in the United Nations and recognized as the representative for the Palestinian people. Arafat argued that diplomacy, not warfare, was the best way to gain the sought-after Palestinian state. His El Fatah and the PLO, however, continued to use both violence and diplomacy to further their goal.

The Intifada in the West Bank. By 1987 the Intifada, a Palestinian youth uprising, was underway in the West Bank. The PLO strongly supported the organization of secret schools and provided other services. Arafat's declared efforts to temper the actions of Intifada, however, were set back by the emergence of Hamas, a PLO terrorist group supported by Iran.

Arafat in the 1970s and 1980s

In the late 1970s, after El Fatah attacks on Israel, the Israelis responded by killing hundreds of Palestinian Arabs. United Nations peacekeepers were called in, and Arafat openly agreed to a cease-fire with Israel. It soon became evident, however, that Arafat would have difficulty controlling all the militant divisions within the PLO.

In the early 1980s, Arafat began to participate in talks with Hussein regarding a joint Palestinian-Jordanian administration in Palestine. His efforts were rejected by various elements of the PLO that remembered its 1970 expulsion by Hussein. In spite of Arafat's diplomatic efforts, Hussein decided to bypass the PLO and deal directly with Israel. Arafat lost support among many Palestinians. To boost his diminishing popularity, he met with Mubarak of Egypt, a country that would become in 1977 the first Arab nation to recognize the state of Israel.

The future state of Palestine. In 1988 the Palestine National Council provisionally declared Arafat the president of the future Palestinian state until elections could be held. Arafat publicly expressed belief in the idea of a joint Jewish-Palestinian state. With the encouragement of the United States and Egypt, he began to negotiate with Israel. The PLO strategy was to trade peace for land—the Gaza Strip and the West Bank.

Israel, however, had been angered by the continuing PLO raids and refused to talk with Arafat. In fact, Israelis were reluctant to deal with anyone in the PLO unless its leadership publicly rejected PLO goals to destroy Israel. In a 1989 French appearance, Arafat took that step, declaring for the first time that the PLO edict that called for the destruction of Israel was void. These diplomatic gains were largely offset in 1990 when Arafat sided with Iraq during the Gulf War in order to gain much-needed funds to continue the efforts of the PLO.

Middle East negotiations. In 1989, before the Gulf War, the joint efforts of Arafat, the United States, Egypt, and Israel had almost reached an accord to ensure transition into Palestinian self-rule. The Middle Eastern leaders agreed on an election in the West Bank and Gaza Strip. However, Israeli leaders gave in at the last minute to pressure from the conservative Likud Party and withdrew from the negotiations.

Following the defeat of Iraq, the PLO lost some of its support from other Arab states, along with its credibility in the West as the spokesman for Palestinians. Always able to snatch opportunities from apparent failure, Arafat now seized a new opportunity. The Gulf War had clearly demonstrated to one Israeli, Foreign Minister Shimon Peres, that standing armies, no matter how great, could no longer protect national borders from missile attacks. Peres could not legally begin talks with Arafat, but the PLO leader had little to lose and much to gain. He initiated discussions with Peres and Israeli prime minister Yitzhak Rabin. The result was a 1993 peace accord signed on the grounds of the White House with U.S. president Bill Clinton presiding over the signing. The agreement stated that Israel would gradually yield authority over the Gaza Strip and most of the West Bank to Arafat and the Palestinians over a five-year period. The transfer of power would begin with Gaza, an ideal starting place because eight hundred thousand Arabs lived there in poverty and it was an area of little interest to other Arab nations. Arafat would have the opportunity to demonstrate his great talents by helping to organize these people and improve their standard of living.

The signing of the peace accord by Arafat, Peres, and Rabin lead to their being named winners of the 1994 Nobel Peace Prize. The announcement of Arafat as co-winner of the prize, however, drew sharp criticism from some circles. Many people around the world protested the bestowing of an award for peace on a man they believe had been responsible for many terrorist activities in the past.

Aftermath

The transition has not been easy for Arafat. He continues to be hampered by militant Arab groups who now terrorize their own people seeking to establish a Palestinian homeland next to the hated state of Israel. Arafat, however, continues to be the international symbol of Palestinian liberation.

For More Information

Hart, Alan. *Arafat: Terrorist or Peacemaker?* London: Sidgwick and Jackson, 1984.

Kiernan, Thomas. *Arafat: The Man and the Myth.* New York: Norton, 1976.

Reische, Diana. *Arafat and the PLO.* New York: Franklin Watts, 1991.

Shimon Peres

1923-

Personal Background

Born in Poland. Shimon Peres was born August 16, 1923, to Itzhak Peres and Sara Persky Peres. His birthplace was Vishniva, a Jewish community in a region of eastern Poland that after World War II became part of the Byelorussian Soviet Socialist Republic and is now in Byelorussia. For the first ten years of his life, Shimon lived among bustling Jewish businesses and factories, thriving synagogues, and a great *yeshiva,* or school, that has been called the "breeding ground for the Jewish national soul" (Peres 1993, p. 2). This place of opportunity and comfort for the Jews who lived there was completely destroyed by anti-Jewish forces in World War II. Fortunately for Shimon, his parents decided, when he was ten or eleven, to leave these pleasant surroundings and move to the region that would eventually become Israel.

Tel Aviv. The Peres family settled in Tel Aviv and Shimon went to school there. Later he would continue his education at the Ben Shemon Youth Village and Agricultural School southeast of Lod on the central plain of ancient Judea. Jews in this region lived under a British mandate and under continuous threats by nearby Arabs who did not want a Jewish presence there. Under those conditions, everyone worked and everyone was concerned with defense. As a high school student Peres joined the Hagenah, a semi-covert Jewish self-defense organization. Then, when he was

▲ Shimon Peres

Event: Forming an Israeli-Palestinian accord.

Role: After serving his country as its president and in other cabinet positions for nearly thirty years, Shimon Peres was Israel's foreign minister when discussions were finally opened directly with Yasir Arafat of the Palestine Liberation Organization. The negotiations initiated by Peres resulted in the promise of a Palestinian homeland in the 1990s and a major step toward peace and cooperation in the Middle East.

▲ David Ben-Gurion; all the time that David Ben-Gurion led Israel, Peres was a member of the governing cabinet.

eighteen, he and other teenagers from the Tel Aviv area decided to start a *kibbutz,* a cooperative farm. The group moved to Lower Galilee and started Kibbutz Alumot. For a few years, Peres was a herdsman for the kibbutz. Later he was elected kibbutz secretary. That same year, 1941, he became active in the Israeli Workers'

Party (Mapai), which was forming even before Israel became a nation. The leaders of Mapai would become officials of the Israeli government from its beginning in 1948 to 1977. Peres also became active in the Histadrut, the umbrella Jewish labor organization. Within the Histadrut, he founded a working-youth organization, Ha-Np'ai Ha-Oved.

Protégé of David Ben-Gurion. All these activities brought Peres to the attention of David Ben-Gurion, then head of the Jewish Agency, a political organization that looked after Jewish interests in the Middle East and pressed for a Jewish homeland. When in 1944 Ben-Gurion, who was always watchful of the Arab neighbors, needed someone to conduct a scouting mission to the town of Eilat on the Red Sea, Peres was chosen for the job. Eilat was later to become Israel's seaport access to the Red Sea. From that mission on, Shimon Peres was David Ben-Gurion's protégé.

Hawk. When Israel became an independent nation in 1948, Ben-Gurion became its first prime minister. (He held that office until 1963.) At the same time, because of the importance of national security in light of the hostile atmosphere generated by the formation of Israel, Ben-Gurion became his own minister of defense. Peres became his deputy minister for naval affairs and then deputy minister of defense. He would soon lead Israel toward developing its own nuclear weapons, establishing a nuclear project at Dimona.

In the Beginning
While still under British management, Israel grew dramatically. In 1933, when the Peres family moved to Tel Aviv, there were fewer than 75,000 Jews among the 1,000,000 Arabs in the area. By the time Israel became a state, 650,000 Jews had purchased land from the Arab owners and settled in Israel along with nearly the same number of Arabs. Four hundred thousand Arabs had sold their land to the Jewish immigrants and moved, and another 400,000 left in panic following Israel's formation. Arab nations all around Israel were angered at this transformation, and Israel was immediately at war with its neighbors.

The new Israel's first line of defense was Hagenah, unofficially organized while the land was under British rule. It was Peres's job to supply these defenders with weapons. This was accomplished and Peres continued to build Israeli armed forces, which became so strong they could resist a threat from Egypt in 1956. In the 1956 fight against Egypt's plan to take over the Suez Canal, Israel occupied the Gaza Strip, a narrow highland overlooking Syria, and the Sinai Peninsula, which bordered the canal. Over the years that followed, many Israelis believed that these lands should be returned to Egypt and Lebanon, but Peres stubbornly refused. Both pieces of land, he claimed, were needed for the defense of Israel. From 1948 to 1963 almost all his attention was devoted to building an Israeli defense machine.

Peres was considerably younger than the other Israeli leaders in the first years of the nation. He and another Mapai member, Moshe Dayan, were part of the "young Mapai," a group that aggressively pursued the defense and military buildup of Israel. Among them, Peres earned a reputation for being the "leading hawk (supporter of a warlike policy)."

Leader of Israel. All the time that David Ben-Gurion led Israel, Peres was a member of the governing cabinet. He resigned his cabinet post when Ben-Gurion resigned but remained in the legislature, the Knesset. Levi Eshkol became prime minister, and almost immediately Ben-Gurion regretted turning the government over to him. The old founder of Israel decided to form a new political party and try to replace Eshkol. Peres joined him as secretary of the new political body, Rafi. The move was unsuccessful, and, for a time, Peres had no other government post than his seat in the Knesset. He had built such a powerful military organization, however, that when, in 1967, Egypt (then united with Syria in the United Arab Republic) tried to reoccupy some of Sinai and close Israeli shipping, the Israeli army needed only six days to defeat the plan. That "Six-Day War" added more territory to Israel: Jerusalem, the Golan Heights, and the West Bank of the Jordan River.

Eshkol died in 1969 and Golda Meir became Israel's prime minister. Peres immediately became part of the governing cabinet again, first as minister of immigration, then in succession as minister without portfolio, minister of transportation and communication, and minister of information. He was minister of information

Peres's Major Defense Activities	
1950-52	Visited the United States to raise money for Israel's defense
1952	Took full control of Israel's armed forces as director-general of the Ministry of Defense
1955	Arranged for France to supply weapons to Israel
1959	Became Ben-Gurion's deputy minister of defense

when Egypt, Syria, and other Arab nations began to mass their military along Israel's borders. Fearing an invasion, Peres was one of those who recommended that Israel strike first, as it had in the Six-Day War. Meir, however, was fearful of world reaction and refused the first-strike idea. The result was an Arab invasion in 1973 during the high Jewish holiday Yom Kippur—an invasion that nearly toppled Israel and required all of Meir's and Peres's influence in the United States to gain the necessary support to win the war.

New guard. The Yom Kippur War broke the hold of the old guard in Israeli politics. Meir resigned. Yitzhak Rabin campaigned to replace her, and the victorious Rabin immediately appointed Peres to his old job as minister of defense. The two men worked together to rebuild the Israeli military, but from the beginning Rabin accused Peres of trying to undermine him. The Yom Kippur War had also begun to draw suspicions of corruption and decadence within the ruling labor party. Rabin remained in office only three years before being replaced by a coalition of small conservative parties (the Likud) led by Menachem Begin. Except for his position in the Knesset, Peres was again out of government. As the "leading hawk," however, he would probably have agreed with Begin policies. Although Begin's rule saw the first break in Israeli-Arab relations when Egypt recognized the state of Israel and a Camp David accord called for Israel to return the occupied territories to their former owners within five years, Begin was for the most part hawkish himself. He persisted in establishing colonies of Jews among the Arabs of the West Bank, Sinai, and the Golan Heights. In 1982 Begin authorized "Operation Peace for Galilee," a military expedition that invaded Lebanon to secure Israeli territory from harassment by six thousand Palestinians based in that country.

More politics. Begin resigned in 1983 to be replaced temporarily by Itzhak Shamir. An election between Shamir and Peres for the next full-term prime ministry resulted in no decision. President Chaim Herzog then proposed that Peres, known for his out-

A Bit of Peres Philosophy

"We must study history to learn its critical lessons, but we must also know when to ignore history. We cannot allow the past to shape immutable [unchangeable] concepts that negate our ability to build new roads. Like the river, we are part of the process of perpetual change: landscapes shift, knowledge widens, and technology expands our horizons" (Peres 1993, p. 3).

▲ In Peres's mind, there was no possibility of peace in the Middle East other than by acknowledging and working with Israel's long-standing adversary, the PLO and Arafat.

standing organizing abilities, try to form a government agreeable to both the labor party and the Likud. The result was a peculiar arrangement: Peres would be prime minister for twenty-five months while Shamir would serve as foreign minister and deputy prime minister. The two would then change roles. The joint effort would begin in 1984. Thus, Peres was Israel's foreign minister in 1987, when **Yasir Arafat** (see entry) and his Palestine Liberation Organization (PLO) were increasing pressure to be given territory and be recognized as the voice of the Palestinians—a role the Israeli government had long refused to concede. When, in 1992, his old adversary Yitzhak Rabin again became prime minister, Peres was again called on to be minister of foreign affairs.

Participation:
Forming an Israeli-Palestinian Accord

A change of policy. Peres was foremost a practical politician. He was prepared to adjust his actions to the changes on the Israeli scene and to the views of the world. In 1990 a world event signaled that it was time to change his hawkish views. That year Iraqi forces invaded the tiny nation of Kuwait. The United States and a United Nations coalition rushed to Kuwait's aid in what became known as the Gulf War. Peres had observed the breakdown of old borders when Iraq and Iran skirmished earlier, but the Gulf War convinced him that guarding national borders with large and expensive standing armies was no longer a practical method of defense. Long-range missiles did not respect boundary lines. Even though the United States had antimissile weapons and had established a front many miles away, Iraqi missiles found their way to Israel.

War, even defensive war, Peres concluded, must give way to agreements between nations, mutual help, and respect. In his mind, there was no possibility of peace in the Middle East other than by acknowledging and working with Israel's long-standing adversary, the PLO and Arafat. But the previous Israeli government had created the structure within which he must work. Discussions were already going on in two forums: Israel and all other interested nations were meeting, and Israel was carrying out individual talks with each nearby Arab country. The PLO was not included in any of these discussions. Few Jews wanted to recognize and talk with Arafat.

Prime Minister Rabin and Foreign Minister Peres agreed to divide the chores; Rabin would lead discussions with individual nations while Peres would lead multinational discussions in Oslo, Norway. An early step was to include the PLO in these discussions, but without recognizing the leadership of Arafat. More and more, though, Peres came to believe that it was absolutely necessary to include Arafat in any Middle East solutions. The only ways to do that were to begin settling issues about the areas least important to the Israeli people and to maneuver in such a way that Arafat himself would extend the invitation to discuss the more important issues. The Gaza Strip was less important to Israel than the West Bank, where the former Israeli government had planted a hundred or more Jewish colonies. Besides, the eight hundred thousand Arabs in the narrow Gaza Strip were very poor; establishing rule there and showing some improvements in living conditions would give Arafat additional strength over the PLO in any negotiations. Peres decided to negotiate the release of the Gaza Strip first.

Peres on Arafat

A major reason for the success of negotiations between the Palestinians and Israelis was the respect Arafat and Peres held for each other. Peres described Arafat with admiration:

"In his twenty-five years of leadership, Arafat has shown both personal courage and manipulative skills. It is not by pure luck that he has managed to survive for so long.... For a quarter of a century he has been leading a national coalition without nationhood, maintaining elections without being elected" (Peres 1993, p. 17).

The plan worked. Negotiations began between PLO agents and Peres to release the Gaza Strip to the PLO. Arafat was a sharp negotiator himself, however. He allowed negotiations to move ahead slightly but never be completed. At the same time, he let it be known that he would be available for conferences and that he was willing to acknowledge the Israeli's right to exist. Finally, a Peres-Arafat conference was arranged. The PLO acknowledged Israel's right to exist as a free state. Israel and the PLO then formed a plan for a peaceful transfer of some of the West Bank and Gaza to Palestinian rule. The change would take place over a five-year period, with periodic and orderly transfer of powers from Israel to the government of the Palestinians.

This momentous agreement was not reached without difficulty. The Egyptian government and the United States stood by to offer help at any time and were often the key to continuing the discussions. On September 13, 1993, with U.S. president Bill Clinton presiding on the lawn of the White House, Israeli prime minister Yitzhak Rabin and PLO leader Arafat signed the historic agreement. It had been accepted by Peres and the PLO earlier—on August 20, 1993, in Oslo. Abu Alaa, a PLO leader, had at that time told Peres that the agreement was a present for his seventy-fifth birthday. With this agreement the nations of the Middle East moved one step closer to peace and to working together for prosperity. For his role in the peace process, Peres, along with Arafat and Rabin, was awarded the 1994 Nobel Peace Prize.

Aftermath

Trouble from Iran. The agreement between Peres and Arafat was not easy to keep. Militant members of both sides immediately began working to undo the arrangement. Israeli colonists in the West Bank region refused to relocate, in fact insisted on building new settlements in this "occupied territory." The main obstacle, however, seemed to be Hamas, a terrorist PLO faction supported by Iran. This group conducted raids on both Israeli lands and on Palestinians suspected of working to make the agreement a success. By the end of 1993, Hamas had been responsible for killing more than a thousand Palestinians. Amid such opposition on both sides, Peres and Arafat continued to work for an orderly establishment of a Palestinian homeland, in harmony with its neighbors, Jordan and Israel.

Within a year, major Western industries began to see the possibilities for creating a prosperous, harmonious Middle East. Some have already invested their resources, gambling that Peres and Arafat have begun the end of a centuries-old dispute.

For More Information

Friedman, Thomas L. *From Beirut to Jerusalem*. New York: Farrar, Strauss and Giroux, 1989.

Peres, Shimon. *Battling for Peace: A Memoir: From Israel's Birth to Today*. New York: Random House, 1995.

Peres, Shimon. *The New Middle East*. New York: Henry Holt, 1993.

Servam-Schreiber. *The Chosen and the Choice*. Boston: Houghton Mifflin, 1988.

Bibliography

Alazraki, Jaime. *Poetica y Poesia de Pablo Neruda*. New York: Las Americas, 1965.

Anderson, Martin. *Revolution: The Reagan Legacy*. Stanford, California: Hoover Institution Press, 1990.

Astrow, Andee. *Zimbabwe: A Revolution That Lost Its Way?* London: Zed, 1983.

Bavly, Dan, and Eliahu Salpeter. *Fire in Beirut: Israel's War in Lebanon with the PLO*. New York: Stein and Day, 1984.

Bly, Robert. *Neruda and Vallejo, Selected Poems*. Translated by Robert Bly, John Knoepfle, and James Wright. Boston: Beacon, 1971.

Brown, L. R. *State of the World, 1986*. New York: W. W. Norton, 1986.

Crozier, Brian. "What Ever Happened to the Red Army?" *National Review,* vol. 47, no. 14 (July 31, 1995), pp. 40-41.

Ehrlich, Anne, and Paul R. Ehrlich. *Earth*. New York: Franklin Watts, 1987.

Ehrlich, Paul R. *Healing the Planet: Strategies for Restoring the Environment*. Reading, Massachusetts: Addison-Wesley, 1991.

Ehrlich, Paul R. *The Population Explosion*. New York: Simon and Schuster, 1990.

Ehrlich, Paul R., and Anne Ehrlich. *Extinction: The Causes and Consequences of Disappearances of Species*. New York: Random House, 1981.

Fromkin, David. *A Peace to End All Peace*. New York: Henry Holt, 1989.

Gastrow. Shelagh. *Who's Who in South African Politics*. 3rd ed. Sevenoaks, England: Hans Zell, 1990.

Glubb, Lieutenant-General Sir John. *Peace in the Holy Land: An Historical Analysis of the Palestine Problem*. London: Hodder and Stoughton, 1971.

Glynn, Patrick. *Closing Pandora's Box*. New York: Basic, 1992.

Hardin, Garrett James. *Exploring New Ethics for Survival: The Voyage of Spaceship Beagle*. New York: Viking, 1972.

Herzog, Chaim. *The Arab-Israeli Wars*. London: Arms and Armour, 1982.

Lewis, William Roger. *The British Empire in the Middle East, 1945-1951*. Oxford: Oxford University Press, 1984.

Malia, Martin. "The Nomenklatura Capitalists." *New Republic,* vol. 212, no. 21 (May 22, 1995), pp. 17-24.

Moody, Fred. *I Sing the Body Electronic: A Year with Microsoft of the Multimedia Frontier*. New York: Viking, 1995.

Morrison, Toni. *Jazz*. New York: Knopf, 1992.

BIBLIOGRAPHY

Morrison, Toni. *Song of Solomon*. New York: Knopf, 1977.

Morrison, Toni. *Tar Baby*. New York: Knopf, 1981.

Nyrop, Richard F., editor. *Guatemala: A Country Study*. Washington, D.C.: American University, 1984.

Peres, Shimon. *David's Sling*. New York: Random House, 1971.

Peres, Shimon. "Let Us All Turn from Bullets to Ballots." *Vital Speeches of the Day,* vol. 59 (October 1993), pp. 739-40.

Peters, Joan. *From Time Immemorial: The Origins of the Arab-Jewish Conflict over Palestine*. Chicago: JKAP, 1993.

Quandt, William B. *Camp David*. Washington, D.C.: Brookings Institution, 1986.

Rabin, Yitzhak. *The Rabin Memoirs*. Boston: Little, Brown, 1979.

Reagan, Ronald. "President's Address, Brandenburg Gate, West Berlin, June 12, 1987." Washington, D.C. Department of State Bulletin, vol. 87, no. 2125 (August 1987), pp. 23-25.

"Reagan: From Actor to Presidential Hopeful." *U.S. News and World Report,* vol. 81, no. 6 (August 9, 1979), pp. 23-25.

Sanchez, Jose, and Antonio Zarate Martin. *Guatemala*. Madrid: Anaya, 1988.

Schwantes, Y. David. *Guatemala: A Cry from the Heart*. Minneapolis, Minnesota: Health Initiative, 1990.

Schweitzer, Peter. *Victory*. New York: Atlantic Monthly Press, 1994.

Wallerstein, Immanuel. *Africa and the Modern World*. New York: Africa World, 1986.

Weitz, Richard. "How the Reagan Doctrine Defeated Moscow in Angola." *Orbis,* vol. 36, no. 1 (Winter 1992), pp. 57-68.

Williams, Walter E. *South Africa's War against Capitalism*. New York: Frederick A. Praeger, 1989,

Wooster, Martin Morse. "The Rest of the Story." *Reason,* June 1990, p. 38.

Worth, Richard. *Robert Mugabe of Zimbabwe*. Englewood Cliffs, New Jersey: J. Messner, 1980.

Cumulative Index

Italic indicates volume numbers;
boldface indicates entries and their page numbers; (ill.) indicates illustrations.

A

Abdullah of Transjordania *7:* 95
Abraham *2:* 128, 133, 136
Abu Bakr *2:* 125, 138, 144, 146-147, 151
Abyssinia *8:* 158
Academy Award *7:* 153
Acampichtli *3:* 202
Achmed *4:* 128
Acquaviva Aragon, Guilio *4:* 106
Action Program *7:* 211-212
Actium, battle of *2:* 52, 52 (ill.)
Acton, John *5:* 57, 60
Adamec, Ladislav *8:* 105-106
Adams, John Quincy *5:* 75
Adi-Granth 4: 43
Adler, Alfred *6:* 61
Advancement of Learning 4: 101
Adventure 5: 12
Afar Triangle *8:* 34
Afghanistan *7:* 72; *8:* 124
Africa *5:* 26-27
African Association *5:* 24, 30
African Independence *8:* 137, 143-144
African Interpreter 7: 63
African National Congress (ANC) *8:*
    137-138, 141, 144, 166-167, 169, 171-
    77
African National Secretariat *7:* 64
Aggrey, Kwegyir *7:* 62
Agrarian Code *6:* 136
Agricultural revolution *4:* 176
Aguirre Cerda, Pedro *8:* 64
AIDS research *5:* 133
Akbar *3:* 188
Akutagawa, Ryunosuke *7:* 153
Alagonakkara *4:* 8
Alam Khan *3:* 187
Alaska *5:* 67, 76, 89, 94

Al-Bakri *3:* 100, **102-109**
Albatross III 7: 132
Albert I *6:* 11
Albert Schweitzer Chair for Humanities
    8: 73
Albert the Great *3:* 69-71
Albigensians *3:* 30-31
Al-Biruni *2:* 162, **176-183**
Albuquerque, Affonso de *4:* 3
Alexander I *5:* 176
Alexander II *5:* 170, **172-179,** 173
    (ill.)
Alexander III *6:* 110
Alexander the Great *1:* 45, 140-142,
    141 (ill.), 145-147, **148-155,** 149
    (ill.), 154 (ill.), 158-159, 161-163, 166-
    168; *2:* 1, 44; *3:* 125
Alexander, William *5:* 71
Alexandria, Egypt *1:* 146, 152; *2:* 127
Alexandrovitch, Alexander *5:* 176
Alexius I *3:* 3, 36
Alexius III *3:* 38-39, 43
Alexius IV *3:* 5, 38-40
Alexius V *3:* 5, **36-43**
Alfonso IX *3:* 27
Alfred the Great *2:* 186, 189, **190-
    197,** 191 (ill.)
Al-Ghazali *3:* 53-54
Ali, Muhammad *8:* 69-70
Aliases *6:* 110
Aljai Khatun Agha *3:* 161
Al-Khwarizmi *2:* 162, 169, **170-175**
"Alleluia" *6:* 156
Allen, Paul *8:* 48-52
Allende, Salvador *8:* 58, 64-66
Allied Control Council *6:* 217
Allied pact *6:* 20
Allied Powers *6:* 11; *7:* 1, 9, 11, 17, 20,
    21, 85, 179

All Is Quiet 7: 150

Allon, Yigal 7: 98

All's Well That Ends Well 4: 119

Almohads 3: 58-59

"Altair" 8: 50

The Amen Corner 7: 169

America, Britain, and Russia: Their Cooperation and Conflict 8: 16

American Central Intelligence Agency 8: 175

American De Forest Wireless Telegraph Company 6: 89

American Legion 6: 194

American Revolution 4: 159, 166; 5: 44

American Telephone and Telegraph Company (AT&T) 6: 92

Amplifying tube 6: 97

Amr ibn al-As 2: 127, 148

Analytical engine 5: 139, 143-144

ANC. See African National Congress (ANC)

Ancestors: In Search of Human Origins 8: 37

Anderson, Alexander 5: 30

Anderson, Allison 5: 29

Andrelinus, Faustus 4: 38

Andromeda galaxy 6: 65

Andropov, Yuri 8: 91

Anger, Per 6: 205

Anglo-Saxons 2: 192, 194, 197-198, 200-201

Angola 8: 176

Annalen der Physik 6: 38

Another Country 7: 169-170

Anthony, St. 2: 57, **58-65,** 59 (ill.), 62 (ill.)

Anthrax 5: 132

Anthropologists 8: 30

Antibiotics 7: 111, 121

Anti-Bolshevik sentiment 7: 12

Anti-Jewish laws 6: 202

Antiochus IV 2: 6, 8, 11, 13

Anti-Semitism 7: 8, 76-78, 100, 101, 156

Anti-Vietnam War movement 6: 197

Antiwar activist 6: 192

Antony, Mark 2: 3, 43, 48-52, 50 (ill.)

The Ants 8: 45

Ants: Their Structure, Development, and Behavior 8: 40

Apartheid 8: 141, 163-166, 171, 177

Apophthegms 4: 102

Appalachian Spring 7: 161

Aquinas, Thomas 3: 47-49, 55, 64, **66-73,** 67 (ill.)

Arab Higher Committee 8: 200

Arabia 2: 125-126, 128, 138, 145-146, 150, 157, 167

Arab-Israeli Wars 7: 96

Arab League 7: 95; 8: 199

Arab Legion 8: 189

Arab nationalism 8: 187, 189-192

Arab Summit 8: 194

Arafat-Peres agreement 8: 185

Arafat, Yasir 8: 181, 185, **196-205,** 197 (ill.), 199 (ill.), 202 (ill.), 207, 213-215

Arden, Mary 4: 112

Argon Khan 3: 134

Aristophanes 7: 159

Aristotle 1: 110-112, 135, **136-143,** 137 (ill.), 141 (ill.), 148, 181; 3: 46, 49-54, 52 (ill.), 60, 63, 68, 70-71; 4: 98, 156

Arkwright, Richard 4: 176, **184-189,** 185 (ill.)

Arouet, François-Marie. See **Voltaire**

Arrow Cross 6: 204-205

Arthur 3: 93

Arthur, John 8: 154

Aryabhata I 2: 94, 95, 117, **118-123**

Ashoka. See **Asoka**

Ashurbanipal 1: 44-45, **46-53,** 47 (ill.), 51 (ill.)

Asoka 1: 147, 169, 173, **174-179**

As-Saheli 3: 121-122

Assembly line factories 4: 188

Assembly of Notables 5: 46

Association of Young Vietnamese Revolutionaries 7: 56

Assyria 1: 3, 44, 46-50, 53-54

Astronomic Instauratae Progymnasmata 4: 82

Astronomy 3: 50-51; 4: 61-63, 77-79, 81-83, 86-88, 90

As You Like It 4: 118

Atahullpa 3: 201

Atatürk, Kemal 3: 171; 7: 2, **14-23,** 15 (ill.), 18 (ill.), 22 (ill.)

Athenaeum 7: 6, 8

Athens 1: 109-110, 122, 126-128, 130-132, 134-136, 138-139, 141-142, 145, 150, 159

Atlantic Charter 8: 159

Atlee, Clement 7: 182

Atomic weight 5: 101, 107

Audion tube 6: 90,92

"Augsburg Letters on the War" 6: 146

Augustine, St. 3: 72

Augustinians 3: 72

Augustus 2: 3, 33, 43, 49-52

Auschwitz (concentration camp) 7: 108

Australia 5: 11

Australopithecines 8: 27, 33

Australopithecus afarensis 8: 35

Austria-Hungary 7: 1-2

Austrian Society for Friends of Peace 6: 7

Austria State Treaty 7: 108

Automatic clock 5: 161

Averroës 3: 46, **48-55,** 49 (ill.), 68, 70

Averroists 3: 71

Avery, Oswald 7: 138

Avesta 1: 86

Avicenna (Ibn Sina) 3: 52-53

Ayyub 3: 6, 8, 11-12

Azcapotzalco 3: 204-205

Aztec Empire 3: 190-192, 192 (ill.), 202-203, 208-210

Aztec relics 3: 203 (ill.)

B

Baal 6: 148

Babbage, Charles 5: 135, **138-145,** 139 (ill.)

Babbage, Henry 5: 145

Babel 7: 163

Babor, Karl 7: 107

Babur 3: 157, **182-189,** 183 (ill.), 184 (ill.)

Babylon 1: 5, 14, 16-19, 17 (ill.), 21, 43-46, 48-50, 52-57, 57 (ill.), 59, 61, 67, 69, 115, 124, 126, 146, 152-153, 155-156, 161-162

Babylonia 1: 3, 15, 44, 59, 61

Bach, Johann Sebastian 4: 153

Bacon, Francis 4: 63, 95, **96-103,** 97 (ill.), 156

Bacon, Nicholas 4: 96, 98

Bacon, Roger 3: 127, 137, 145

Bacteria 7: 116-118

A Bad Lot 6: 7

Baghdad 2: 162, 164, 167, 170, 172

Baghdad Pact 8: 189

Baldwin, James 7: 145, 147, **164-171,** 165 (ill.), 167 (ill.)

Baldwin, Stanley 7: 180

Balfour, Arthur 7: 83; 8: 182, 198

Balfour Declaration 7: 81, 87-88, 95

Balkan States 6: 183

Balkan wars 6: 172

Ballet d'action 6: 166

Ballet Russe 6: 166

Ballistic missile defense (BMD) 8: 123

Baltic Committee for Free and Independent Trade Unions 8: 110

Banks, Joseph 5: 24, 26, 112

"Barbarity in the Skies" 6: 11

Barbarossa 4: 132

Bardeen, John 7: 124-126

Barlow, Arthur 8: 154

Barnham, Alice 4: 101

Barrier Treaty 4: 180

Bassarion, Cardinal 3: 179

Bastille 4: 162-163, 163 (ill.); 5: 34 (ill.), 45 (ill.), 48

Batista, Fulgencio 7: 200-202

Batu Khan 3: 138, 140-141, 143

Bayazid, Sultan 3: 163

Bayeux Tapestry 2: 212, 211 (ill.)

Bayezid 4: 126, 128, 132

Bay of Pigs 7: 194, 204

H.M.S. *Beagle* 5: 120-123; 8: 43

Beaupry, Captain 5: 202

Beauttah, James 8: 155

Becket, Thomas 3: 76, **78-87,** 79 (ill.), 85 (ill.)

Becquerel, Henri 6: 32, 48, 51

Beethoven, Ludwig van 6: 164; 7: 161

Before the Storm 6: 7

Begin, Menachem 8: 211

Beijing, China 7: 42, 48

Bell, Alexander Graham 5: 136; 6: 73

Beloved 8: 59, 74

Benedictine Code 2: 57

Benedictine Order *2:* 86

Benedictines *3:* 66, 68-69

Benedict of Nursia *2:* 57, 86, 90

Benes, Eduard *7:* 10, 11, 13, 208

Bergen-Belsen (concentration camp)
7: 108

Ben-Gurion, David *7:* 93-94, 96-98; *8:*
182, 208 (ill.), 209-210

Beria, Lavrenti *7:* 189 (ill.), 190

Berlin Wall *7:* 193; *8:* 86, 94

Bernard, Susanne *4:* 168, 170

Bernays, Martha *6:* 56, 58

Bernstein, Eduard *6:* 27

Bernstein, Leonard *7:* 145-146, **156-163,** 157 (ill.), 158 (ill.), 162 (ill.)

Bessemer, Henry *5:* 136, **146-151,**
147 (ill.)

Bethmann-Hollweg, Theobald von *6:*
183, 185-186

The Bible *1:* 34, 59; *2:* 58, 60-61

Big-bang theory *6:* 63, 67, 70

Biodiversity *8:* 29, 44

Birth control *8:* 12

Birth of African Nations *8:* 138

Bismarck, Otto von *5:* 178; *6:* 171, 178,
180 (ill.)

Black Friday *6:* 19

Black Holes *6:* 71

Black "homelands" *8:* 164-166

Blackhouse, Edmund *5:* 190

The Black Race 7: 54

Black September *8:* 202

Bloody Sunday *6:* 27

Blue Period *6:* 156, 160

The Bluest Eye 8: 58, 71

Board of Poor Law Guardians *6:* 14

Boccaccio, Giovanni *4:* 93

Boer War *8:* 164

Bohemia *7:* 5, 9, 11

Bolívar, Simón *5:* 85

Bolshevik People's Commissar of
Nationalities *7:* 11

Bolsheviks and Bolshevism *6:* 115,
210; *7:* 2, 10-12, 25-29, 180, 188

Bolshoi Nakaz 4: 146

Boniface VIII *4:* 32

*The Book of Marco Polo Concerning the
Kingdoms and Marvels of the East 3:*
137

The Book of Roads and Kingdoms 3:
103, 105

Booth, John Wilkes *5:* 93

"The Borderers" *5:* 205

Borgia, Cesare *4:* 72

Boston Symphony Orchestra *7:* 159,
161

Botha, Pieter W. *8:* 141, 165, 176

Boulton, Matthew *4:* 194

Bourtai *3:* 17-18, 23

Boxer Rebellion *5:* 194-195; *6:* 126

Boxer Rising *7:* 38, 42

Bragadino, Pietro *4:* 131

Brahe, Jorgen *4:* 74

Brahe, Tycho *4:* 63-64, **74-83,** 75
(ill.), 85, 87-90

Braque, Georges *6:* 158

Brattain, Walter *7:* 124-126

Brecht, Bertolt *6:* 143, **144-151,**
145 (ill.), 150 (ill.)

Breuer, Joseph *6:* 57-59

Brezhnev Doctrine *8:* 94

Brezhnev, Leonid *7:* 194; *8:* 86, 91, 129

Briand, Aristide *6:* 194

British Broadcasting Corporation
(BBC) *6:* 213

British navy *5:* 2 (ill.)

Brito, Richard *3:* 86

Bronson, Charles *7:* 152

Brooks, F. T. *7:* 68

The Brothers Karamazov 5: 179

Brown, Edmund G. "Pat" *8:* 119

Brown, William *8:* 41

Brownian motion *6:* 40

Brush, Charles F. *5:* 156

Brutus, Marcus *2:* 33, 50

Bryant, William Cullen *4:* 110-111

Brynner, Yul *7:* 152

Buddha. See **Siddhartha Gautama**

Buddhism *1:* 80, 88-95, 100, 173, 175-177; *2:* 93-94, 102, 107, 109, 110, 112-114, 116-117; *4:* 137; *5:* 185

Bukharin, Nikolai *7:* 30

Bunin, Ivan *6:* 165

Burgos Debray, Elisabeth *8:* 83

Burke, Edmund *5:* 17

Burns, Robert *5:* 17

Bush, George *8:* 124-125

Bushido 7: 46

Byron, Lord (George Gordon) *5:* 144, 207

Byzantine Empire *2:* 57, 75, 83, 87, 126, 132, 146, 152, 154-159, 167

C

Cabot, John *4:* 3, 22

Caesar, Julius *2:* 3, 23, **24-33,** 25 (ill.), 31 (ill.), 40-42, 47, 49

Calculating machines *5:* 141

Calfa, Marian *8:* 106

Callas, Maria *7:* 162

Calles, Plutarco *6:* 133, 135-136

"Call to Honor" *6:* 213

Calonne, Charles de *5:* 45

Calvert, Raisley *5:* 203

Campbell, Archibald *5:* 68

Camp David *8:* 184

"Canción de la Fiesta" *8:* 62

Candide *4:* 161, 164, 164 (ill.)

Candragupta. See **Chandragupta**

Cannes Film Festival *7:* 154

Canning, George *5:* 75

Canterbury Cathedral *3:* 81 (ill.)

Cantlie, James *6:* 124

Canute the Great *2:* 186, **198-205,** 199 (ill.), 203 (ill.)

Capital *5:* 217

Capitalism *5:* 197, 199, 217; *7:* 1, 30-31, 174

Carchemish, battle of *1:* 56

Cárdenas, Lázaro *6:* 107, **130-139,** 131 (ill.), 135 (ill.), 137 (ill.)

Carnegie Hall *7:* 160

Caroline Matilda *5:* 38-41

Carpini, John *3:* 126

Carranza, Pedro *6:* 133

Carson, Rachel *7:* 113, **128-135,** 129 (ill.)

Carter, Jimmy *8:* 121, 194

Carthage *1:* 171, 186, 188, 190-191, 193-195; *2:* 152, 154-155

Cartier, Jacques *4:* 3, **22-29,** 23 (ill.), 26 (ill.), 28 (ill.)

Caruso, Enrico *6:* 92

Cas *7:* 6, 8

Cassius, Gaius *2:* 33, 50

Castel Nuovo *5:* 58 (ill.)

Castriota, George *3:* 173

Castro, Fidel *7:* 175, 194, **196-205,** 197 (ill.), 199 (ill.), 203 (ill.)

Castro, Raul *7:* 201

Cathay *3:* 21

Catherina de Ataíde *4:* 21

Catherine des Granches *4:* 22

Catherine the Great *4:* 125, **142-149,** 143 (ill.)

Cathode ray tube *6:* 97

Catholic Church *4:* 35-37

Catiline, Lucius Sergius *2:* 39-40

Ceauçescu, Nicolae *8:* 94

Cecil, Robert *4:* 99

Celestine III *3:* 26

Central Committee Secretariat *7:* 209

Central Kikuyu Association (CKA) *8:* 155-156, 159

Central Powers *7:* 9, 16, 85

Cepheid Variables *6:* 65

Cervantes, Miguel de *4:* 95, **104-108,** 105 (ill.), 110-111

Ch'in dynasty *1:* 173, 196-199, 201

Ch'ing dynasty *6:* 105, 121-122, 127

Chagatai Khan *3:* 158

Chain, Ernst *7:* 119, 121

Chalchiuhtlatonac. See **Moctezuma I**

Chalco *3:* 208

Chamberlain, Neville *7:* 180

Chandragupta *1:* 146, 163, **164-169,** 173-174

Chandragupta II *2:* 96, 98, 101, 113

Chanute, Octave *6:* 78

Charcot, Jean-Martin *6:* 58

Charles I *4:* 103, 154

Charles V *4:* 46, 57, 131

Charpentier, Antoinette *5:* 44

"Charter 77" *8:* 99, 101-102

Charter Oath *5:* 171, 183, 186-187

Chechnya *8:* 135

Cheng Ho *4:* 2, **4-11**

Chen-Tsu-i *4:* 8

Chernenko, Constantin *8:* 91

Chesme, battle of *4:* 147

Chiang Kai-shek *6:* 129; *7:* 38-39, 44 (ill.), 45-46

Chikerema, James *8:* 145

Children's Crusade *3:* 30 (ill.), 31

Chile *8:* 58, 62-66

China *1:* 4, 6, 8-13, 10 (ill.), 80, 81 (ill.), 96-97, 100, 102-105, 107, 111, 171, 173, 177-178, 180-185, 196-199, 201; *2:* 1, 4, 5, 16-21, 93-95, 102-109, 110-117; *7:* 36, 37-49, 55-58, 175

China under the Empress Dowager 5: 190

Chinese Communist Party *7:* 43-48

Chinese Nationalist Party *7:* 43

Chinese Revolution *6:* 121

Chirac, Jacques *6:* 218

Chopin, Fréderic *6:* 165

Chou dynasty *1:* 80, 96, 103-104

Christian August *4:* 142

Christianity *2:* 55-58, 61, 63-65, 68, 72, 74-76, 78, 80-83, 88, 91, 132, 136, 145, 156, 195, 202; *3:* 45; *4:* 123

Christian Reformed Church *8:* 162

Christian VII *5:* 38, 40

The Christian Soldier's Manual 4: 49

Chronicle of English History 4: 114

Church of the Cordeliers *5:* 46

Churchill, Randolph *7:* 176

Churchill, Winston *6:* 174 (ill.), 175, 196, 213-214; *7:* 33, 87, 89, 173, **176-185,** 177 (ill.), 179 (ill.), 181 (ill.); *8:* 159

Chu Ti *4:* 4

Chu Yun-Wen *4:* 6

Cicero, Marcus Tullius *2:* 3, 33, **34-43,** 35 (ill.), 40 (ill.), 49

Citlalcohuatzin *3:* 206

Civic Forum *7:* 213; *8:* 104, 106

Civil disobedience *7:* 72; *8:* 174

Civil rights movement *7:* 127

Cixi. See **Tz'u-hsi**

CKA. See Central Kikuyu Association (CKA)

Clay, Cassius M. *5:* 94

Clement III *3:* 24

Clement V *4:* 32

Clement, Joseph *5:* 143

Clementis, Vladimir *7:* 209

Cleopatra VII *2:* 3, 31, 43, **44-53,** 45 (ill.), 46 (ill.), 50 (ill.)

Clinton, Bill *8:* 168 (ill.), 177, 204, 215

Clodius, Publius *2:* 41, 42

Club of the Cordeliers *5:* 49

Club of the Jacobins *5:* 49

Coateotl *3:* 202

Cocteau, Jean *6:* 169

Codio Agrario. See Agrarian Code

Coetsee, Hendrik J. *8:* 176

Coke, Edward *4:* 100-102

Coke, Thomas *4:* 182

Cold War *7:* 34, 47, 173-175, 177, 181, 187, 190, 204; *8:* 85, 92, 121

Coleridge, Samuel *5:* 203, 207

Collective farming *7:* 30, 32-34

Colloquia 4: 38

Colonialism *7:* 52

Color blindness *5:* 104

Columbus, Christopher *3:* 137, 193; *4:* 3, 14

The Comedy of Errors 4: 116

Comite Unidad Campesina (CUC) *8:* 80

Committee for the Defense of the Unjustly Prosecuted *8:* 102

Committee for Workers Defense *8:* 113

Commonwealth of Independent States *8:* 134

Communism *6:* 106; *7:* 3, 12, 46, 54, 179; *8:* 57, 65, 99, 100-101, 105, 115, 192

Communist Correspondence Committee *5:* 215

Communist League *5:* 215

Communist Manifesto 5: 209, 215-216

Communist Party *6:* 148-149; *7:* 2, 27, 41, 45, 187, 189, 192, 208; *8:* 64-65, 91, 94, 101, 126, 129, 133-134

Computer chip *7:* 126

Computers *7:* 126

Concentration camps *6:* 187, 204

Condell, Henry *4:* 120

Confederation Regional Michoacana del Trabajo (Michoacan Confederation of Workers) *6:* 134

Conference of Versailles *7:* 42

Confessions 4: 173

Confucianism *2:* 5, 109-110

Confucius *1:* 6, 80, 96, 99, 101, **102-107,** 103 (ill.), 106 (ill.), 111, 173, 181-185; *2:* 18, 95, 102, 103 (ill.), 107, 110, 117; *7:* 40

Congress of People's Deputies *8:* 133

Congress of Victors *7:* 192

Congress Party *7:* 72

Congress Working Committee *7:* 72

Conservation in Action 7: 132

Constance *3:* 27

Constantine XI *3:* 168, 170

Constantine the Great *2:* 56-57, 65, **66-75,** 67 (ill.), 71 (ill.), 76, 78, 86, 152, 156

Constantinople *2:* 75-76, 86-88, 152, 154-156; *3:* 36 (ill.), 38-43, 167-172, 169 (ill.)

Constitutionalists *7:* 180

Constitution of 1889 *5:* 187

Constitution of Clarendon *3:* 82

Contras *8:* 124

Convention People's Party (CPP) *7:* 39, 64-66

Cook, James *5:* 2, **4-13,** 5 (ill.)

Copernican theory *4:* 82

Copernicus, Nicolaus *4:* 84, 151; *6:* 70

Copland, Aaron *7:* 159, 161

Coppola, Francis Ford *7:* 154

Coronet 7: 202

Cortés, Hernando *3:* 123, 210

Corvilhan, Pedro de *4:* 16

Cosmology *6:* 33, 68

Cossacks *3:* 177 (ill.); *4:* 148 (ill.)

Cottle, Joseph *5:* 203

Coulomb, Charles de *5:* 113

Council of Trent *4:* 33

Count of Lemos *4:* 110

CPP. See Convention People's Party (CPP)

"The Cradle Will Rock" *7:* 159

Crane, Charles *7:* 9

Crassus, Marcus Licinius *2:* 28-30, 41

Crick, Francis *7:* 112, 137-143

Crime and Punishment 5: 179

Crimean War *5:* 148, 170, 174

"The Crisis of Social Democracy" *6:* 28

Croesus *1:* 66

Crop rotation *4:* 181-182

Crusades *3:* 1-4, 2 (ill.), 125

Crying Holy 7: 166-168

Crystals *7:* 122

Cuba *7:* 196-204

Cuban Revolution *7:* 200

Cubism *6:* 153, 157-159

CUC. See Comite Unidad Campesina (CUC)

Cultural Revolution *7:* 49

Cuneiform *1:* 3, 52, 54, 70

Curie, Bronia *6:* 44

Curie, Irene *6:* 48

Curie, Marie *6:* 32, **44-53,** 45 (ill.), 46 (ill.), 49 (ill.)

Curie, Pierre *6:* 45-53, 46 (ill.)

Curzon, George Nathaniel *7:* 88

Cyrus the Great *1:* 45, 61, **62-69,** 63 (ill.), 64 (ill.), 66 (ill.), 68 (ill.), 83, 86, 110, 156

Czech National Council *7:* 11

Czechoslovak Central Committee *7:* 211

Czechoslovak Communist Party *7:* 206-207, 211

Czechoslovak Federal Republic *8:* 106

Czechoslovak republic *7:* 10

Czechoslovakia *7:* 2, 4-13; *8:* 87, 99, 102-103, 106, 110

Czech Republic *8:* 107

D

Daimyo 4: 139

Dalindyebo, David *8:* 170

Dalton, John *5:* 98-99, **100-107,** 101 (ill.)

Dalton, Jonathan *5:* 102

Dalton's law *5:* 106

D'Amboise, Charles *4:* 73

Dandolo, Enrique *3:* 38-39, 42

Daniela Dormes 6: 7

Dante, Alighieri *4:* 93

Danton, Georges *5:* 35, **42-53,** 43 (ill.)

Daoguang *5:* 190

Daoism. See Taoism

Darius III *1:* 146-147, 151-152, **156-163,** 157 (ill.)

Darius the Great *1:* 45, 69, **70-77,** 71 (ill.), 73 (ill.), 74 (ill.), 83, 110, 122, 151, 156

Darlan, Francois *6:* 215

Dart, Raymond *8:* 33

The Daruma Temple 7: 150

Darwin, Charles *5:* 99, **116-125,** 117 (ill.), 118 (ill.); *6:* 141; *8:* 43-44
Darwin, Erasmus *5:* 116
Darwin, Robert *5:* 116
Das Kapital *5:* 199, 209, 216; *6:* 149; *7:* 200
Davidoff, Monte *8:* 50
Davis, Angela *8:* 69-70
Davis, Nancy. See Reagan, Nancy
Davy, Humphry *5:* 110-112, 111 (ill.), 154-155
Dawkins, Richard *8:* 44
Dayan, Moshe *7:* 98; *8:* 210
D-Day *6:* 215
DDT *7:* 112-113, 133-134
Death Valley Days *8:* 119
Debussy, Claude *6:* 143, 166
Decameron *4:* 93
Declaration of Independence *4:* 159
"The Declaration of the Rights of Man" *5:* 47 (ill.), 48
De Forest, Lee *6:* 74, **87-93,** 86 (ill.), 91 (ill.)
De Gaulle, Charles *6:* 175, **208-219,** 209 (ill.), 212 (ill.), 216 (ill.)
De Klerk, F. W. *8:* 140 (ill.), 141, 149 (ill.), **162-169,** 163 (ill.), 168 (ill.), 171, 176-178
Delaney, Beanford *7:* 166
Delian League *1:* 128
Delphic oracle *1:* 131
Democratic Republic of Vietnam *7:* 57-58
Democritus *5:* 212
De Nova Stella *4:* 79
Dersu Uzala *7:* 153
Descartes, René *4:* 65, 156
"Descriptive Sketches" *5:* 203
Desmoulins, Camille *5:* 48-50, 52
De-Stalinization *7:* 209
Deutsches Theater *6:* 149
Dharma *1:* 177
Diaghilev, Sergei *6:* 165-166, 169
Dias, Bartolomeu *4:* 3, 14
Dias, Diego *4:* 17
Díaz, Porfiro *6:* 107, 138
Diaz-Balart, Mirta *7:* 200
Dickson, James *5:* 24
Diderot, Denis *4:* 153, 171

Die Gesellschaft *6:* 6
Difference Engine *5:* 139, 141, 142 (ill.), 144
Diocletian *2:* 66, 68-69, 78
Discourse on Method *4:* 65
Discourse on the Origin of Inequality *4:* 169, 171
Discourse on the Sciences and the Arts *4:* 171
Disputed Questions on Truth *3:* 70
Divine Comedy *4:* 93
Divine right of kings *4:* 159
Djenné, Mali *3:* 119 (ill.)
DNA (deoxyribonucleic acid) *7:* 112, 136-143
Domagaya *4:* 25
Dominic, St. See Guzmán, Dominic
Dominicans *3:* 68, 70
Donata *3:* 136
Donnacona *4:* 25-28
Don Quixote *4:* 95, 107-110, 107 (ill.), 109 (ill.)
Dostoyevsky, Fyodor *5:* 177, 179
The Double Helix *7:* 139, 142
"Dove" *5:* 204
Drake, Francis *4:* 116
The Dream and the Lie of Franco *6:* 160
Dreams *7:* 155
Drunken Angel *7:* 151
Dubcek, Alexander *7:* 174, **206-213,** 207 (ill.), 210 (ill.); *8:* 101
Duc d'Aquitaine *5:* 7
Dulles, John Foster *7:* 191
Dunant, Jean Henri *6:* 10
Dunbar, Paul Lawrence *6:* 78
Dutch Reformed Church *8:* 141, 162
Dynamite *6:* 9
Dynamo *5:* 114

E

Eagle *5:* 7
Eastern European Mutual Assistance Treaty *7:* 213
East India Islands (ill.) *4:* 10
Eastwood, Clint *7:* 152
Economic Revolution *5:* 19-21
The Edge of the Sea *7:* 133

Edict of Milan *2:* 72

Edison and Swan United Electric Light Company *5:* 156

Edison Electric Company *5:* 167

Edison, John *5:* 158

Edison, Mary *5:* 163, 167

Edison, Thomas Alva *5:* 136-137, 153, 155-156, **158-167,** 159 (ill.), 164 (ill.); *6:* 73, 90

E=mc2 *6:* 39

Egypt *1:* 3, 5, 22-26, 33, 35-38, 40, 44-45, 50, 56, 75, 115, 123-126, 146, 152, 156; *2:* 31-32, 44, 47-49, 51-53, 57-58, 63, 127, 149-150, 155, 157, 159; *3:* 121; *8:* 189, 192, 194, 200, 211

Ehrlich, Anne *8:* 2-3, 21 (ill.), 22

Ehrlich, Paul *8:* 2-3, **20-25,** 21 (ill.)

Eichmann, Adolf *6:* 202, 205; *7:* 107-108

Einstein, Albert *5:* 116; *6:* 32, **34-43,** 35 (ill.), 37 (ill.), 41 (ill.), 67; *7:* 84 (ill.)

Einstein, Elsa *6:* 42

Eisenhower, Dwight D. *6:* 215, 216; *7:* 193; *8:* 119

Eisner, Tom *8:* 41

Ejidos 6: 136-137

Elam *1:* 16, 21, 43-45, 50, 52, 62

Eleanor of Aquitaine *3:* 88

Electromagnetic field *5:* 114

Electromagnetic tube *6:* 97

Electromagnetic waves *6:* 31

Electromagnetism *5:* 109

Electron microscopy *6:* 101-102

Electron optics *6:* 101

Electroplating *5:* 115

El Fatah *8:* 184, 192, 200-201, 203

Elizabeth I *4:* 96, 101, 112, 115 (ill.), 116, 119 (ill.)

Elizabeth (of Russia) *4:* 142, 144, 146

Emerillion 4: 25

Émile, or On Education 4: 172-173

Empiricism *4:* 158

Enchiridion Militis Christiani 4: 38

Endeavor 5: 9, 11

Engels, Friedrich *5:* 209, 213-217, 213 (ill.)

Enlightenment *4:* 146, 151-153, 156, 161, 163-164, 166, 171; *5:* 33-38, 59, 170

Environmental movement *7:* 112, 129, 131-135

Epic theater *6:* 143, 145, 147, 149

Epicurus *5:* 212

Epistolarum 4: 80 (ill.)

Equal Franchise Society *6:* 190

Equal Rights for Women *6:* 16

Erasmus, Desiderius *4:* 32, **34-39,** 35 (ill.), 37 (ill.), 49

Erdeni-Tsu monastery *3:* 144 (ill.)

An Essay Concerning Human Understanding 4: 155, 157

Eshkol, Levi *7:* 98; *8:* 210

Estonia *7:* 2

Ethelred *2:* 198, 200-201

Ethiopia *8:* 34

Euclid *6:* 34

Eudocia *3:* 38, 43

Euphrates River *1:* 14-16, 32, 46, 58-59

The Evening Item 6: 78

"An Evening Walk" *5:* 202, 204

The Evidence of Things Not Seen 7: 147, 171

"Evolutionary biology" *8:* 44

"The Excursion" *5:* 102, 205

Experimental Researches in Electricity 5: 115, 161

Experiments in Aerodynamics 6: 78

Extractor's Club *5:* 140

F

Facing Mount Kenya 8: 158

Falsafah *3:* 51

Fancy Free 7: 160

Faraday, James *5:* 108

Faraday, Michael *5:* 98-99, **108-115,** 109 (ill.), 161; *6:* 31

Faraday, Sarah *5:* 113

Fascist dictatorships *8:* 57

Fasti 4: 114

Fatimid Caliph *3:* 10

Fatwa 7: 20

Feminist Federation *6:* 134

Fenwick, Isabelle *5:* 207

Ferdinand I *5:* 86

Ferdinand II *4:* 14, 48
Ferdinand IV *5:* 35, 56-57, 62
Ferdinand, Francis *6:* 172, 182, 184
Ferdinand of Habsburg *4:* 131
Fermentation *5:* 130
Fernandez de Avellanda, Alonso *4:* 110
Feudalism *2:* 19; *5:* 185, 187
Feu d'artifice 6: 165
Field effect *7:* 125
Fifth Crusade *3:* 33-34
Fifth Pan-African Congress *7:* 64
Fifth Republic *6:* 218
Filament *6:* 90
Final Solution *6:* 199, 204; *7:* 105
Finland *7:* 2
The Firebird 6: 166
The Fire Next Time 7: 170
First Crusade *3:* 39
A Fistful of Dollars 7: 152
Fitzroy, Robert *5:* 119, 120
FitzUrse, Reginald *3:* 86
Five-Year Plan *7:* 32, 194
"The Flag Cadet" *6:* 146
Fleming, Alexander *7:* 111, **114-121,** 115 (ill.), 120 (ill.)
Fleming valve *6:* 92
Florey, Howard *7:* 112, 119, 121
The Flower of the Saints 4: 48
Flyer III *6:* 83
Fontenelle, Bernard de *4:* 151
Ford, Gerald *8:* 119
Ford, Henry *4:* 189
Fourth Republic *6:* 218
Francis I *4:* 25, 27, 29, 73
Francis I *5:* 54, 56
Francis II *5:* 83
Franciscans *3:* 70; *4:* 140
Francis of Assisi *3:* 31, 33-34, 70
Franco, Francisco *6:* 160; *8:* 63
Frank, Anne *7:* 108
Franklin, Benjamin *5:* 100
Frederick I *3:* 13
Frederick II *3:* 27, 33-34, 68; *4:* 81-82
"Freedom Charter" *8:* 174
Freedom of the press *5:* 177
Free Economic Society *4:* 146
Free French *6:* 213-216
Freelove 5: 6
Free Trade Union *8:* 111

Frei Montalva, Edward *8:* 64
French Committee of National Liberation *6:* 215
French Communist Party *7:* 54
French, Melinda *8:* 54
French North Africa *6:* 214
French Revolution *4:* 173; *5:* 35, 43, 55, 57, 62, 80
French Socialist Party *7:* 54
Freud, Anna *6:* 61
Freud, Jacob *6:* 54
Freud, Sigmund *6:* 33, **54-61,** 55 (ill.), 60 (ill.)
Friedman, Aleksandr *6:* 68
Fulton Speech *7:* 183

G

Gahagan Douglas, Helen *8:* 118
Galapagos Islands *5:* 122 (ill.)
Galatea 4: 107
Galera 8: 78
Galich *3:* 174
Galilei, Galileo *4:* 64, 87, 91, 151
Gallic War *2:* 29
Gama, Estevao da *4:* 12
Gama, Vasco da *4:* 3, 8, **12-21,** 13 (ill.), 20 (ill.)
Gamow, George *6:* 68
Gandhi, Mohandas *7:* 38, 69, 71-73, 73 (ill.); *8:* 144
Gang of Eight *5:* 193
Gao *3:* 118
Gaozu. See **Kao Tsu**
The Garden Party 8: 100
Garrigue, Charlotte *7:* 6
Gasparri, Pietro *8:* 7
Gates, Bill *8:* 28, **46-55,** 47 (ill.), 49 (ill.), 51 (ill.)
Gatsha Buthulezi, Mangosuthu *8:* 170, 178
Gaugamela, battle of *1:* 152, 162
Gaul *2:* 26, 29-30, 80
Gaza Strip *8:* 185, 204, 209, 214
Gazeta Ludova 6: 26
Gebhard, Henrich *7:* 158
Gelignite *6:* 9
General Electric *5:* 167
General Electric Theater 8: 118

Genes *7:* 138

Genetics *7:* 138

Genghis Khan *3:* 5, **14-23,** 15 (ill.), 22 (ill.), 28, 34, 127-128, 133

Geoffrin, Marie-Thérèse de *4:* 153

Geometry of space *6:* 41, 67

George I *4:* 180

George III *4:* 189

George III *5:* 8, 38-39, 41

George, David Lloyd. See Lloyd George, David

Georgia Peace Society *6:* 194

Germ theory *5:* 127

German SPD *6:* 27, 28

German tanks *6:* 201 (ill.)

German Workers' Association of Brussels *5:* 215

Germany *7:* 1

Gestapo *6:* 187, 215; *7:* 102, 106

Ghana *3:* 99-101, 106-108; *7:* 60

Ghettos *6:* 203, 206; *7:* 104

Gierek, Edward *8:* 110, 111

Gil, Fray Juan *4:* 107

Giocondo, Francesco del *4:* 71

Giovanni's Room *7:* 169

Giraud, Henri *6:* 215

Girina, Naya *8:* 128

Girondists *5:* 202

Glasgow University *5:* 16 (ill.)

Glasnost *8:* 93-94, 124, 129-130

Globe *6:* 126

Globe Theatre *4:* 118

Glubb, John *8:* 189

Godwin, William *5:* 203

Goebbels, Joseph *7:* 102

Golan Heights *8:* 200-201, 211

Gold Coast *7:* 37, 39, 60-61, 63-65

Golden Laurel award *7:* 153

Golden Palm Award *7:* 154

Goldwater, Barry *8:* 119

Golos, Danuta *8:* 108

Gomulka, Waldyslaw *8:* 110

Gonzáles Videla, Gabriel *8:* 64-65

Gorbachev, Mikhail *8:* 86-87, **88-97,** 89 (ill.), 92 (ill.), 95 (ill.), 113, 124, 129-131, 134

Gorbachev, Raisa *8:* 90

Gordon, Aaron David *7:* 93

Go Tell It on the Mountain *7:* 147, 168

Gottwald, Clement *7:* 208

Gough, John *5:* 102

"Government of National Unity" *8:* 178

Gqozo, Oupa *8:* 167

Grand Alliance *7:* 180

Grand National Assembly *7:* 20-21

Grande Hermine *4:* 25

Grant, Robert *5:* 119

Grant, Ulysses S. *5:* 67, 94

Gray, Tom *8:* 35

Great Barrier Reef *5:* 11

Great Depression *7:* 130

Great Leap Forward *7:* 49

Great Northern War *4:* 147

Great Rift Valley *8:* 36

Great Wall of China *2:* 18; *3:* 156 (ill.)

Greed Dilemma: War and Aftermath *8:* 16

Greenberg, Stan *8:* 177

Greene, Robert *4:* 117, 118

Greer, Frank *8:* 177

Gregorian chant *2:* 90

Gregory IX *3:* 34

Gregory the Great *2:* 57, 83, **84-91,** 85 (ill.), 89

Grenada *8:* 124

Grenville *5:* 8

Grigg Bill *8:* 156

Grigg, Edward *8:* 156

Gromyko, Andrei *8:* 93

Grossman, Marcel *6:* 36

Guangzu *5:* 195

Guatemala *8:* 58, 79-80, 82-83

Guatemalan Forestry Commission (INAFOR) *8:* 79

Guatemalan National Institute for Agrarian Transformation *8:* 79

Guernica *6:* 159 (ill.), 160

"Guevara, Ernesto "Che" *7:* 201

Guide for the Perplexed *3:* 47, 57, 63-64

Gulag *7:* 32-34

Gulbehar *4:* 132

Gulf of St. Lawrence *4:* 24

Gulf War *8:* 185, 204, 213

Gupta dynasty *2:* 93-94, 96, 98-99, 113

Gutenberg, Johannes *4:* 93

Guzmán, Dominic *3:* 31, 33-34

H

The Hague Conference 6: 10
Hague Peace Conference 6: 9
Hajj 3: 146
Halaby, Lisa 8: 189
Hale, George Ellery 6: 64, 70
Hale telescope 6: 70
Hamas 8: 215
Hamid, Abdul (sultan) 7: 16
Hamilton, Alexander 5: 21
Hamilton, William 8: 44
Hamlet 4: 118-119
Hammurabi's code 1: 19-21, 20 (ill.)
Hammurabi 1: 3, **14-21,** 15 (ill.), 18 (ill.), 44
Han dynasty 1: 173, 178, 185, 197, 199-201; 2: 5, 16, 18-22
Ha-Np'ai Ha-Oved 8: 209
Han Wu Ti. See **Wi Ti**
Handel, George 4: 153
Hanging Gardens of Babylon 1: 61, 127
Hanna 6: 10
Hannibal 1: 171, 172 (ill.), 185, **186-195,** 187 (ill.), 192 (ill.); 3: 186
Hanukkah 2: 12
Hardie, Keir 6: 16
Hardin, Garrett 8: 2, 24
"A Hard Kind of Courage" 7: 170
"Harlem Ghetto: Winter 1948" 7: 168
Harlequin 6: 157
Harold Godwinsson 2: 188, 210-211, 213 (ill.)
Hart, Robert 5: 190
Haruko 5: 187
Harvey, Gabriel 4: 117
Hashimite Kingdom of Jordan 8: 186
Hastings, battle of 2: 189, 212-214, 213 (ill.)
Hathaway, Anne 4: 114, 117 (ill.), 120
Hatikvah 7: 96
Hat law 7: 23
Hatshepsut 1: 5, **22-27,** 23 (ill.)
Hatti 1: 3, 28-32, 44
Hattin, battle of 3: 12
Hattusas 1: 28, 31, 33, 45
Hauptmann, Elisabeth 6: 149

Havel, Vaclav 8: 87, **98-107,** 99 (ill.), 103 (ill.), 105 (ill.)
Hawaii 5: 13
Haydn, Joseph 6: 164; 7: 161
Hayfron, Sally 8: 145
Hebrews 1: 4 (ill.), 5, 34-38, 40, 45, 67, 73; 2: 1
Hegel, Georg Wilhelm Friedrich 5: 210-212, 211 (ill.), 214
Hegira 2: 134
Heidenstam, Jeannette von 6: 203
Heminge, John 4: 120
Hemingway, Ernest 8: 74
Henry I 3: 75
Henry II 3: 76, 79-80, 82, 84; 4: 29
Henry III 3: 90, 96, 164
Henry IV, Part 1 4: 116, 119
Henry VI 3: 27
Henry VIII 3: 86
Henry, Duke of Saxony 3: 27
Henry the Navigator 4: 3, 12
Henslow, John Stevens 5: 119
Heraclius 2: 126, 147, 151, **152-159,** 153 (ill.), 157 (ill.)
Hero and Leander 4: 118
Herodotus 1: 62, 70, 72, 110, 112, 119, **120-127,** 121 (ill.), 125 (ill.), 130
Herschel, John 5: 140, 141
Hertz, Heinrich 6: 88
Herzl, Theodor 7: 78, 82-83
Herzog, Chaim 8: 211
Heydrich, Reinhard 7: 105
Hideyoshi, Toyotomi 4: 125, **134-141,** 135 (ill.)
Higgins, Elmer 7: 130, 131
High Life 6: 6
High-vacuum pump 6: 90
Hill, Anita 8: 74
Hilsner, Leopold 7: 8
Himmler, Heinrich 7: 102, 105
Hinckley, John, Jr. 8: 122
Hindenburg, Paul von 6: 185-186
Hinduism 1: 80, 91-93, 95, 173-174, 177; 2: 93, 98-99; 4: 42; 7: 71
Hippocrates 4: 156
Hirohito 5: 187
Histadrut 7: 94; 8: 209
Histories (Herodotus) 1: 120-124, 126-127

History Handbook of Western Civilization 8: 16

History of the English-Speaking Peoples 7: 185

Hitler, Adolf 6: 42, 149-150, 160, 173, 187, 196, 202, 213; 7: 13, 34, 77-79, 101-102, 105, 119, 173, 180, 208

Hittites 1: 3, 28-29, 31-33, 44

Ho Chi Minh 7: 39, **50-59,** 51 (ill.), 55 (ill.)

Hodges, Joy 8: 118

Holinshed, Raphael 4: 114

Holocaust 6: 42, 206; 7: 79, 101, 107-108

Holt, Patience 4: 184

Holy Alliance 5: 74, 176

The Holy Family 5: 215

Holy Roman Emperor Francis II 5: 80

Holy Trinity Church 4: 120 (ill.)

Hominids 8: 33

Homo erectus 8: 28, 33

Homo habilis 8: 27-28, 33

Homo sapiens 8: 27-28, 33

Honecker, Erich 8: 94

Honey and Rue 8: 74

Horace 4: 114; 6: 147

Horthy, Miklós 6: 204

Hottentots 4: 17

Ho Tzu-chen 7: 43

Hough-Guldberg, Ové 5: 41

Houghton, Daniel 5: 25-26

Houlun 3: 14, 16-17

House Un-American Activities Committee 6: 151

Howe, Richard 5: 158

Howell, Clark 8: 33

How to Know the Butterflies 8: 22

Hoyos, López de 4: 104, 106

Hozier, Clementine 7: 178

Hsia dynasty 1: 12-13

Hsüan-tsang 2: 94, 107, **110-117**

Hsün-tzu 1: 111, 173, 179, **180-185**

Huáscar 3: 201

Huayna Cápac 3: 195, 200

Hubble, Edwin 6: 33, **62-71,** 63 (ill.), 66 (ill.), 69 (ill.)

Hubble's law 6: 67

Hubble Space Telescope 6: 71

Huckins, Olga 7: 112, 133

Huehue. See **Moctezuma I**

Huerta, Victoriano 6: 132-133

Hughes, Charles Evans 6: 93

Huitzilhuitl 3: 202

Huitzilopochtli 3: 204-205

Humanae Vitae 8: 3, 12

Human Genome Project 7: 143

Humayun 3: 186-187

Huns 2: 18

Huntsman, Benjamin 5: 149

Hunyadi, Janos 3: 173

Hunyadi, John 3: 166

Husák, Gustav 8: 101

Huss, John 4: 32

Hussayn, Amir 3: 161-162

Hussein I 8: **186-195,** 187 (ill.), 190 (ill.), 193 (ill.)

Hussein, Sharif 8: 186

Hutcheson, Francis 5: 16

Hutchinson, Mary 5: 207

Huxley, Thomas Henry 5: 125

Hwang Ho (Yellow River) 1: 8, 8 (ill.), 11

Hysteria 6: 59

I

I, Rigoberta Menchu: An Indian Woman in Guatemala 8: 77, 83

Ibáñez del Campo, Carlos 8: 64

Ibn Battutah 3: 116, 127, **146-153,** 147 (ill.); 4: 7

Ibn Khaldun 3: 114

Ibn Tufayl 3: 50, 53-54

Ibrahim Lodi 3: 187

I-chu 5: 188, 190

The Idiot 7: 155

Ieyasu Tokugawa 4: 125, 139, 141

If Beale Street Could Talk 7: 171

Ignatius of Loyola 4: 32, **46-51,** 47 (ill.)

Ikiru 7: 153

Ilhiucamina. See **Moctezuma I**

Imam El Shafei cemetery 3: 149 (ill.)

Imperialism 7: 19, 36-39, 60, 71, 169

Inca Empire 3: 190-193, 192 (ill.), 194-201

Incandescent light 5: 157

The Incoherence of the Incoherence 3: 54

The Increased Difficulty of Concentration 8: 100

The Independent 7: 71

Independent Students' Organization 8: 104

India 1: 80, 89-95, 146, 149, 153, 164-168, 171, 173-176, 178; 2: 93-96, 98-101, 110, 112-116, 118, 120, 167, 174, 180-182; 7: 38, 68-75

Indian National Congress 7: 68-73

Indochinese Communist Party 7: 56

Induction 5: 114

Industrialization 5: 199; 6: 2

Industrial Revolution 4: 175-177, 179, 195; 5: 98, 103, 148, 150, 197, 205; 6: 1, 171

Information Superhighway 6: 103

Inkatha Freedom Party 8: 170, 178

Innocent III 3: 4, **24-35,** 25 (ill.), 39, 93

Inoculation 7: 116

An Inquiry into the Nature and Causes of the Wealth of Nations 5: 19

Institutional Revolutionary Party (PRI) 6: 136

Inter-enterprise Strike Committee 8: 111

International African Service Bureau 8: 158

International Arbitration and Peace Association (IAPA) 6: 7-8

International Friends of Abyssinia 8: 158

International Friends of Ethiopia 8: 158

International Ghetto 6: 206

International Journal of Environmental Science 8: 25

International Peace Organization 6: 8

International Psycho-Analytical Association 6: 61

International Socialist Bureau 6: 26

International Working Men's Association 5: 209, 216

The Interpretation of Dreams 6: 60

Intifada 8: 203

Inventarium einer Steele 6: 10

Iñigo. See **Ignatius of Loyola**

Ionia 1: 109-110, 114-115, 120, 122-124, 146, 173

Iquehuacatzin 3: 206

Iran-contra affair 8: 124

Iraq 8: 185, 191

Irene 4: 166

Iron curtain 7: 173, 182-183; 8: 87, 94

Iroquois 4: 25, 27

Isaac 3: 38, 42

Isaac II 3: 39

Isabella I 4: 48, 106

Isabella of Angouléne 3: 90

Isabella of Gloucester 3: 90

Iskra 6: 113-114

Islam 1: 80; 2: 124-127, 132-138, 142-150, 157, 159, 161-163, 166-167, 176; 3: 45, 120-121

Islamic pact 8: 192

Israel 7: 78-79, 81-82, 86, 89, 91, 94, 96-98; 8: 182, 189, 192-194, 209-211, 213-215

Israeli-Palestinian Accord 8: 207, 213

Israeli Philharmonic Orchestra 7: 162

Israeli-PLO agreement 8: 194

Issus, battle of 1: 147, 147 (ill.), 151, 161

Itzcóatl 3: 191, 202-204, 206, 208

Ivan III 3: 176

Ivan IV. See **Ivan the Great**

Ivan the Great 3: 157, **174-181,** 175 (ill.); 5: 172

J

Jablochkov, Paul 5: 156

Jackson, Andrew 5: 73

Jacob, Max 6: 156-157

Jagielski, Mieczslaw 8: 111

Jakes, Milos 8: 104

Janissaries 4: 128

Japan Proletariat Artists Group 7: 148

Japanese film 7: 149, 151

Jaruzelski, Wojciech 8: 94, 113

Jazz 8: 74

Jefferson, Thomas 5: 21, 71, 75

Jeremiah 7: 160-161

Jerome, Jennie 7: 176

Jerusalem 2: 1, 7, 10-12, 148-149, 155-156, 158; 3: 4 (ill.), 5; 8: 194

Jesus Christ *2:* 60, 72, 132-133, 156

Jeugbond *8:* 162

Jewish Agency *7:* 94-95

Jewish Central Committee *7:* 107

Jewish Labor Party *7:* 94

Jewish Workers Union *6:* 25

Jews *2:* 6-13, 15, 134, 136, 145

Jiang Jieshi. See Chiang Kai-shek

Jiang Qing *7:* 43

Jihad 3: 12

Jim Crow laws *7:* 166

"Jirous, Ivan Martin ("Magor") *8:* 101

Jogiches, Leo *6:* 25

Johannesburg, South Africa *8:* 172

Johanson, Donald *8:* 27, **30-37,** 31
   (ill.)

John XXIII *8:* 10

John (of Portugal) *4:* 14-16

John, King *3:* 27, 77, 86, **88-97,** 89
   (ill.), 92 (ill.), 95 (ill.)

Johnny Carson Show 8: 24

John Paul II *8:* 113

Johnson, Andrew *5:* 89, 93-95

John the Baptist 4: 73

Johst, Hanns *6:* 147

Joliot, Fredrick *6:* 48

Jonson, Ben *4:* 118, 121

Jordan *8:* 182, 187, 189, 191-192, 194,
   215

Jordan-Iraqi pact *8:* 190

Josef, Franz *6:* 183

Journal of Friar William of Rubrouck: A
   Frenchman of the Order of the Minor
   Friars, to the East Parts of the World,
   in the Years 1253 to 1255 3: 145

Journey to Parnassus 4: 110

Juarez, Benito *6:* 132

Judah *1:* 5, 44-45, 56-57, 67

Judaism *2:* 8, 9, 132

Judea *2:* 6-7, 10-12, 14

Julian the Apostate *2:* 56, 75, **76-83,**
   77 (ill.), 79 (ill.)

Jung, Carl *6:* 61

"Junius Pamphlet." See "Crisis of Social
   Democracy"

Junzi *1:* 183-184

Just above My Head 7: 171

K

Kabal Khan *3:* 16

Kadar, Janos *8:* 93

Kádár, János *7:* 193

Kaganovich, Lazar *7:* 28

Kagemusha 7: 154

Kaiser Wilhelm. See **Wilhelm II**

Kalafaty, Vassily *6:* 164

Kalidasa *2:* 94-95, **96-101**

Kalinga War *1:* 176

Kamenev, Lev *7:* 30, 33

Kant, Immanuel *4:* 151

KANU. See Kenyan African National
   Union (KANU)

Kao Tsu *1:* 173, 178, 195, **196-202**

Karaits *3:* 18

Katane, Moses *8:* 173

KAU. See Kenyan African Union
   (KAU)

Kaul, Kamala *7:* 72

Kay, John *4:* 186

Kazgan, Amir *3:* 158, 161

Keats, John *5:* 207

Kelley, Renee *8:* 42, 43

Kelley, William *5:* 149

Kellogg-Briand pact *6:* 194

Kellogg, Frank *6:* 194

Kennedy, John F. *7:* 135, 193-194, 204

Kenney, Annie *6:* 17

Kenya *8:* 140, 153, 158, 160

Kenyan African National Union
   (KANU) *8:* 160

Kenyan African Union (KAU) *8:* 139,
   159

Kenyan Peoples Union *8:* 160

Kenyatta, Jomo *8:* 139, **152-161,**
   153 (ill.), 155 (ill.), 157 (ill.)

Kepler, Johannes *4:* 64, 75, 82-83,
   84-91, 85 (ill.), 151

Kerensky, Alexander *6:* 115

KGB *8:* 134

Khrushchev, Nikita *7:* 174, **186-**
   195, 187 (ill.), 191 (ill.), 204, 209; *8:*
   91, 100

Kibbutz *7:* 93

Kidnapped in London 6: 124

Kikuyu *8:* 154, 156, 158

Kinescope *6:* 75, 101

King Lear 4: 120; 7: 154
Kinsky, Franz 6: 6
Kirov, Sergei 7: 33
Kissinger, Henry 8: 148
Kitchener, Horatio H. 7: 85
Kitty Hawk, North Carolina 6: 80-82
Kleist Award 6: 149
Knights of St. John 4: 129, 133
Knights of the Order of Chivalry 3: 33
Knute Rockne: All American 8: 118
Koch, Robert 5: 132
Kolkhozes 8: 88
Kolon, Ali 3: 121
Komsomol 8: 88
Koran 2: 127, 136, 142, 149, 151, 161
Korkud 4: 128
Körner, Theodor 6: 6
Kortright, Elizabeth 5: 72
Kosice Agreement 7: 210
Koumintang 7: 45-46, 48
Koussevitzky, Sergei 7: 159, 161
Krenz, Egon 8: 94
Krieg und Frieden 6: 10
Kruger, Paul 6: 181
Kruger Telegram 6: 182
Krupskaya, Nadezhda 6: 111, 113
Krzysztof Bielecki, Jan 8: 115
Kublai Khan 3: 23, 128-130, 132 (ill.), 133, 136
Kuchachin (Cocacin) 3: 134
Kucuk Kainarji, Treaty of 4: 148
Kulakov, Fyodor 8: 91
Kulaks 7: 32
Kuraish 2: 125, 130, 140, 144, 145
Kurosawa, Akira 7: 145, 146 (ill.), **148-155,** 149 (ill.)
Kurosawa, Heigo 7: 150
Kuwait 8: 185
Kuyuk Khan 3: 127
Kyd, Thomas 4: 118
Kyushu 5: 186

L

Lacroix, Sylvestre 5: 140
La Giaconda 4: 71
Laidley, John 5: 26, 27, 29
Lake District 5: 200, 203-206
Lakhmi Das 4: 44

Lamarck, Jean-Baptiste 5: 119, 121, 123
Lamentations for Jeremiah 7: 159
Lander, John 5: 31
Lander, Richard 5: 31
Langevin, Paul 6: 97
Langley Aerodrome 6: 84
Langley, Samuel P. 6: 81
Lansing, Robert 7: 88
Lao-tzu 1: 80-81, 95, **96-101,** 97 (ill.), 98 (ill.)
Laozi. See **Lao-tzu**
The Last Supper 4: 70 (ill.), 71
Lateran Council 3: 32 (ill.), 33
Latin 3: 45
Latvia 7: 2
Lauer, Koloman 6: 201, 203
Laugerud Garcia, Kjell 8: 79
Law of Partial Pressures 5: 106
Lay Down Your Arms 6: 7-8
League Against Imperialism 8: 156
League of Nations 6: 3, 11; 7: 72, 88, 95
League of Oppressed Peoples of Asia 7: 56
Leakey, Louis 8: 32-33, 32 (ill.), 36
Leakey, Mary 8: 32-33, 32 (ill.), 36
Leakey, Richard 8: 28, 33, 37
Leavitt, Henrietta 6: 33, 65
Leda 4: 73
Ledyard, John 5: 24
Lee, Spike 7: 171
Lefferts, Marshall 5: 163
Lehna 4: 44
Leibniz, Gottfried 5: 144
Lemaitre, Georges 6: 68
Le Monnier, Frantisek 7: 4, 6
Lenin 5: 179, 217-218; 6: 106, **108-118,** 109 (ill.), 112 (ill.), 117 (ill.); 7: 2, 12, 25, 27-30, 29 (ill.)
Leninism 5: 217
Lenin Peace Prize 8: 65
Lenin Shipyard 8: 111
Leo X 4: 32
Leonardo da Vinci 4: 63-64, **66-73**
Leone, Sergio 7: 152
Leopold II 5: 80
Les Demoiselles d'Avignon 6: 143, 158
Leser, Paul 8: 30
Les Noces 6: 169

Les Sylphides 6: 165
Letters Concerning the English Nation 4: 153
"A Letter to the Bishop of Landoff" 5: 203
Le Vasseur, Thérèse 4: 171
Levin, Joseph 7: 153
Lewis, Elizabeth 7: 142
Li (ritual) 1: 105, 183-184
Liadov, Anatol 6: 166
Liberal Party 6: 12; 7: 178
"Liberté, Egalité, Fraternité" 5: 49, 72-73
Libya 8: 124
Licinius 2: 72
Liebknecht, Karl 6: 29
The Life of Christ 4: 48
Light Quanta (Photons) 6: 40
Likud Party 8: 204, 211-212
Lilienthal, Otto 6: 78, 81
Lincoln, Abraham 5: 67, 89, 91-93, 91 (ill.)
"Lines Written in Early Spring" 5: 205-206
Lippmann, Walter 8: 85
Liquid nitroglycerin 6: 9
Liquid rocket propellants 6: 75
Lithuania 7: 2
Lloyd George, David 7: 85-87, 178
Locke, John 4: 151, **154-159,** 155 (ill.), 164-165
Lodge, Thomas 4: 117
Lombards 2: 87
The London Times 6: 124
Long March 7: 45
Lord Chamberlain's Men 4: 118, 120
Lord Randolph Churchill 7: 183
Lothar, Klemens Wenzel Nepomuk. See **Metternich, Klemens**
Louis IX 3: 127, 138-139
Louis XIV 4: 162
Louis XV 4: 162
Louis XVI 5: 43-51, 59
Louisiana Purchase 5: 70-71
Louis Napoléon 5: 148
Lovers of Zion 7: 82
Love's Labour's Lost 4: 118
Lowther, James 5: 202
Lubeck, Gustav 6: 26

Lubeck, Karl 6: 25
Lucas, George 7: 154
Lucas, Simon 5: 25
Lucas Garcia, Fernando 8: 80
Lucy 8: 28, 31, 35-36
"Lucy in the Sky with Diamonds" 8: 35
"Lucy Lyrics" 5: 204
Ludendorff, Erich 6: 185-186
Luder, Hans 4: 52, 54
Luria, Salvador 7: 136, 138
Lusitania 6: 185
Luther, Martin 4: 32, 38, **52-59,** 53 (ill.), 56 (ill.), 59 (ill.)
Luxemburg, Rosa 6: 3, **22-29,** 23 (ill.), 28 (ill.)
Lyceum 1: 141-142
Lydia 1: 65-66
Lyly, John 4: 117, 118
Lyly, William 4: 114
Lyrical Ballads 5: 203-207
Lysozyme 7: 117, 118, 199

M

Mabovitch, Sheyna 7: 92
Macbeth 7: 155
Maccabees 2: 10-11, 14
Maccabeus, Judas 2: 1, 5, **6-15,** 7 (ill.), 12 (ill.)
Macedonia 1: 136, 138, 141, 145, 148-150, 158-159, 173
Machina coelestis 4: 62 (ill.)
Madero, Francesco 6: 132
Madison, James 5: 75
Madizekela, Winnie. See Mandela, Winnie
Maginot Line 6: 211
Magna Carta 3: 77, 89, 94-97, 95 (ill.)
The Magnificent Seven 7: 146, 152
Magnus, Albertus 3: 64, 70
Mahim 3: 186
Maimon 3: 58-59
Maimonides 3: 47, **56-65,** 57 (ill.), 61 (ill.), 68, 70
Malcolm X 7: 171
Malenkov, Georgi 7: 189 (ill.), 190
Mali 3: 111-118, 119 (ill.), 121, 123
Malindi 4: 18
Malleable iron 5: 147

Malta, siege of *4:* 133
A Man's a Man 6: 149
Man's Noblest Thought 6: 11
Manchester Guardian 7: 87; *8:* 156
Manchester Literary and Philosophical Society *5:* 103
Manchu government *7:* 38, 41
Manco Cápac *3:* 194
Mandela, Nelson *8:* 140 (ill.), 141, 144, 166-168, 168 (ill.), **170-79,** 171 (ill.), 178 (ill.)
Mandela, Winnie *8:* 173, 176
Mangu Khan *3:* 127, 139, 142-144
Manifesto to the Europeans *6:* 40
Mann, William *8:* 42
Manuel I *4:* 16
Mao Tse-tung. See **Mao Zedong**
Mao Zedong *6:* 129; *7:* 38, **40-49,** 41 (ill.), 47 (ill.), 56
Marat, Jean-Paul *5:* 48, 50
Marconi, Guglielmo *6:* 88-89
Maria Carolina *5:* 35, **54-63,** 55 (ill.)
Maria Theresa *5:* 54
Maric, Mileva *6:* 37 (ill.), 38
Marie-Antoinette *5:* 54-56, 59, 60 (ill.), 61, 63
Marlowe, Christopher *4:* 116-118
Marshall Plan *7:* 174, 184
Martyr Abu Khalid Society *8:* 196
Marx, Heinrich *5:* 208, 210
Marx, Jenny *5:* 212
Marx, Karl *5:* 199, **208-218,** 209 (ill.); *6:* 3, 27, 105-106, 111, 141, 143, 145, 149, 210; *7:* 1, 3, 43, 54, 150, 200; *8:* 57
Marxism *6:* 24, 27, 118, 141; *7:* 27, 31, 148; *8:* 58, 61-63, 65, 150, 156-157, 184
Marxist-Leninist doctrine *7:* 203
Mary, Queen of Scots *4:* 116
Masaryk, Jan *7:* 9, 13
Masaryk, Tomás Garrigue *7:* 2, **4-13,** 5 (ill.), 7 (ill.); *8:* 100
Masur, Norbert *6:* 202
Materialism *5:* 212, 214
Mathematical Principles of Natural Philosophy 4: 151
Matilda *3:* 75
Matlalxochitl *3:* 202
Maurya *1:* 146, 169, 173-179

Mawema, Michael *8:* 145
Mawson, John *5:* 152
Maxentius *2:* 70-72
Maximilian (Austria) *6:* 107
Maximilienne Wilhelmine Marie *5:* 175
Maxims of the Law 4: 100
Maxtla *3:* 204-205
Maxwell, James Clerk *5:* 114; *6:* 31
Mboya, Tom *8:* 160
McCoy, Elijah *5:* 136
McLeod, Iain *8:* 160
McNeill, William *8:* 2-3, **14-19**
McQueen, Steve *7:* 152
Measure for Measure 4: 120
Mecca *2:* 125, 128, 130-134, 136, 138, 140-145, 161
Media *1:* 45, 53-56, 62, 64-65
Medina *2:* 125, 134, 136, 144-146, 148-151, 161
Mehmed II *3:* 157, **166-173,** 167 (ill.)
Meiji Tenno. See **Mutsuhito**
Mein Kampf 7: 77
Meir, Golda *7:* 79, **90-99,** 91 (ill.), 97 (ill.); *8:* 194, 210-211
Meister, Joseph *5:* 133
Memoiren 6: 10
The Memorandum 8: 100
Menchu, Petrocinio *8:* 81
Menchu, Rigoberta *8:* 58-59, **76-83,** 77 (ill.)
Menchu, Tum *8:* 58, 76, 82
Menchu, Vicente *8:* 58, 76, 79-80, 82
Mendelssohn, Felix *6:* 164
Mengele, Josef *7:* 107
Menlo Park, New Jersey *5:* 163-165
Mensheviks *6:* 115
Mercantilism *5:* 19
The Merchant of Venice 4: 118
The Merry Wives of Windsor 4: 119
Mesopotamia *1:* 1, 14, 152
Mestizo 6: 130
Metamorphoses 4: 114
Meteorological Observations and Essays 5: 103
Meteorology *5:* 103
Metternich, Klemens *5:* 65-66, 74, **78-87,** 79 (ill.), 84 (ill.)

Mexican Department of Indian Affairs (DIA) *6:* 138

Mexican Revolution *6:* 107, 131

Mickiewicz, Adam *6:* 22

Middle Ages *4:* 31, 123-125, 175

Middle East *8:* 180-215

Midget 6: 76

A Midsummer Night's Dream 4: 118

"A Mighty Fortress Is Our God" *4:* 57

Military potential *6:* 84

Milky Way *6:* 63-66

Miller, Frances *5:* 88

Miller, Mina *5:* 167

Milvian Bridge, battle of the *2:* 72

Ming dynasty *6:* 120

Mingrelia, Princess von *6:* 6

Mishnah *3:* 58, 60

Mishneh Torah 3: 62, 64

Missouri Compromise *5:* 74

Mitropoulos, Dimitri *7:* 159

Moctezuma I *3:* 191, 193, **202-210**

Moctezuma II *3:* 210

Molotov, Vyachislav *7:* 28

Mombasa *4:* 18

Mona Lisa 4: 73

Monasticism *2:* 57, 60, 64

Mongol Empire *3:* 157-160, 183

Mongols *3:* 1, 5, 14, 19 (ill.), 21, 23, 126-127, 160, 163

Monophysites *2:* 156

Monroe Doctrine *5:* 66-69, 75-76, 79, 81, 86, 89, 92-94

Monroe, James *5:* 66, **68-77,** 69 (ill.), 70 (ill.), 79, 81, 85

Montagu, Edwin *7:* 85

Monte Cassino *3:* 69 (ill.)

Monteux, Pierre *6:* 168

Montfort, Simon de *3:* 90, 97

Monti, Jorge *8:* 64

Montreux Convention *7:* 22

Morelos, José *6:* 132

Morgan, John *4:* 190

Morrison, George *5:* 190

Morrison, Harold *8:* 70

Morrison, Toni *8:* 58, **68-75,** 69 (ill.), 71 (ill.), 73 (ill.)

Morse, Samuel *5:* 136; *6:* 73

Morville, Hugh de *3:* 86

Moses *1:* 5, **34-41,** 35 (ill.), 39 (ill.)

Mosquini, Marie *6:* 93

Mother and Child at the Seashore 6: 160

Motion Picture Artists Association *7:* 151

Moudros Armistice *7:* 17

Mozambique *4:* 18; *8:* 147, 176

Mozart, Wolfgang Amadeus *4:* 153; *6:* 164; *7:* 161

Mt. Palomar Observatory *6:* 66 (ill.)

Mt. Sinai *1:* 40-41

Mt. Wilson Observatory *6:* 70

Mt. Wilson telescope *6:* 64, 65

Mubarak, Muhammad Hosni *8:* 184

Mugabe, Robert *8:* 141, **142-151,** 143 (ill.), 146 (ill.), 149 (ill.), 170

Muhammad *2:* 124-127, **128-139,** 129 (ill.), 137 (ill.), 140, 142, 144-146, 151, 157, 161, 167; *3:* 50, 55, 60

Muhammad II. See **Mehmed II**

Muir, John *7:* 132

Mujahideen *8:* 124

Müller, David *5:* 14

Müller, Hermann *7:* 136

Müller, Rezso *6:* 206

Murad II *3:* 166, 168

Murer, Franz *7:* 107

Murtzuphlus. See **Alexius V**

Musa, Mansa *3:* 101, 115, **116-123,** 117 (ill.)

Muslim Brotherhood *8:* 198

Muslims *2:* 126-127, 134-138, 142, 144-147, 150, 157, 161, 173, 179-182; *4:* 42; *7:* 71-73

Mustapha *4:* 132

Mutsuhito *5:* 171, **180-187,** 181 (ill.), 184 (ill.)

Muzorewa, Abel *8:* 148

My Early Life: A Roving Commission 7: 183

Myerson, Goldie. See **Meir, Golda**

Myerson, Morris *7:* 93-94

My Life 7: 90

Mysterium Cosmographicum 4: 87

N

Naboulsi, Suleiman *8:* 191

Nader, Ralph *6:* 197

Nanak, Guru *4:* 33, **40-45**

Napoleon III *5:* 131

Napoléon Bonaparte *5:* 35, 53, 61-62, 65-66, 74, 78-79, 81, 82 (ill.), 83, 94, 176, 206, 208

Nashe, Thomas *4:* 117

Nasser (President of Egypt) *8:* 192, 198

Nathanson, Amalie *6:* 54

National Assembly *7:* 213

National Book Critics Circle Award *8:* 72

National Congress of Solidarity *8:* 112

National Council of Christians and Jews *7:* 169

National Democratic Party (NDP) *8:* 145-146

National Fellowship Award *7:* 163

National Front Coalition *7:* 208

National Geographic *8:* 42

Nationalists, Chinese *7:* 45

Nationalists, Turkish *7:* 19

National Organization for Women (NOW) *8:* 58

National Pact *7:* 19-20

National Party *6:* 193

National Revolutionary Party (PNR) *6:* 135

National Security Council *8:* 124

National Woman Suffrage Association *6:* 190

Native Son *7:* 167-168

Natural selection *5:* 117, 120, 123-124; *8:* 43

The Nature of the Chemical Bond *7:* 140

Nazi Party *6:* 150, 199, 201-206, 213, 215

Nazis and Nazism *7:* 13, 101-106, 108-109

NDP. See National Democratic Party (NDP)

Nebuchadnezzar II *1:* 21, 45, **54-61,** 55 (ill.), 67

Nebula *6:* 64

Necho *1:* 56

Need, Samuel *4:* 187

Negro Anthology *8:* 158

Neher, Rudolph Ludwig Casper *6:* 146, 148

Nehru, Jawaharlal *7:* 38, **68-75,** 69 (ill.), 73 (ill.), 74 (ill.)

Neruda, Pablo *8:* 58, **60-67,** 61 (ill.)

Nestorians *3:* 143

Nestorius *3:* 125

New Astronomy *4:* 82

New Atlantis *4:* 101

Newcomb, Simon *6:* 81

Newcomen, Thomas *4:* 176, 192-193

New Economic Policy (NEP) *7:* 30

Newfoundland *4:* 24

New Leader *7:* 168

New Republic of China *6:* 127

New System of Chemical Philosophy *5:* 105 (ill.), 106

Newton, Isaac *4:* 63, 85, 91, 151; *5:* 125, 140-141, 144, 161; *6:* 31

New York Philharmonic Orchestra *7:* 146, 160

New York Symphony Orchestra *7:* 161

New Zealand *5:* 11-12

Neyrum *3:* 14, 16-17

"Nguyen Ai Quoc ("Nguyen the Patriot") *7:* 54

Nicaea, Council of *2:* 57, 73 (ill.), 74

Nicene Creed *2:* 74

Nicholas I *5:* 148, 172, 174, 176-177

Nicholas II *6:* 165

Niger *5:* 31

Night vision *6:* 102

Nihon Eiga contest *7:* 150

Nijinsky, Vaslav *6:* 167 (ill.), 168

Nika Exhibition *7:* 148

Nikolayevich, Aleksandr. See **Alexander II**

Nile River *1:* 22, 25, 36, 38, 75, 115, 124, 146; *3:* 151 (ill.)

95 theses *4:* 55

Nineveh *1:* 45-50, 52-53

Ninth Moscow International Film Festival *7:* 153

Nipkow, Paul *6:* 97

Nixon, Richard M. *6:* 197; *8:* 119

Nkomo, Joshua *8:* 145-146, 148, 150

Nkrumah, Kwame *7:* 39, **60-67,** 61 (ill.), 66 (ill.); *8:* 145, 158

Nobel, Alfred *6:* 5-7, 10, 52

Nobel Foundation *6:* 9
Nobel Peace Prize *6:* 5, 10; *8:* 59, 69, 77, 83, 89, 94, 113, 168, 171, 177, 205, 215
Nobel Prize *6:* 32, 51-52; *7:* 121, 142
Nobody Knows My Name 7: 170
Nobunaga Oda *4:* 125, 134-140
Non-Cooperation Movement *7:* 71
Norman Conquest *2:* 212
Normandy *2:* 186, 196, 200-201, 206, 208-211, 213-214
Normans *2:* 208, 212, 214
North Atlantic Treaty Organization (NATO) *7:* 184
North Vietnam *7:* 51, 56-58
Northwest Passage *5:* 12
Nossenko, Catherine *6:* 165
Notaras *3:* 168-169, 171
Notes of a Native Son 7: 166, 169
Nova 8: 37
Novgorod *3:* 176, 178
Novotny, Antonin *7:* 209, 211; *8:* 101
Novum Organum 4: 101
NOW. See National Organization for Women (NOW)
Nuclear threat *7:* 194
Nur al-din *3:* 6, 8-12
Nuremberg laws *7:* 102
Nuremberg trials *7:* 107

O

Obregón, Alvaro *6:* 133
Ocllo, Mama *3:* 195, 200
O'Connor, James *6:* 195
Odinga, Oginga *8:* 160
Oedipus Complex *6:* 33, 59
Oedipus 4: 163
Oersted, Hans Christian *5:* 113
The Old Guitarist 6: 156
Olivier, Fernande *6:* 157
Olsen, Iver *6:* 202
Olszewiski, Jan *8:* 115
On Being and Essence 3: 70
On Contempt for the World 3: 24
One Day, When I Was Lost 7: 171
On Human Nature 8: 45
On Protracted War 7: 45

On the Economy of Manufactures and Machinery 5: 143
On the Heavens 3: 50-51
On the Holy Trinity 3: 70
"On the Manufacture of Cast Steel, Its Purposes and Employment" *5:* 150
On the Origin of Species and the Descent of Man 5: 99, 117
On the Principles of Nature 3: 70
On the Town 7: 160
Operation Margarethe *6:* 202
"Operation Peace for Galilee" *8:* 211
Operation Torch *6:* 214
Opium Wars *5:* 188, 190
Opletal, Jan *8:* 103
Order of Jesuits *4:* 47, 50-51, 140
Order of the Red Banner of Labor *8:* 90
Ordoric of Pordenone *4:* 7
Organization of Nonaligned Nations Movement *7:* 204
The Origin of Inequality 4: 172
Orlov, Aleksei *4:* 146
Orlov, Grigori *4:* 146
Orthodoxy *4:* 144
Ortodoxo Party *7:* 200
Othello 4: 120
Ott, John *5:* 165
Otto IV *3:* 27
Ottoman Empire *3:* 157, 166; *6:* 172; *7:* 1, 2, 14, 16, 22
Our Palestine 8: 200
Overseas Workers Association *7:* 54
Ovid *4:* 114

P

PAC. See Pan-Africanist Congress (PAC)
Pachacútec *3:* 194-195, 199
Pacifism *7:* 9
Padmore, Gregory *8:* 157
Paganism *2:* 78-79, 82
Paine, Thomas *5:* 203
Palacios, Catalina de *4:* 107
Palestine *2:* 126, 149-150, 157-158; *7:* 78, 81-83, 89; *8:* 182, 189, 191, 197-198, 200, 204, 215

Palestine Liberation Organization (PLO) *8:* 181, 184, 192-194, 197, 200, 202-204, 207, 213-214
Palestine National Council *8:* 204
Palingenus *4:* 114
Palliser, Hugh *5:* 7, 9
Pallit, Edward *4:* 184, 188
Palma, Arturo Alessandri *8:* 64
Pan-African Freedom Conference *8:* 175
Pan-Africanist Congress (PAC) *8:* 174
Pankhurst, Adela *6:* 14, 21
Pankhurst, Christabel *6:* 14, 16-17, 21
Pankhurst, Emmeline *6:* 2, **12-21,** 13 (ill.), 15 (ill.), 18 (ill.)
Pankhurst, Richard *6:* 12, 14
Pankhurst, Sylvia *6:* 14, 21
Pappenheim, Anna *6:* 58
Pappenheim, Bertha *6:* 57
Paradise 8: 75
Paris Commune *5:* 48, 50
Paris Manifesto *7:* 9-10
Park, Mungo *5:* 1-2, **22-31,** 23 (ill.), 25 (ill.)
Parsberg, Marderup *4:* 77
Pasha, Damad Ferid *7:* 17, 19
Passages from the Life of a Philosopher 5: 145
Past and Future 8: 16
Pasteur Institute *5:* 133
Pasteur, Jean-Baptiste *5:* 128
Pasteur, Louis *5:* 99, **126-133,** 127 (ill.), 129 (ill.); *7:* 116
Pasteur, Marie *5:* 128
Pasteur, Marie-Louise *5:* 128
Pasteurization *5:* 99, 127, 132
Patent Office Official Gazette 6: 86
Patocka, Jan *8:* 102
Paul III *4:* 33, 50
Paul VI *8:* 2-3, **4-13,** 5 (ill.), 9 (ill.), 11 (ill.)
Paul, St. *3:* 72
Paul, Lewis *4:* 186
Paulet, Amias *4:* 98
Pauling, Linus *7:* 138-141
Pauling, Peter *7:* 140
Peace Movement *6:* 5-6
Peacock, George *5:* 140-141
Pearl Harbor *6:* 196

Peasant International Organization *7:* 54
Peele, George *4:* 117, 118
Pelham, Elizabeth *4:* 180
Peloponnesian War *1:* 127, 132, 135
Pembroke 5: 7
Penaud, Alphonse *6:* 78
Penicillin *7:* 111, 115-119
The People 7: 54
People's Enlightenment and Propaganda *7:* 102
The People's Journal 6: 126
People's Republic of China *5:* 189, 195; *7:* 39, 41, 45, 48
The People's Will 6: 24
Peres-Arafat conference *8:* 214
Peres, Shimon *8:* 182, 184-185, 204-205, **206-216,** 207 (ill.), 212 (ill.)
Perestroika 8: 93-95, 124, 129-130, 133
Pericles *1:* 126, 130, 132
Perpetual motion machines *6:* 86
Pershing II missiles *8:* 93
Persia *1:* 45, 61, 63, 65-67, 69-70, 72, 75-77, 79-80, 82-83, 85-86, 110, 115, 122-124, 126, 128, 146-147, 149-153, 156, 158-159, 161-163; *2:* 127, 146-148, 150, 152, 154-156, 158-159, 161, 167, 170, 172
Persian Wars *1:* 122
Persiles y Sigismunda 4: 110
Personal Narrative 5: 119
Pesticides *7:* 134
Petain, Philippe *6:* 210-211
Peter III *4:* 145 (ill.), 146
Peter, St. *3:* 72
Peter the Great *4:* 125, 143, 147
Peter the Hermit *3:* 3
Petite Hermine 4: 25
Petrarca, Francesco *4:* 93
Petrograd, Russia *6:* 116 (ill.)
Petroleum *5:* 136
Petrushka 6: 168
Pham Van Dong *7:* 58
Philip II *1:* 138, 140, 145, 148-150, 158
Philip IV *4:* 32
Philip Augustus *3:* 27
Philip of Swabia *3:* 27
Philippines *7:* 39
Philosophes 4: 153

Phonofilm *6:* 93
Phonograph *5:* 159, 164 (ill.)
Photoelectric cells *6:* 97
Pianotype machine *5:* 149
Picasso, Pablo *6:* 141, **152-161,** 153 (ill.), 166, 169
Pierce, John R. *7:* 125
Pierne, Gabriel *6:* 166
Piero da Vinci *4:* 66
Pinochet Ugarte, Augusto *8:* 66
Piston, Walter *7:* 159
Pitchblende *6:* 48, 49
Pius XI *8:* 7
Pius XII *8:* 7, 10
Pizarro, Francisco *3:* 123, 201
Pizzardo, Guiseppe *8:* 7
Plagues and Peoples *8:* 19
Planck, Max *6:* 32
Plato *1:* 110-111, 118-119, 128, 130, 132, 134, 136, 138-140, 142; *4:* 156
Plautus *4:* 114
Playing in the Dark *8:* 74
PLO. See Palestine Liberation Organization (PLO)
PNR. See National Revolutionary Party
Poe, Edgar Allan *8:* 74
Pokrovsky, Ivan *6:* 164
Poland *7:* 2; *8:* 110-115
Polarized light *5:* 128-129
Polish Communist Party *8:* 113
Politburo *8:* 91, 130-131
Pollaiuolo, Antonio *4:* 68
Polo, Maffeo *3:* 128, 130-132, 131 (ill.), 136
Polo, Marco *3:* 126 (ill.), 127, **128-137,** 129 (ill.), 131 (ill.); *4:* 7
Polo, Nicolo *3:* 128, 130-132, 131 (ill.), 136
Pompey *2:* 3, 28, 30, 38, 41, 43, 47-49
Pope, Franklin *5:* 162
Popham, Alexander *4:* 154
The Population Bomb *8:* 3, 24
Population Registration Act *8:* 167
Powered Flight *6:* 77, 81
"Power of the Powerless" *8:* 102
Prague Spring *7:* 207, 209, 212; *8:* 99-101, 110
Pratt, Hodson *6:* 8
"The Prelude" *5:* 204

Presidium *8:* 94, 133
"Previous Condition" *7:* 168
Principia *5:* 161
Principles of Geology *5:* 121
Progress in Flying Machines *6:* 78
Progymnasmata *4:* 83
Proletariat *7:* 31
Protestantism *4:* 32, 33, 55-58
Protestant Reformation *4:* 53, 98
Provisional Vietnamese Republic *7:* 57
Psyche *6:* 57
Psychiatry *6:* 57
Psychoanalysis *6:* 33, 55, 59, 61
Psychoanalytic theory *6:* 60
Psychology *6:* 61
Ptolemaic dynasty *2:* 44, 47, 53
Public Against Violence *8:* 104
Pugachev, Yemelian *4:* 147
Pugo, Boris *8:* 96
Pulitzer Prize *8:* 45, 56, 59, 74
Punic War, First *1:* 171, 186, 188
Punic War, Second *1:* 171, 190, 193-195
Punic War, Third *1:* 172
Punjab *1:* 166-168
Pushkin, Aleksandr *5:* 179
Pu Yi *5:* 195
Pydna, battle of *2:* 44
Pythagoras *1:* 111, **112-119,** 113 (ill.), 116 (ill.)
Pythagorean Order *1:* 116
Pythagorean theorem *1:* 113, 119

Q

Qin dynasty. See Ch'in dynasty
Quadrant *4:* 78 (ill.)
Quadruple Alliance *5:* 74, 83
Quanta *6:* 32
Quantum physics *6:* 32
Quarterly Review of Biology *8:* 41
Quinn, Anthony *8:* 190 (ill.)
Quraysh. See Kuraish
Qutluq-nigar Khanim *3:* 184

R

Rabies *5:* 132
Rabin, Yitzhak *8:* 204-205, 211, 213-215

Race-ing Justice, En-gendering Power: Essays on Anita Hill 8: 74
Radiation *6:* 50
Radio *6:* 87
Radio Corporation *6:* 101
Radioactivity *6:* 32, 45, 50-51, 96
Radium *6:* 51
Radium Institute *6:* 53
Rally for the People of France *6:* 218
Ran 7: 154 (ill.)
Rankin, Jeannette *6:* 175, **188-197,** 189 (ill.), 195 (ill.)
"The Rape of Lucrece" *4:* 114
Rashomon 7: 153
Ravel, Maurice *6:* 166
Reagan Doctrine *8:* 86, 93, 124
Reagan, Maureen *8:* 118
Reagan, Michael *8:* 118
Reagan, Nancy *8:* 118
Reagan, Patty *8:* 118
Reagan, Ronald *8:* 86, 93, 95 (ill.), **116-125,** 117 (ill.), 120 (ill.), 122 (ill.), 194
Reagan, Ronald, Jr. *8:* 118
The Realm of the Nebulae 6: 70
Rebozos *6:* 130
Recalde, Iñigo López de. See **Ignatius of Loyola**
Red Army (Chinese) *7:* 30, 48-49
Red Army (Soviet) *7:* 183, 188; *8:* 90
Red Cross *6:* 10, 207
The Red Flag 6: 29
Red Guard *7:* 49
Red shift *6:* 66
Reflections on the Decline of Science in England 5: 145
Reformation *4:* 33, 39, 54-58
Reginald of Piperno *3:* 72
Reign of Terror *5:* 52-53
Renaissance *4:* 39, 61, 73; *5:* 1
Renard 6: 169
Republic 6: 208
Republican National Convention *8:* 119
Republican Party *5:* 90
Republic of Czechoslovakia *7:* 11
Republic of Ghana *7:* 66
Republic of Turkey *7:* 15, 17
Resolution 5: 12
Revolution of 1917 *5:* 173-174; *7:* 2

Reynaud, Paul *6:* 211-212
Rhapsody in August 7: 155
Rhazes *2:* 162, 163, **164-169,** 178, 181
Rheinische Zeitung 5: 213
Rhodes, siege of *4:* 129
Rhodesia *8:* 147
Ricardo, David *8:* 116
Richard I, the Lion-Hearted *3:* 7, 13, 27, 77, 86, 90, 92 (ill.)
Riebau, George *5:* 110
"The Rights of Man" *5:* 203
"The Rime of the Ancient Mariner" *5:* 203
Rimsky-Korsakov, Nikolai *6:* 164
Rinehardt, Max *6:* 149
Rio dos Bons Sinaes 4: 18
Rios, Juan Antonio *8:* 64-65
The Rise of the West: A History of the Human Community 8: 2, 16-17, 19
The Rite of Spring 6: 168
The River War 7: 183
Rivonia Trial *8:* 175
RNA (Ribonucleic acid) *7:* 140
Road to Survival 8: 20
Robbins, Jerome *7:* 163
Robert A. Milliken Distinguished Service Professor *8:* 16
Robert F. Cohen Chair in the Council of Humanities *8:* 73
Roberts, Ed *8:* 50
Roberval, Jean-Francois de la Rocque de *4:* 27
Robespierre *5:* 49, 52-53
Robinson, Elihu *5:* 100, 103
Rockets *6:* 74
Rodriguez, Jorge Alessandri *8:* 64
Roebuck, John *4:* 193
Roentgen, Wilhelm *6:* 32, 47-48, 74
Roman Catholic Church *3:* 24, 26
Roman Catholicism *4:* 56
Romance under the Waters 7: 131
Roman Empire *2:* 55-56, 66, 68, 72, 75-76, 86
Rome *1:* 171, 186, 188-191, 193-195; *2:* 1-4, 24-30, 32-34, 37-44, 47-51, 53, 56, 84, 86-88, 152, 190
Romeo and Juliet 4: 118
Roncalli, Angelo *8:* 10

Roosevelt, Franklin D. *6:* 42, 175, 194, 202, 214, 217; *7:* 132, 180-182
Rose Period *6:* 156-157
Rosenwald fellowship *7:* 168
Rosing, Boris *6:* 96
Roteiro 4: 17
Rothchild, Walter *7:* 87
Rousseau, Isaac *4:* 168, 170
Rousseau, Jean-Jacques *4:* 152 (ill.), 153, **168-173,** 169 (ill.); *5:* 33, 35, 38, 59
Roxas, Manuel *7:* 39
Roxelana *4:* 132
Royal Academy of Science *6:* 52
Royal Institution *5:* 98, 110, 112
Royal Society of London *5:* 8-9, 24, 112, 141, 143-144, 157
Rubenstein, Anton *6:* 164
Rudolf II *4:* 82, 90
Rudolphine Tables 4: 83, 88, 91
"The Ruined Cottage" *5:* 205
Ruiz, José *6:* 152, 154
The Runaway Train 7: 153
Rush, Richard *5:* 73
Rush-Bagot Agreement *5:* 73
Russell, Bertrand *7:* 70
Russia *5:* 169-170; *7:* 1, 24-34, 186-194
Russian American Company *5:* 67, 94
Russian Ballet *6:* 159
Russian Empire *3:* 157, 175-180; *5:* 172
Russian Federation *8:* 87
Russian Orthodox Church *5:* 172
Russian Revolution *5:* 173-174; *6:* 74, 98, 106 (ill.), 109, 169, 210; *7:* 10
Russo-Japanese War *6:* 183
Rutherford, Ernest *6:* 32, 50

S

Sacher, Henry *7:* 87
SACP. See South African Communist Party (SACP)
Sadat, Anwar *8:* 184
Saigo *5:* 186
Saladin *3:* 4, **6-13,** 7 (ill.), 9 (ill.), 62, 64
Samarkand *3:* 185
Samos *1:* 112, 114, 115, 123
Samuel, Herbert *7:* 85, 88

Samurai *5:* 185
Samurai films *7:* 145, 151
Samurai revolution *5:* 171
Samurai swords *4:* 136, 136 (ill.)
Sandeman, Robert *5:* 108
San Gabriel 4: 16
San Jacinto 5: 92
Sanko Seisako 7: 46
San Rafael 4: 16
Sanshiro Sugata 7: 151
Sanskrit *2:* 94, 99-101, 110, 112-116, 120, 180-181
Sarnoff, David *6:* 101
Sartak *3:* 138, 140-141
Scheiman, Arthur *7:* 106
Scherzo fantastique 6: 165
Scheutz, Georg *5:* 145
Scholasticism *4:* 156
Schumann, Robert *7:* 161
Science *5:* 96-99; *7:* 111-143
Scientific American 6: 83
Scomber, A Young Mackerel 7: 131
Scott, C. P. *7:* 87
Scott, Henry *5:* 18
Screen Actors' Guild *8:* 118
SDI. See Strategic Defense Initiative (SDI)
SDKP. See Social Democracy for the Kingdom of Poland Party
The Sea around Us 7: 133
Second Industrial Revolution *5:* 135; *6:* 73
Second Opium War *5:* 190-191
Second Symphony 7: 159
Secret codes *6:* 111
Secret Session speeches *7:* 184
Sectarianism *5:* 185
Sekigahara, battle of *4:* 141
Seleucia *1:* 146, 168
Seleucids *2:* 1, 6, 9-11, 13-14
Self-analysis *6:* 59
"Self-Government Now" *7:* 64
The Selfish Gene 8: 44
Selfridge, Thomas *6:* 84
Selim the Terrible *4:* 126, 128, 132
Selznick, David O. *7:* 153
Semiconductors *7:* 124-125
Separate Amenities Act *8:* 166
Serfdom *5:* 170, 172

Seton-Watson, Robert *7:* 9

The Seven Samurai 7: 146, 152 (ill.)

Seven Years' War *5:* 2

Seville *3:* 104 (ill.)

Seward, William *5:* 67, 76, **88-95,** 89 (ill.)

"Seward's Folly" *5:* 94

Sextant *4:* 76 (ill.), 78

Sforza, Ludovico *4:* 69-71

Shakantula *2:* 97 (ill.)

Shakespeare, John *4:* 112

Shakespeare, William *4:* 95, 110, **112-121,** 113 (ill.), 119 (ill.); *7:* 154-155

Shamir, Itzhak *8:* 211

The Shape of European History 8: 19

Sharpesville massacre *8:* 174

Shelley, Percy Bysshe *4:* 103; *5:* 207

Shemyaka, Dimitri *3:* 174

Shevardnadze, Eduard *8:* 93, 95-96

Shiite Islam *2:* 139; *3:* 11

Shikai, Yuan *6:* 127-128

Shintoism *5:* 185

Shirkuh *3:* 8-11

Shirley, Jon *8:* 54

Shockley Semiconductor Laboratories *7:* 126

Shockley, William *7:* 112, **122-127,** 123 (ill.)

Shogun *5:* 171, 180, 182

Shogun 4: 137

Shona nation *8:* 144

Siberia *6:* 113

Sibling rivalry *6:* 33

Siddhartha Gautama *1:* 80, 87, **88-95,** 89 (ill.), 90 (ill.); *2:* 113 (ill.)

Sikhism *4:* 41-45

Silberbauer, Karl *7:* 109

Silent Spring 7: 113, 129, 134

Silicon Valley *7:* 126

Silkworms *5:* 131

Siloti, Alexander *6:* 165

Sinai *8:* 200-211

Sino-Japanese War *5:* 187, 194

Sisulu, Walter *8:* 166, 172-173, 175

Six Day War *7:* 98; *8:* 200-211

Skanderberg *3:* 173

Skinker, Mary *7:* 130

Slovakia *8:* 106-107

Smalley, John *4:* 187

Smith, Adam *5:* 3, **14-21,** 15 (ill.), 18 (ill.); *8:* 116

Smith, Ian *8:* 147-148

Smith, Marion *8:* 40

Smithsonian Institution *6:* 78, 84-85

Smuts, Jan C. *7:* 88

The Social Contract 4: 169, 172

Social Democracy for the Kingdom of Poland Party (SDKP) *6:* 25-27

Social Democrats *7:* 27

Socialism *5:* 214, 217; *6:* 21; *7:* 39, 43, 174, 200, 206

Socialist Labor Party *7:* 92

Society for the Revival of China *6:* 122

Society of Jesus *4:* 50-51

Society of the Friends of the Rights of Man *5:* 49

The Sociobiology: New Synthesis 8: 44-45

Socrates *1:* 110-111, 127, **128-135,** 129 (ill.), 142

The Soldier's Tale 6: 169

Solel Boneh *7:* 94

Solidarity *8:* 87, 94, 109, 111-113, 112 (ill.), 115, 124

Solovyov, Vladimir *5:* 177

Something Like an Autobiography 7: 155

Sondheim, Stephen *7:* 163

Song of Solomon 8: 72

South Africa *8:* 141, 144, 163-165, 172, 174-175

South African Communist Party (SACP) *8:* 168, 172-174, 177-178

Southern Rhodesia African National Congress *8:* 145

Southey, Robert *5:* 207

Soviet International Peace Prize *8:* 65

Soviet Marxism *7:* 12

Spaghetti westerns *7:* 145, 151

Spanish Armada *5:* 1

Spanish Civil War *6:* 159

Spark gap *6:* 90

Sparta *1:* 109-110, 122, 127, 132-133, 135, 145, 159

Spartacides *6:* 148

Spartacist League *6:* 29

Spartacist Movement *6:* 29

Spartacus *6:* 29, 148
Spartacus Letters 6: 28
Spenser, Edmund *4:* 117
Spinning jenny *4:* 176, 186, 187 (ill.)
Spiral galaxies *6:* 65
Spiritual Exercises 4: 51
Sprengel, Herman *5:* 155
Sputnik 7: 193
Sri Chand *4:* 44
SS (Schutzstaffel) troops *7:* 102, 104,
    105 (ill.)
Staite, W. E. *5:* 154
Stalin, Joseph *6:* 29, 117-118, 173, 217;
    7: 2, 11, **24-35,** 25 (ill.), 26 (ill.), 29
    (ill.), 31 (ill.) 181, 187, 189-190, 192,
    209; *8:* 88, 90-91, 100-101, 126
Stalin Peace Prize *8:* 65
Stangl, Franz *7:* 107
St. Anne 4: 73
"Star Wars" *8:* 117, 123
Starr, J. W. *5:* 154
Staupitz, John (Johann von) *4:* 55
Steam engine *4:* 191-192, 192 (ill.), 194
    (ill.)
Steam power *5:* 103
Stearn, Charles *5:* 155
Steed, Henry Wickham *7:* 9
Stefanik, Milan *7:* 11
Stein, Gertrude *6:* 155 (ill.), 157
Stepan, Miroslav *8:* 104
Stephen I of Serbia *3:* 38
St. Nicholas 7: 128
Stoeckl, Edouard de *5:* 94, 95
The Story of Mankind 7: 131
Stowe, Harriet Beecher *7:* 168
Strategic Defense Initiative (SDI) *8:*
    93, 123
*Strategic Problems in the Anti-Japanese
    Guerrilla War 7:* 45
Stravinsky, Igor *6:* 143, 159, **162-
    169,** 163 (ill.), 167 (ill.)
Stray Dog 7: 151
Struensee, Johann Friedrich *5:* 34,
    36-41, 37 (ill.)
Strut, Jedediah *4:* 187
St. Sophia Church *3:* 171
Studies in Hysteria 6: 59
Suffragette movement *6:* 13
Sula 8: 72

Sulakhni *4:* 40
Suleiman the Magnificent *4:* 124-
    125, **126-133,** 127 (ill.), 130 (ill.)
Sultan Abu Inan *3:* 152
Sumanguru *3:* 101, 112-114, 116
Summa contra gentiles 3: 73
Summa Theologica 3: 73
Sumner, Charles *5:* 67, 95
Sundiata *3:* 101, **110-115,** 111 (ill.)
Sunni Islam *2:* 139; *3:* 11
Sun Yat-sen *6:* 107, **120-129,** 121
    (ill.), 123 (ill.); *7:* 38, 43, 45
Suppululiumas I *1:* 5, **28-25**
Suppression of Communism Act *8:* 173
Supreme Soviet *8:* 94, 133
Su Shun *5:* 193
Suttner, Arthur von *6:* 6
Suttner, Bertha von *6:* 2, **4-11,** 5 (ill.)
Swan, Joseph Wilson *5:* 137, **152-
    157,** 153 (ill.)
Sykes, Mark *7:* 87
Sykes-Picot agreement *8:* 186
Syria *2:* 147, 150, 157-158, 161; *8:* 192,
    200
A System of Moral Philosophy 5: 17
Szalasi, Ferenc *6:* 204

T

Tahiti *5:* 9
Taidjuts *3:* 17-18
Taieb, Maurice *8:* 34
Taignoagny *4:* 25
Taiping Rebellion *6:* 120
T'ai Tsung *2:* 94, 101, **102-109,** 112,
    114, 116-117
Taizong. See **T'ai Tsung**
Takuwera, Leopold *8:* 145
Talmud *3:* 58
Tambo, Oliver *8:* 172
Tamburlaine. See **Timur Lenk**
Tamerlane. See **Timur Lenk**
T'ang dynasty *2:* 93-94, 105, 109, 112,
    117
Tao-te ching *1:* 81, 100
Taoism *1:* 80, 99-101; *2:* 110
Targoutai *3:* 19
Tatars *3:* 18
The Tatler 6: 78

Taylor, Charley *6:* 80-81

Taylor, Zachary *5:* 90

Tell Me How Long the Train's Been Gone *7:* 169

The Tempest *4:* 120

Temujin. See **Genghis Khan**

Ten Commandments *1:* 35, 39 (ill.), 40

Tenochtitlán *3:* 202, 204-205, 207 (ill.), 209, 209 (ill.)

"Ten Points" petition *8:* 101

Tensai Sana. See **Mutsuhito**

Terra Australis Incognita *5:* 8, 10, 12

Texcoco *3:* 206

Thatcher, Margaret *8:* 148

Theater of the Absurd *6:* 143

Thebes *1:* 150, 152

Theobald, Archbishop of Canterbury *3:* 78, 82

The Theory of Moral Sentiments *5:* 17

Theory of Relativity *6:* 32, 37-38

Third Crusade *3:* 13

Third Estate *5:* 46

Third Republic *6:* 208, 218

"Thirty-sixers" literary circle *8:* 100

Thomas, Clarence *8:* 74

Thomas Aquinas, St. See **Aquinas, Thomas**

Thompson, Randall *7:* 159

Thoreau, Henry David *7:* 132

Thorez, Maurice *6:* 217

Thornley, David *4:* 187

The Threepenny Opera *6:* 150

The Throne of Blood *7:* 155

Thuku, Harry *8:* 154, 156, 158

Thutmose II *1:* 22, 27

Thutmose III *1:* 24-25, 27

Ticker tape machine *5:* 159, 162

Tigris River *1:* 15-16, 32, 46, 48

Timbuktu *3:* 118, 121, 123

Timur Lenk *3:* 155, **158-165,** 159 (ill.), 182, 185, 188

Tirpitz, Alfred von *6:* 182

Titarenko, Raisa. See Gorbachev, Raisa

Tito, Marshal *8:* 13

Tolstoy, Leo *6:* 165; *7:* 9

Tong Meng Hui. See United League

Tongzhi. See Tsai-ch'un

Tora! Tora! Tora! *7:* 153

Tordesillas, Treaty of *4:* 14, 15 (ill.), 17

Tories *4:* 180

Toure, Sekou *7:* 67

Tower of Babel *1:* 59

Tower of London *4:* 102 (ill.)

Townshend, Charles *4:* 176, **178-183,** 179 (ill.); *5:* 17-18

Townshend, Horatio *4:* 178

Tracy, William de *3:* 86

Transfer resistor *7:* 125

Transformer *5:* 114

Transistor *7:* 112, 122-125

Trasmund of Segni *3:* 24

Travels in the Interior Districts of Africa *5:* 29

Treatment on Armament Technology *4:* 9

Treaty of Lausanne *7:* 21

Treaty of Nanking *5:* 190

Treaty of Sevres *7:* 20

Treaty of Tianjin *5:* 191

Treaty of Versailles *6:* 172, 194; *7:* 54

Trevino, Perez *6:* 135

Triumvirate, First *2:* 28-30, 41

Triumvirate, Second *2:* 43, 49, 51

Troilus and Cressida *4:* 119

Trotsky, Leon *6:* 7, 114, 117-118; *7:* 30

Trujillo, Rafael L. *7:* 200

Truman Doctrine *7:* 174, 184

Truman, Harry S *6:* 217-218; *7:* 174, 182-183; *8:* 85

Tsai-ch'un *5:* 191, 193

Tsiolkovsky, Konstantin *6:* 74

Tughluq Temur *3:* 161-162

Tull, Jethro *4:* 182

Turgenev, Ivan *5:* 177

Turkey *7:* 2, 14-23

Tvar *8:* 100-101

Twentieth Party Conference *7:* 192

Twentieth Party Congress *7:* 209

26th of July Movement *7:* 201

The Two Gentlemen of Verona *4:* 116

Two Treatises of Civil Government *4:* 157-159

Tychonic system *4:* 81-82, 88

Tyson, Anne *5:* 200

Tz'u-hsi *5:* 170, **188-195,** 189 (ill.), 192 (ill.)

U

Uganda *7:* 83
Ukrainian nationalists *7:* 189
Ulyanov, Alexander *6:* 108, 110
Umar I *2:* 127, 138, 139, **140-151**
Umar Shaik Mirza *3:* 182
"Uncle Ho" *7:* 58
Uncle Tom's Cabin *7:* 168
Under the Sea-Wind *7:* 132-133
"Undersea" *7:* 131
Union of Soviet Socialist Republics
    (U.S.S.R.) *6:* 118, 207; *7:* 2, 25, 28,
    30, 43, 55, 90, 97, 187, 208; *8:* 85-86,
    90-97, 100, 110, 117, 121-129, 133-
    134, 182, 200
Union Treaty *8:* 133
United Arab Republic *8:* 190
United Gold Coast Convention
    (UGCC) *7:* 64
United League *6:* 126
United Nations *6:* 11
United Nations Resolution 242 *8:* 192,
    194
United Nations Resolution 338 *8:* 194
United Nations Resolution 3236 *8:* 203
United Nations Security Council *6:* 11
United Party (UP) *7:* 67
United States *8:* 85, 184
United States Constitution *4:* 159
Uraniborg *4:* 78 (ill.), 79 (ill.), 81, 82
Uranium *6:* 48
Urban II *3:* 3, 36, 38-39
Urban VI *3:* 71
Urbanek, Karel *8:* 104
USSR. See Union of Soviet Socialist
    Republics (U.S.S.R.)
Ustad Ali *3:* 186

V

Vacuum tube *6:* 90
Vahideddin VI, Mehmed *7:* 17
Valdés, Miguel Alemán *6:* 139
Vallery-Radot, Rene *5:* 128
Van Buren, Martin *5:* 90
Van Loon, Hendrik Willem *7:* 131
Vasily II *3:* 174

Vasilyevich, Ivan III. See **Ivan the
    Great**
Vassilievna, Anna *3:* 178
Vauxcelles, Louis *6:* 158
Vedel, Anders Sorensen *4:* 77
Vega, Lope de *4:* 95
Velasquez, Juan *4:* 46, 48
Velvet Revolution *7:* 213; *8:* 87, 99, 102,
    106
Venice Film Festival *7:* 153
Venizelos, Eleutherios *7:* 20
Venus and Adonis *4:* 116-118
Verdun, battle of *6:* 210
Verrazano, Giovanni da *4:* 22
Verrocchio, Andrea del *4:* 66-69
Versailles Peace Conference *7:* 54, 88
Victoria *5:* 148, 157, 207
Vienna Psycho-Analytical Society *6:* 61
Vietminh *7:* 56-57
Vietnam *7:* 39, 50-59; *8:* 57, 121
Vikings *2:* 184-189, 187 (ill.), 192, 194-
    196, 198, 200-202, 206, 208, 210, 212
Villa, Pancho *6:* 133
Villon, François *6:* 148
Vindication of the Rights of Women *6:* 2
Virgil *4:* 114
Vladimir I *5:* 217
Vogt, William *8:* 20
Voice of Palestine *8:* 200
"Voice of Revolution" *7:* 67
Voltaire *4:* 146-147, 151, **160-168,**
    167 (ill.); *5:* 33, 35, 37-38, 40, 59
Von Bora, Katharina *4:* 57
Von Humboldt, Alexander *5:* 119
Von Kunitz, Eleanore *5:* 80
Von Lerchenfeld, Frau *5:* 57
Voroshilov, Dmitri *7:* 28
Voroshilov, K. E. *7:* 189 (ill.)
Vorster, John *8:* 147-148
Votes for Women *6:* 17
Vperyed *6:* 115

W

Walentynowicz, Anna *8:* 111
Walesa, Lech *8:* 87, **108-115,** 109
    (ill.), 114 (ill.)
Wallace, Alfred Russell *5:* 124
Wallenberg, Gustav *6:* 198

Wallenberg, Raoul *6:* 175, **198-207,** 199 (ill.)

Wallerstein, Immanuel *8:* 2

Walpole, Dorothy *4:* 180

Walpole, Robert *4:* 178, 181

Walsh, Thomas J. *6:* 193

Walter, Bruno *7:* 160

War Guilt Clause *6:* 194

Warner Brothers *8:* 118

War of 1812 *5:* 65, 85

War of Liberation *7:* 47-48

War Refugee Board *6:* 202

Warring States period *1:* 180

Warsaw Pact *8:* 94, 110

Washington Declaration *7:* 11

Washington, George *5:* 71

Water frame *4:* 176, 186

Watergate hearings *6:* 197

Watson, James *7:* 112, **136-143,** 137 (ill.), 141 (ill.)

Watt, James *4:* 176, **190-196,** 191 (ill.)

The Wealth of Nations 5: 15, 21

Wedgwood, Emma *5:* 124

Wedgwood, Josiah *5:* 116

Wedgwood, Susannah *5:* 116

Weed, Thurlow *5:* 90

Weigel, Helene *6:* 150 (ill.), 151

Weill, Kurt *6:* 150

Weizmann, Chaim *7:* 78, **80-89,** 81 (ill.), 84 (ill.), 86 (ill.), 94

Weltpolitik 6: 179, 181-182

West Africa *5:* 23

West Bank *8:* 185, 192-193, 200-201, 203-204, 211, 214-215

West Side News 6: 76

West Side Story 7: 146, 163

Western allies *7:* 34, 47, 183, 194

Western Electric *6:* 92

Western European Youth Orchestra *7:* 163

Western Union *5:* 163

Westminster School *4:* 156

Weston, Richard *4:* 182

Westphalen, Frieherr Ludwig von *5:* 211, 212

Wheeler, William Morton *8:* 40

Whig Party *4:* 180; *5:* 90

White Paper *7:* 95

White, Tim *8:* 36

Whitman, Walt *6:* 148

Whitmore, Georgiana *5:* 143

Wiese, Kurt *7:* 107

Wiesenthal, Simon *7:* 79, **100-109,** 101 (ill.), 106 (ill.)

Wilhelm I *6:* 176

Wilhelm II *6:* 29, 171, **176-187,** 177 (ill.), 179 (ill.), 181 (ill.)

Wilhelm, August *6:* 187

Wilkins, Maurice *7:* 138

William of Moerbeke *3:* 71

William of Rubrouck *3:* 127, **138-145**

William the Conqueror *2:* 186, 189, 205, **206-214,** 207 (ill.), 211 (ill.); *3:* 75-76, 80, 82

Wilmo Central Organization *6:* 25

Wilson, Edward O. *8:* 29, **38-45,** 39 (ill.), 42 (ill.)

Wilson, Woodrow *6:* 93, 192; *7:* 9, 54, 86

Winestine, Belle Fligelman *6:* 193

Wireless telegraph *6:* 74, 88

Wojtila, Karol. See John Paul II

Wollstonecraft, Mary *6:* 2

Women's Franchise League *6:* 14

Women's Freedom League *6:* 19

Women's International Congress for Permanent Peace *6:* 193

Women's International League for Peace and Freedom *6:* 193

The Women's March to Versailles 4: 172 (ill.)

Women's Parliament *6:* 19

Women's Social and Political Union (WSPU) *6:* 2, 16-17, 19-21

Women's suffrage *6:* 16, 19, 190

Wonderful Town 7: 163

Wordsworth, Anne Cookson *5:* 200

Wordsworth, John *5:* 200, 202

Wordsworth, William *5:* 102, 199, **200-207,** 201 (ill.)

Worker's Cause 6: 25

World Bank *8:* 160

World Council of Churches *8:* 13

The World Crisis 7: 183

World Festival of Youth *7:* 193

A World History 8: 19

World Peace Congress *6:* 197
World War I *4:* 125; *6:* 11, 20, 23, 27,
    29, 40, 42, 64, 98, 105, 115, 148, 159,
    169, 171-172, 182, 191, 210; *7:* 1-2, 5,
    9, 11, 15-17, 21, 37-38, 42, 52, 54, 71,
    85, 100, 117, 188
World War II *6:* 11, 42, 70, 102, 151,
    160, 175, 187, 193, 195, 199, 202,
    209, 211; *7:* 13, 33-34, 37, 39, 46, 54,
    56, 63, 74, 79, 112, 124, 132, 151,
    163, 174, 181; *8:* 1, 110
World Zionist Organization *7:* 94
Wright, Almroth *7:* 116-117
Wright Flyer I biplane *6:* 82, 84
Wright, Orville *6:* 74, **76-84,** 77 (ill.),
    79 (ill.), 82 (ill.)
Wright, Richard *7:* 167, 168
Wright, Wilbur *6:* 74, **76-84,** 77
    (ill.), 79 (ill.), 82 (ill.)
Wriothesley, Henry *4:* 117
WSPU. See Women's Social and
    Political Union
Wudi. See **Wu Ti**
Wu Ti *2:* 5, 15, **16-23,** 17 (ill.)
Wyatt, John *4:* 186; *5:* 197
Wycliffe, John *4:* 32
Wyman, Jane *8:* 118

X

X *7:* 171
Xerxes *1:* 120, 122, 151, 156
Xia dynasty. See Hsia dynasty
X'ing Zhong Hui. See Society for the
    Revival of China
X-ray crystallography *7:* 140
X-rays *6:* 32, 47-48, 51, 74
Xuanzang. See **Hsüan-tsang**
Xunzi. See **Hsün-tzu**

Y

Yalta Conference *6:* 217
Yanaev, Gennadi *8:* 96
Yang Ch'ang-chi *7:* 42
Yang Kai-hui *7:* 43
Yaqui Indians *6:* 133, 139
Yassa *3:* 21

Yat-sen, Sun. See **Sun Yat-sen**
Yehenera. See **Tz'u-hsi**
Yelachich, Alexander *6:* 162
Yeltsin, Boris *8:* 87, 94-96, **126-135,**
    127 (ill.), 130 (ill.), 132 (ill.)
Yesukai *3:* 14, 16-17
Yojimbo *7:* 152
Yom Kippur War *7:* 98; *8:* 194, 211
Yose *7:* 150
Young Czech Party *7:* 8
Yuan Shi Kai *5:* 195
Yugoslavia *7:* 2
Yupanqui, Topa Inca *3:* 193, **194-
    201**
Yurt *3:* 141 (ill.)
Yury of Zvenigorod *3:* 174
Yu the Great *1:* 5, **6-13,** 7 (ill.)

Z

Zahir-ud-Din Muhammad. See **Babur**
ZANU. See Zimbabwe African National
    Union (ZANU)
Zapata, Emiliano *6:* 133
Zapolya, John *4:* 131
Zapotocky, Antonin *7:* 209
ZAPU. See Zimbabwe African People's
    Union (ZAPU)
Zengi *3:* 6
Zero Population Growth *8:* 24
Zhao dynasty. See Chou dynasty
Zheng He. See **Cheng Ho**
Zimbabwe *8:* 143, 146, 149-150
Zimbabwe African National Union
    (ZANU) *8:* 146-148
Zimbabwe African People's Union
    (ZAPU) *8:* 146, 150
Zinoviev, Grigori *7:* 30
Zinoviev, Nikolai *7:* 33
Zionism *7:* 78, 82-83, 87-88, 92, 94, 96
Zionist Congress *7:* 83
Zionist Organization *7:* 88
Zoroaster *1:* 70, 79-81, **82-87,** 83 (ill.)
Zoroastrianism *1:* 79, 82-86; *2:* 109
Zulus *8:* 167
Zworykin, Vladimir *6:* 74, **94-103,**
    95 (ill.), 99 (ill.), 100 (ill.)

PROFILES IN WORLD HISTORY

Significant Events and the People
Who Shaped Them

Volume 5: *British World Influence to Seeking Alternatives to Capitalism, 1750-1900*

Beginning of British World Influence
James Cook, Adam Smith, Mungo Park
Revolution in Europe
Johann Friedrich Struensee, Georges Danton, Maria Carolina
Rise of the United States
James Monroe, Klemens Metternich, William Seward
Rise of Professional Science
John Dalton, Michael Faraday, Charles Darwin, Louis Pasteur
Technological Breakthroughs
Charles Babbage, Henry Bessemer, Joseph Wilson Swan, Thomas Alva Edison
Attempting to Modernize Governments
Alexander II, Mutsuhito, Tz'u-hsi
Seeking Alternatives to Capitalism
William Wordsworth, Karl Marx

Volume 6: *Social Reform to World Wars, 1880-1945*

Social Reform
Bertha von Suttner, Emmeline Pankhurst, Rosa Luxemburg
Science Exploring the Unseen World
Albert Einstein, Marie Curie, Sigmund Freud, Edwin Hubble
Expanding Global Communications
Wilbur and Orville Wright, Lee De Forest, Vladimir Zworykin
Twentieth-Century Revolutions
Lenin, Sun Yat-sen, Lázaro Cárdenas
Experimentation in the Arts
Bertolt Brecht, Pablo Picasso, Igor Stravinsky
World Wars
Wilhelm II, Jeannette Rankin, Raoul Wallenberg, Charles de Gaulle